Alternate Americas

Science Fiction Film and American Culture

M. Keith Booker

PRAEGER

**Westport, Connecticut
London**

Library of Congress Cataloging-in-Publication Data

Booker, M. Keith.
    Alternate Americas : science fiction film and American culture / M. Keith Booker.
      p. cm.
    Includes bibliographical references and index.
    ISBN 0–275–98395–1 (alk. paper)
    1. Science fiction films—United States—History and criticism. I. Title.
    PN1995.9.S26B56 2006
    791.43'615—dc22   2005032303

British Library Cataloguing in Publication Data is available.

Library of Congress Catalog Card Number: 2005032303
ISBN: 0–275–98395–1

First published in 2006

Praeger Publishers, 88 Post Road West, Westport, CT 06881
An imprint of Greenwood Publishing Group, Inc.
www.praeger.com

Printed in the United States of America

The paper used in this book complies with the
Permanent Paper Standard issued by the National
Information Standards Organization (Z39.48–1984).

10 9 8 7 6 5 4 3 2 1

For Benjamin Booker

Contents

Photo essay follows chapter 7.

Introduction

Science fiction film is essentially as old as film itself. It was, for example, central to the work of the pioneering French filmmaker Georges Méliès, who found in the genre a perfect opportunity for the exploration of his belief that the true potential of film lay not in the simple photographic representation of reality but in illusion and visual trickery. A magician by trade, Méliès made dozens of films that relied centrally on what would now be referred to as special effects to create worlds of visual fantasy for his audiences. By 1902, he had made what is still his best-known film, the fourteen-minute *Voyage dans la Lune (A Trip to the Moon)*. This work of whimsical imagination, based on a novel by Jules Verne, was a major milestone in cinema history and still has the ability to entertain and fascinate audiences even today.

Following the work of Méliès, films that might be described as science fiction quickly became a staple of the new industry, though many of these early works might equally well be described as horror films, establishing a generic uncertainty that continues to the present day. Thus, the Edison studio had, by 1910, produced the first film adaptation of *Frankenstein*, and, in 1920, German expressionism came to the screen with the production of *Das Kabinett des Doktor Caligari (The Cabinet of Dr. Caligari)*, which deals with a sort of mad scientist but which, more importantly, features extreme lighting and distorted sets that effectively combine to create a mood of strangeness and horror.

Similar techniques were put to good use in Fritz Lang's *Metropolis* (1927), in many ways the culmination of German expressionist cinema and a film that is widely regarded as the first truly great work of science fiction cinema. *Metropolis* involves a towering futuristic city in which the rich live in utopian luxury while legions of poor workers slave away like automatons beneath the surface, tending the gigantic machines that power the golden world above. The film includes numerous visions of advanced technology, the most important of which is the humanoid robot developed by the inventor Rotwang (Rudolf Klein-Rogge), which is used to impersonate the woman Maria (Brigitte Helm), spiritual leader of the workers. The ersatz Maria leads the workers in a doomed rebellion, presumably to preclude the possibility of a more genuine (and successful) revolution, though she is ultimately destroyed by the rioting workers. The real Maria is saved from the clutches of the deranged Rotwang by Freder Fredersen (Gustav Fröhlich), son of the city's ruler, who then serves as a mediator between his father and the workers, heralding a new era of cooperation between the classes.

Many critics have complained about the facile ending of *Metropolis*, which certainly makes it weak as a film about a class-based revolution, but this is a film in which image and atmosphere are far more important than plot or characterization. The special effects (especially those involved in the scene in which the metallic robot is transformed into a Maria look-alike) are quite impressive and have been widely imitated. However, the real secret to the success of *Metropolis* is the ability of the expressionist lighting and sets to convey effectively the feeling of a machine-dominated urban future, even if the actual details are not particularly convincing or realistic.

Envisioning the future is very much the project of the British-produced *Things to Come* (1936), which is probably the first truly important science fiction film of the sound era. Scripted by science fiction pioneer H. G. Wells and based on his book *The Shape of Things to Come* (1933), this film well illustrates Wells's belief late in his life that a utopian future was attainable, but only after the current order of civilization had been destroyed. The film is a speculative "history" of the future that projects the development of human civilization over the next hundred years, beginning with a thirty-year-long world war that begins in 1940 and eventually leaves civilization in ruins, largely as the result of bioweapons that trigger a deadly plague that sweeps the globe. It focuses on the city of Everytown, which begins as a

London-like metropolis, but which, by the end of the war, is in decay, ruled by a warlord engaged in primitive warfare with the surrounding "Hill People." The city, like the rest of civilization, is then rebuilt under the leadership of a visionary group of aviators and engineers who use technology (and superior air power) to enforce their vision of an enlightened world government.

By the year 2036, Everytown is a high-tech paradise, a futuristic city of light and open spaces, almost entirely lacking in the ominous undertones that inform the city of *Metropolis*. The city's leaders, however, are not content to rest on their accomplishments but now set their sights on outer space in the belief that humanity as a species must face continual challenges in order to flourish and prosper. Some in the population bitterly oppose this new project, believing that the insatiable drive for progress only threatens to undermine what is already an idyllic life for the citizens of Everytown. However, these protestors are unable to stop the initial launch in the new space program. As the film ends, they angrily look on as a rocket is fired toward the moon from a giant "space gun," ushering in a new era of exploration. "All the universe or nothing!" cries the leader of the city's ruling council. "Which shall it be?"

Directed by William Cameron Menzies and produced by Alexander Korda, *Things to Come* was a big-budget film whose impressive scenes of a futuristic city made it in many ways the direct forerunner of later science fiction blockbusters from *Star Wars* to *The Matrix*. Its images of the urban future (and the costumes of its future citizenry) would set the style for any number of future films, just as its basic faith in technology and its vision of a humanity that could never rest until it had explored the stars would remain crucial components of science fiction in both the cinema and television for the rest of the century.

Other than monster movies such as James Whale's *Frankenstein* (1931), American science fiction film of the 1930s was largely confined to low-budget serials, such as those featuring Flash Gordon and Buck Rogers as the protagonists, all of which starred Buster Crabbe in the central roles. These serials were based on popular syndicated comic strips, and they definitely had a comic-strip quality to them. Produced in episodes of 15–20 minutes in length, each serial ran for 12–15 episodes that were shown weekly in theaters in an attempt to attract young audiences. By today's standards (or even in comparison to a contemporary film such as *Things to Come*), the special effects of these serials were extremely crude. However, to a generation of young Americans, they offered thrilling images of other planets and other times that presented an exciting alternative to a dreary Depression-era world that was drifting toward global war.

American science fiction came of age as a film genre in 1950 with the release of *Destination Moon*, directed by Irving Pichel and produced by George Pal, who would go on to become one of the leading figures in SF (science fiction) film in the next decade, when his productions included such films as *When Worlds Collide* (1951), *War of the Worlds* (1953), *Conquest of Space* (1955), and *The Time Machine* (1960), the last of which he also directed. The Hungarian-born Pal, who had worked as a production designer for Germany's UFA Studios (makers of *Metropolis*) before fleeing Germany when the Nazis came to power in 1933, served as a sort of transition between the early achievement of European SF films and the later dominance of American SF films. Pal's films typically feature higher budgets, better special effects, and better acting than most other SF films of the 1950s. In addition, several of Pal's films gained respectability by drawing on the works of major science fiction writers, as in the case of *War of the Worlds* and *The Time Machine*, both based on novels by Wells, still at that time the best known international writer of science fiction.

Destination Moon was based on *Rocket Ship Galileo*, a 1947 juvenile novel by Robert A. Heinlein, who also co-wrote the script. Heinlein himself would go on to become one of the best-known novelists in SF history, though he had not yet written any of the classic novels (*The Puppet Masters*, *Double Star*, *The Door into Summer*, *Starship Troopers*, *Stranger in a Strange Land*, *The Moon Is a Harsh Mistress*) on which his later fame would be based. Filmed in brilliant Technicolor, *Destination Moon* projects the first American trip to the moon. It includes a number of realistic details that combine to convey a very believable picture of future space travel. Meanwhile, the film clearly shows its Cold War context, while strikingly anticipating the coming space race. In particular, the American mission is propelled by the perceived urgency to reach the moon before some less scrupulous nation (obviously meant to be the Soviet Union) can establish a base there. The success of the American effort is a distinct victory for free-market capitalism, not only over communism, but over government in general. The mission is a purely private affair, funded and carried out by enlightened capitalists, who in fact are forced to overcome opposition from the United States government in order to complete the mission.

Destination Moon ends with the vaguely utopian message "THIS IS THE END OF THE BEGINNING" displayed on the screen, suggesting that this mission has initiated a new era in human endeavor. In retrospect, the message also announces the way in which the success of the movie would usher in the 1950s craze for science fiction films, many of which seemed to go out of their way to reproduce various elements of *Destination Moon*. The Pal-produced *Conquest of Space* (directed by Byron Haskin) may be the best example of a film that attempted a realistic portrayal of space travel in the manner of *Destination Moon*, but there were many others. Indeed, Kurt Neumann's *Rocketship X–M* was rushed through production and released slightly before *Destination Moon*, attempting to ride on the coattails of the advance publicity of the latter film. This attempt was so blatant that *Rocketship X–M*, originally conceived as a story about a trip to the moon, was reformulated as the story of a trip to Mars after a threatened lawsuit from Pal.

Fred Wilcox's **Forbidden Planet**★ (1956), one of the most stylish SF films of the decade, also drew upon interest in the future possibilities of space travel. Memorable for the technological marvel of Robby the Robot, this film nevertheless warns against the dangers of science and technology, which in this case threaten to unleash sinister and devastating forces. Indeed, the SF films of the 1950s were remarkable for the way in which they reflected the various anxieties and tensions of the era. A large number of alien–invasion films addressed the widespread sense among Americans of the time of being surrounded by powerful and sometimes mysterious enemies. Meanwhile, a side genre of monster movies reflected a similar fear, while often directly dealing with the threats posed by the nuclear arms race. Finally, a plethora of postapocalypse films also spoke to the decade's fears of potential nuclear holocaust. At the same time, looked at more carefully, most films in all three categories reflected not only anxieties over international threats to the American way of life but concerns that the American way itself might have a decidedly dark and dehumanizing side.

Some SF films of the 1950s, including *Invasion U.S.A.* (1952), *Red Planet Mars* (1952), and *The 27th Day* (1957) overtly promoted a paranoid fear (and hatred) of communism as a dehumanizing force, often with aliens

---

★ Boldface titles indicate films that are discussed at length in their own individual chapters later in this volume.

standing in for communists. On the other hand, Jack Arnold's *It Came from Outer Space* (1954) features benevolent aliens who stop off on Earth simply to make repairs and find themselves confronted by hysterical violence at the hands of humans. Meanwhile, Robert Wise's **The Day the Earth Stood Still** (1951) is essentially a plea for global peace and understanding. Here, in one of the first alien-invasion films of the decade, the Christ-like alien Klaatu (Michael Rennie) is essentially benevolent, though he also issues a stern warning: Earth will be destroyed if it seeks to extend its violent ways beyond Earth. This rejection of the Cold War arms race was a courageous gesture in a film that was produced at the height of American Cold War hysteria and at a time when Hollywood itself was under siege by anti-communist zealots in Washington. The success of the film thus demonstrated the way in which science fiction, because it is perceived by many as divorced from contemporary reality, can serve as a venue for trenchant social and political commentary that might have been judged too controversial in a more "mainstream" form.

Christian Nyby's *The Thing from Another World* (also 1951) was more prototypical of the alien-invasion films to come in the next decade. It was also more representative of American paranoia in the early 1950s, when Americans felt threatened not only by the Soviet Union but also the impoverished masses of the Third World, with which America was increasingly coming into contact as a result of the global politics of the Cold War. In this case, the eponymous Thing, a sort of vegetable creature (it is described at one point in the film as "some form of super carrot"), has come to Earth to colonize the planet for itself and its kind, planning to use the human race as a source of their favorite plant food, blood. The Thing is powerful, highly intelligent, and able to multiply rapidly, thus posing a very serious threat to Earth, though it is, in fact, defeated relatively easily. Then again, the most important and interesting battle in the film is not between the Thing and the humans, but among the humans themselves. In this sense, the primary opposition is between the military men and the scientists, with the film ultimately siding with the former, though only after Captain Patrick Hendry (Kenneth Tobey) defies the military bureaucracy and obeys his own judgment in destroying the Thing.

Even more paranoid about alien threats is Menzies's much-admired *Invaders from Mars* (1953, remade with tongue-in-cheek in 1986 by Tobe Hooper), though there is a vague suggestion that the invasion of that film is really a defensive measure designed as a preemptive strike against the U.S.

space program to prevent the earthlings from reaching Mars. In the film, young David Maclean (Jimmy Hunt) can initially get no one to believe that he has seen a Martian saucer land, especially as the saucer has taken refuge underground, doing its work there by sucking anyone who approaches down through the sand that covers it. David watches in horror as his parents and various other adult authority figures turn into robot-like zombies, controlled by the Martians. Luckily, he is eventually able to get the authorities to believe his story, and the U.S. military quickly dispatches the invaders, thus providing audiences with at least some assurance that the military would be able to repel whatever threats that might arise. Perhaps the most memorable thing about *Invaders from Mars*, however, was the design of its aliens. In particular, the head Martian is a metallic-looking creature that is essentially all brain, living in a glass globe, waving its weird tentacles, and controlling, through telepathy, a troop of drone-like mutant slaves, who do all of its physical work.

Haskin's *The War of the Worlds*, again based on a Wells novel, was probably the slickest and most technically impressive of all of the science fiction films produced by Pal during the 1950s. In the film, the Martian invaders are quickly opposed by conventional military forces after scientist Clayton Forrester (Gene Barry), a famous "astro- and nuclear physicist," learns of their existence and alerts the authorities, who quickly mobilize. Unfortunately, the Martians prove invulnerable to conventional attack, surrounding their hovercraft with force fields that are impermeable to the bombs and bullets that are launched against them. Desperate, the top American brass order an atomic attack, but the Martians prove impervious even to a bomb that is "ten times more powerful than anything used before." All seems lost, when the Martians suddenly die off due to their lack of resistance to the germs that inhabit Earth's atmosphere. This is literally a *deus ex machina* ending, the Martians having been destroyed by what is essentially presented as divine intervention. As the film closes, church bells ring and a chorus sings "amen," while the narrator informs us that the Martians have been killed by "the littlest of things, which God in His wisdom had put upon this Earth."

If *War of the Worlds* privileges religion over science, *This Island Earth* (1955) is far more positive in its figuration of science, though its alien invaders are themselves scientists. These aliens, from the besieged planet of Metaluna, have come to Earth, not to colonize the planet or to prevent the evolution of Earth's technology, but to recruit Earth scientists to help them develop better sources of nuclear power so they can fight off their enemies on the neighboring planet of Zahgon. We are told that this recruitment is necessary because most of the Metalunan scientists have already been killed in the war, but it is fairly clear that the depiction of the Metalunans picking the brains of American scientists in this film heavily partakes of the same mindset that convinced Americans in the 1950s that the primitive Soviets could not possibly have developed nuclear weapons without somehow stealing the technology from their more advanced American rivals (who had boosted their own scientific advancement by importing former Nazi scientists after World War II). In the film, he-man scientist Cal Meacham (Rex Reason) and beautiful female scientist Ruth Adams (Faith Domergue) are able to escape from the Metalunans and return to Earth, where they will no doubt get married and breed several beautiful and intelligent American children.

Scientist Russell Marvin (Hugh Marlowe) and new wife Carol (Joan Taylor) have a similarly bright future at the end of *Earth vs. the Flying Saucers* (1956), but only after helping to mobilize the American military-industrial complex to defeat an invasion of aliens, who again do not seem all that evil, other than the fact that they hope to come to Earth to live, their own planet having been rendered uninhabitable. But this in itself is a frightening prospect, just as Americans of the 1950s were widely hostile to the idea of all those Third World masses moving here to take our jobs and use up our resources. So the relatively peaceful aliens are greeted with military force, resulting in an all-out war. The Earthlings win, again providing a reassuring ending.

If the aliens of *Earth vs. the Flying Saucers* are forced to turn to violence largely because of the belligerence of the Earthlings who greet them, there is no such ambivalence in the depiction of the aliens of **Invasion of the Body Snatchers** (1956), perhaps *the* signature alien-invasion film of the 1950s. Here, alien replicants begin replacing the inhabitants of a small California town, with the clear implication that they plan eventually to take over the entire country and perhaps the entire world. While this film is particularly easy to read as an allegory about the threat of communist infiltration in the United States, it is also a complex film that can be read as a commentary on a variety of domestic threats, including conformism and McCarthyism.

Gene Fowler's *I Married a Monster from Outer Space* (1958) resembles *Invasion of the Body Snatchers* in its paranoia about aliens who look just like us, but also indicates the extent to which anxieties over gender roles were central to the decade. In fact, in its focus on male aliens who have come to Earth to mate with human women in order to save their species from dying out, this film addresses a number of concerns surrounding the centrality of marriage and family to American life in the 1950s. It was unusual for the time in that the lone individual who warns of the alien invasion is a woman, who thereby finds herself aligned against Norrisville's masculine authorities, most of whom are already aliens. Nevertheless, the film, despite its apparent suggestion that you never know when your spouse might be an alien, or a communist, or something similarly sinister, ultimately makes a statement in favor of the conventional nuclear family. Indeed, the aliens are finally routed by a group of responsible males who have recently performed their familial duties by producing offspring.

In some cases, such as *The Blob* (1958), the alien invaders in 1950s SF films do not resemble humans but are quite clearly monstrous. Here, the line between alien invasion and monster films often becomes quite thin. Also notable are films in which the monsters were created by radiation, addressing the decade's fear of nuclear catastrophe. One of the earliest of these films was Sam Newfield's *Lost Continent* (1951), in which a team of scientists and soldiers goes to a remote Pacific island to try to retrieve some crucial data from an experimental rocket that has crashed there. Not only are the prehistoric monsters that inhabit the island apparently the result of the high levels of radiation on the island, but the team is also racing to retrieve the top-secret rocket before the Russians can get to it. The monsters of *The Beast from 20,000 Fathoms* (1953), *Them!* (1954), *It Came from Beneath the Sea* (1955), *Tarantula* (1955), *Attack of the Crab Monsters* (1957), and *Attack of the Giant Leeches* (1960) are all either produced or stirred to aggressive action as a result of nuclear testing or radiation experiments.

One of the most interesting sequences of monster films from the 1950s was the trilogy *The Creature from the Black Lagoon* (1954), *Revenge of the Creature* (1955), and *The Creature Walks among Us* (1956), the first two directed by Arnold, one of the most prolific directors of the decade. Clearly reptilian and thus seemingly just as foreign to the human species as the insects and spiders of *Them!* and *Tarantula*, the creature is nevertheless a biped, essentially humanoid in its overall shape, as is indicated by the tendency of the humans in the films to refer to it as the "Gill Man." It is, in fact, an evolutionary missing link between reptiles and mammals, discovered in the remote Third World setting of the Amazon. The basic primitive-critter-from-the-Third-World premise of the creature sequence also places those films in the tradition of *King Kong*. Moreover, the creature itself follows very much in the huge footsteps of Kong in that it is ultimately more sinned against than sinning, so sensitive to the cruel treatment meted out to it by its human captors that audiences could not avoid feeling a certain sympathy with it.

If the Gill Man is almost human, it is also the case that many films of the 1950s blurred the boundary between humans and monsters in general. In particular, unrestrained scientific research always threatens, in the science fiction films of the 1950s, to deprive humans of their humanity in one way or another. In Kurt Neumann's *The Fly* (1958), for example, well-meaning scientist André Delambre (David Hedison) develops a teleportation apparatus, then teleports himself as an experiment. Unfortunately, a common housefly accidentally gets into the machine with him and when they come out on the other end their atoms have become intermixed. Though a somewhat silly film, *The Fly* supplied one of the iconic moments of 1950s science fiction film in a scene near the end in which the fly with a human head, trapped in a spider web, cries out "Help me!" in a tiny voice—only to be smashed with a rock by Police Inspector Charas (Herbert Marshall). The film became a cult classic and was eventually remade into a much more interesting film by David Cronenberg in 1986. In Arnold's *The Incredible Shrinking Man* (1957), radioactive pollution causes protagonist Robert Scott Carey (Grant Williams) to shrink continually, until he literally fades out of existence. This film, however, stands out among the SF films of the decade in its focus on the psychic impact on Carey of his gradually decreasing size. At the other end of the size spectrum was Glenn Manning (Glenn Langan), the protagonist of Bert I. Gordon's *The Amazing Colossal Man* (1957), who grew to colossal size (but also experienced 1950s-style existential trauma), as did Nancy Fowler Archer (Allison Hayes) in Nathan Juran's cult classic *Attack of the 50 Foot Woman* (1958).

Roger Corman, whose trademark campy, low-budget films would make him an important force in American cinema, began his SF film career with the post-apocalypse film *The Day the World Ended* (1955), which also featured a humans-into-monsters motif. Like most of the films directed (or produced) by Corman, *The Day the World Ended*, however silly, has its interesting moments. In a graphic reminder of the horrors of radiation, the film suggests that radiation poisoning can transform humans into monstrous mutant cannibals. In the end, one man and one woman survive, preparing to restart the human race, Adam-and-Eve style. Hackneyed plot, stock characters, and cheesy-looking monster aside, *The Day the World Ended* is still notable as one of the few films of the 1950s that actually showed the effects of radiation on humans, however unrealistic its depiction of those effects might have been. It thus differs from the most popular post-holocaust film of the 1950s, Stanley Kramer's *On the Beach* (1959), which shows no such effects. Here, a global nuclear war has apparently destroyed all human life everywhere on earth, except Australia, which has been spared because of its remote location. Unfortunately, the clouds of deadly radiation that cover the rest of the globe are headed for Australia as well, so the Australians themselves have only a few months before what seems to be inevitable death. The film concentrates on the attempts of the various characters to cope with their impending doom. Indeed, while the how–could–we–be–so–stupid senselessness of the nuclear war looms in the margin as a message throughout, Kramer also seems to have wanted to make the film a sort of universal commentary on how human beings come to grips with the realization of their own certain mortality.

Other post-holocaust films of the long 1950s were even more indirect in their representation of nuclear war and its aftermath. For example, in Edward Bernds's *World without End* (1956), the nuclear holocaust is projected hundreds of years into the future, and the film itself is set hundreds of years after that, when radiation levels have essentially returned to normal. Pal's 1960 film adaptation of Wells's classic 1895 novel *The Time Machine* also focuses on a far-future post-apocalyptic world. At one point, Pal has his time traveler (who begins his journey on New Year's Eve, 1899) stop off in 1966, where he is nearly killed in a nuclear assault on London, placing the nuclear holocaust itself in the near future of the film. Then, he travels into the far future (he ends up in the year 802,701, just as in Wells's book), where the human race has evolved (actually, devolved) into two separate species. The passive Eloi live on the garden-like surface of the planet, enjoying lives of mindless leisure. They are completely indolent, illiterate, and incapable of creative thought or action. Meanwhile, the aggressive and animalistic Morlocks live beneath the surface, where they still have at least some operating technology. It turns out that they are raising the Eloi essentially as cattle, taking them, at full maturity, beneath the surface to be slaughtered for food. The time-traveling protagonist (Wells himself, played by Rod Taylor) stirs the Eloi to revolt, destroying the Morlocks. As the film ends, he returns to 802,701 to help lead the Eloi in their attempt to build a new world and regenerate their ability for creative action.

By 1962, science fiction films began to deal a bit more directly (and less optimistically) with nuclear holocaust, though a film such as Ray Milland's *Panic in Year Zero* still resembles *On the Beach* in its focus on the human drama of the survivors of the disaster, not the human tragedy of the victims. There are again no actual signs of nuclear destruction, though the film does depict certain negative consequences, such as the looting, rape, and murder that occur in the wake of a nuclear attack. By and large, however, *Panic in Year Zero* is essentially a survivalist adventure, in which the resourceful Baldwin family meet all challenges and ultimately survive the nuclear war unscathed.

The cycle of post-apocalyptic films that marked the 1950s came to a close in 1964 with Stanley Kubrick's *Dr. Strangelove, or How I Learned to Stop Worrying and Love the Bomb.* This highly effective absurdist farce brilliantly captures the insanity of the mutually-assured-destruction mentality of the arms race and may very well have made a significant contribution to the easing of the anti-Soviet hysteria that had marked the 1950s. On the other hand, by providing a sort of final word on this hysteria, the film also brought to a halt the Golden Age of SF film production that had marked the earlier decade, though it was certainly the case that numerous other aspects of American life in the 1960s created an environment in which SF film did not thrive. The decade's emphasis on "relevance," and the clear importance of such phenomena as the anti-war movement, the Civil Rights movement, and the women's movement, made SF film seem frivolous to many.

Some SF films of the 1960s, such as Roger Vadim's sex farce *Barbarella* (1968), attempted to appeal to the ethos of the decade in intentionally frivolous ways. On the other hand, films such as François Truffaut's *Fahrenheit 451* (1966) and Franklin Schaffner's **Planet of the Apes** (1968), the latter of which would become one of the signature films of American popular culture, attempted seriously to engage the issues of the day. Meanwhile, Kubrick's **2001: A Space Odyssey** (1968) strove more for artistic seriousness, bringing unprecedented critical attention and respect to the genre of science fiction film.

In the wake of the success of such films, SF cinema made something of a comeback in the early 1970s. A cycle of SF films in the first half of that decade continued to strive for relevance and artistic seriousness, usually with a dark tone that reflected the era's growing skepticism and increasing sense (driven by such events as the Watergate scandal) that the new and better world envisioned by the political movements of the 1960s didn't seem that different from the old and darker world that had preceded it. In 1971 alone, several films projected a dystopian future, including Kubrick's *A Clockwork Orange* (1971), Wise's *The Andromeda Strain* (1971), and Boris Sagal's *The Omega Man* (1971). Other dark visions of the future followed, including Douglas Trumbull's *Silent Running* (1972), Richard Fleischer's *Soylent Green* (1973), Norman Jewison's *Rollerball* (1975), and Michael Anderson's *Logan's Run* (1976). These dystopian visions of the future set a precedent for important films such as Michael Radford's 1984 adaptation of George Orwell's *Nineteen Eighty-Four* (1949), perhaps the most important of all dystopian novels. By contrast, Woody Allen's *Sleeper* (1973) was a farcical parody of the dystopian genre, while former Monty Python member Terry Gilliam followed in 1985 with *Brazil*, which also presented what was essentially a parodic dystopia, though one that continued to make many of the same serious satirical points for which the sub-genre is well known. Films such as John Carpenter's *They Live* (1988), Andrew Niccol's *Gattaca* (1997), Alex Proyas's *Dark City* (1998), and Kurt Wimmer's *Equilibrium* (2002) continued this tradition into the twenty-first century.

One of the most visually effective dystopian films of the early 1970s was *THX 1138* (1971), the first film by *Star Wars* creator George Lucas. Then, in 1977, **Star Wars** itself took science fiction film in whole new directions. *Star Wars* appealed greatly to the sensibilities of a late-1970s America that, after the disappointments of Vietnam and Watergate, was hungry for a rousing, old-fashioned adventure in which good triumphed over evil. Moreover, *Star Wars* defined "good" in traditional American terms in which individual conscience trumped obedience to official authority. In addition to its charming optimism (and its targeting of juvenile audiences, which was also a key to its commercial success), *Star Wars* was a technical triumph that wowed audiences with its unprecedented special effects. In many ways the most successful SF film of all time, *Star Wars* began one of the most important phenomena in the history of science fiction cinema. For one thing, *Star Wars* inspired no fewer than five sequels (so far), including *The Empire Strikes Back* (1980), *The Return of the Jedi* (1983), *The Phantom Menace* (1999), *Attack of the Clones* (2002), and *Revenge of the Sith* (2005). *Star Wars* also took the phenomenon of merchandising to unprecedented levels, as a seemingly limitless array of related books, toys, and various kinds of collectibles produced even more income than the blockbuster films themselves.

Star Wars appeared at the beginning of a several-year period that was the richest in the history of SF film, while its old-fashioned, nostalgic appeal also marked the beginning of a rightward turn in American politics that would lead to the election of Ronald Reagan to the presidency in 1980. Indeed, looking at the Cold War years of the 1950s, then at the late 1970s and early 1980s, some critics have concluded that science fiction film seems particularly to flourish in conservative times, perhaps because of their escapist appeal to audiences appalled by contemporary reality. Even seemingly "liberal" SF films of this period—such as Steven Spielberg's **Close Encounters of the Third Kind**, released the same year as *Star Wars*—contained a strong escapist component. Here, however, the escape is not from what many saw as the leftist drift of global politics but from the soul-destroying nature of life in modern capitalist America. The box-office success of the more adult-oriented *Close Encounters* verified the commercial potential of SF film that had been suggested by *Star Wars*, while demonstrating that such film could appeal to a variety of ages and ideologies. On the other hand, Spielberg's **E.T. the Extra-Terrestrial** (1982) turned back to a more youthful audience, aiming more at the sentiments than the intellects of its viewers—and with hugely successful commercial results.

Partly inspired by the recent commercial and technical success of *Star Wars*, Wise's *Star Trek: The Motion Picture* (1979) was an attempt to update the *Star Trek* franchise for a new generation of fans, building upon recent dramatic advances in special effects technology. With nearly three times the budget of *Star Wars* and with special effects wizards such as Douglas Trumbull and John Dykstra on board, *Star Trek* is indeed an impressive-looking film, even if it is not really groundbreaking in the way *Star Wars* had been. It is grander than *Star Wars* (and intended for a more adult audience), but the plot is a bit weak, and the interpersonal relationships (especially among Kirk, Spock, and McCoy) that had provided so much of the energy of the original television series never really quite come off in the film. Still, the built-in audience from fans of the series made the first *Star Trek* film a substantial commercial success, leading to the longest series of sequels in SF film history. For most fans (and critics), *Star Trek: The Wrath of Khan* (1982) was a great improvement over the first film, returning more to the spirit of the original series. *Star Trek III: The Search for Spock* (1984), *Star Trek IV: The Voyage Home* (1986), *Star Trek V: The Final*

Frontier (1989), and *Star Trek VI: The Undiscovered Country* (1991) found fans as well, though the aging original cast was beginning to creak a bit by the last film. *Star Trek: Generations* (1994) handed the mantle over to the younger cast of television's *Star Trek: The Next Generation*, who continued the film series in *Star Trek: First Contact* (1996), *Star Trek: Insurrection* (1998), and *Star Trek: Nemesis* (2002). Together, these films represented a rare example of SF crossover from television to film (the reverse is more common), though one might also mention Rob Bowman's *The X-Files: Fight the Future* (1998) as a fine SF thriller based on the popular *X-Files* television series. That series, incidentally, drew much of its inspiration from the same 1960s-style oppositional politics that had fueled the original *Star Trek*, except that *The X-Files* series and film were both heavily influenced by the greater cynicism and skepticism of the 1990s.

1979 also saw the beginning of another major SF film franchise with the release of Ridley Scott's **Alien** (1979). Mixing the genres of horror and science fiction with an unprecedented sophistication—and presenting film audiences with a dark, but detailed vision of future technology that they had never before seen—*Alien* was a genuine breakthrough in SF film, not the least because of the effectiveness of its presentation of a tough female heroine, the formidable Ellen Ripley (Sigourney Weaver). Meanwhile, the titular alien was one of the most effective-looking SF film monsters of all time, impacting the look of any number of future alien creatures in SF film. James Cameron's *Aliens* (1986) was in many ways an even greater success, while David Fincher's *Alien*³ (1992) and Jean-Pierre Jeunet's visually striking *Alien: Resurrection* (1997) were solid efforts as well, with the latter adding new touches of irony and humor to the sequence.

Blade Runner (1982), Scott's own follow-up to *Alien*, was perhaps the most visually influential SF film of all time, rivaled only by *2001: A Space Odyssey*. Together with *Alien* it ushered in the postmodern era in SF film, a phenomenon that has drawn substantial attention from academic critics, who have found science fiction film (and science fiction in general) to be among the paradigmatic cultural expressions of postmodernism. *Blade Runner* was distinctive for its blurring of the boundary between detective fiction and science fiction, both in its plot and its visual style, while its interrogation of the distinction between humans and the products of their technology addressed numerous contemporary concerns about human identity. Meanwhile, the dark, oddly indeterminate, multicultural city of the film provided some of the most striking visuals in the history of cinema.

Based on a novel by Philip K. Dick, *Blade Runner* also announced a new level of maturity for SF film in which the genre felt able to tackle some of the same kinds of serious issues that had long been the stuff of science fiction novels and stories. Dick's stories, for example, provided the basis for such successful later films as Paul Verhoeven's *Total Recall* (1990) and Steven Spielberg's *Minority Report* (2002). On the other hand, the adaptation of serious SF literature to film is a difficult project that has generally met with relatively little success. Even David Lynch's *Dune* (1984), which provides some striking examples of the director's unique visual style, was largely reviled by fans of the classic Frank Herbert novel—and ultimately rejected as a failure by Lynch himself.

The year 1984 also saw the release of James Cameron's **The Terminator**, another key example of postmodern SF cinema. This film made Arnold Schwarzenegger a star, made the SF action film a major genre, and triggered any number of imitations, including its own two sequels, *Terminator 2: Judgment Day* (1991) and *Terminator 3: Rise of the Machines* (2003). One of the films influenced by *The Terminator* was Paul Verhoeven's **Robocop** (1987), a work that included a substantial amount of social satire but also provided ironic commentary on the science fiction genre itself. Both *The Terminator* and *Robocop* showed a fear of the dehumanizing potential of technology that was typical of the Reagan years, in which nostalgic visions of a return to a simpler past were prominent in the popular American imagination. Indeed, by the end of the 1980s, SF film itself had begun to take a new kind of nostalgic turn enabled by the fact that the genre had become so well established that all subsequent works inevitably entered into dialogues with their predecessors. Even a film as innovative as Cameron's **The Abyss** (1989) had underwater adventure predecessors such as Disney's *20,000 Leagues under the Sea* (1954) and Irwin Allen's *Voyage to the Bottom of the Sea* (1961), while reaching back to *The Day the Earth Stood Still* in the way its alien visitors use their advanced technology to try to put a stop to the Cold War arms race.

The Abyss, however, went well beyond its undersea predecessors in the quality of its special effects, which among other things pioneered computer generated imaging (CGI), leading into a new era of special effects–driven films that relied heavily on such techniques. Though itself a thoughtful film, *The Abyss* in this sense continued the movement toward increased emphasis on special effects that had been a key factor in the evolution of SF film from *Star Wars* onward. This tendency reached new levels in the

1990s with the production of a number of big-budget, high-profit special-effects spectaculars, including Spielberg's *Jurassic Park* (1993), Roland Emmerich's *Stargate* (1994) and **Independence Day** (1996), and Verhoeven's *Starship Troopers* (1997).

The latter two films were indicative of other new trends in SF film in the 1990s as well. Featuring advanced aliens who warn Earth of the follies of the Cold War arms race, *The Abyss* joins *The Day the Earth Stood Still* as anti-war SF films that bracket the Cold War years. Meanwhile, the Cold War had provided background for any number of science fiction films during those years, suggesting that the genre might move in new directions after the end of the Cold War at the beginning of the 1990s. For example, cultural historians such as Richard Slotkin and Tom Engelhardt have argued that the national identity of the United States has from the beginning been defined in opposition to enemies who could be construed as savage and evil.★ With the loss of the Soviet bloc as such an enemy, American culture seemed to be seeking new enemies to be defeated, as reflected in such films as *Independence Day* and *Starship Troopers*.

The computer simulation of reality was the other major new trend in SF film in the 1990s. While the video-game inspired *Tron* had explored virtual reality as early as 1982, the growing importance of computers and the Internet as part of the texture of everyday life in America in the 1990s led to the production of a number of virtual-reality films, taking SF film in genuinely new directions. Such films included *Johnny Mnemonic* (Robert Longo, 1995), *Strange Days* (Kathryn Bigelow, 1995), and *Virtuosity* (Brett Leonard, 1995). Films such as Alex Proyas's *Dark City* (1998), David Cronenberg's *eXistenZ* (1999), and Josef Rusnak's *The Thirteenth Floor* (1999) took such films to a new level of sophistication in the late 1990s, though by far the most important of such films was Andy and Larry Wachowski's **The Matrix** (1999), which was followed by two sequels in 2003, *The Matrix Reloaded* and *The Matrix Revolutions*. Appropriately enough, virtual-reality films (especially the *Matrix* trilogy) were among those that made the best and most innovative use of computer generated imagery in the production of special effects.

★ See Tom Engelhardt, *The End of Victory Culture* (Basic Books, 1995) and Richard Slotkin, *Gunfighter Nation: The Myth of the Frontier in Twentieth-Century American Culture* (University of Oklahoma Press, 1988).

If such films were made possible by advances in computer technology in Hollywood, they were made popular by computer advances in the world at large, in which the growth of the Internet and video gaming spurred a popular fascination with the possibilities of virtual reality. This fascination also grew out of a growing sense of the unreality of reality itself. As described by cultural theorists such as Jean Baudrillard, life in the postmodern era (especially in the United States) has been characterized by a growing sense of unreality and by a collapse of the once seemingly-solid boundary between fiction and reality, between authenticity and simulation.

This phenomenon would only become more prominent in the early years of the twenty-first century, just as CGI became increasingly important in SF film. Computer simulation is especially important in a series of films in which the technology allowed comic books to come to life. Many of the latter were semi-SF superhero films such as Sam Raimi's hugely successful *Spider-Man* (2002) and *Spider-Man 2* (2004), though films such as Bryan Singer's *X-Men* (2000) and *X2* (2003) fit more comfortably into the category of science fiction. CGI was also ideal for the conversion of popular video games into film, among which Paul W. S. Anderson's *Resident Evil* (2002) and Alexander Witt's *Resident Evil: Apocalypse* (2004) were particularly interesting. Films such as Alex Proyas's *I, Robot* (2004) drew upon the classic science fiction of the past (in this case the robot stories of Isaac Asimov from the 1950s) as material for special-effects extravaganzas. Kerry Conran's *Sky Captain and the World of Tomorrow* (2004), like *Star Wars*, looked back to the 1930s, while introducing new CGI techniques in which virtually everything except the human actors themselves (and even one of the actors) was computer-generated.

The campy nostalgia of *Sky Captain* also placed it in the tradition of films that have played with science fiction convention, sometimes in highly ironic ways. Of course, the addition of an element of camp to SF films goes back at least to the 1950s, when campiness in the films of directors such as Corman sometimes compensated for budget shortages. Campiness in SF film reached its zenith in Jim Sharman's ultra-campy cult classic *The Rocky Horror Picture Show* (1975), a comic rock sendup of the horror genre that includes numerous science fictional elements as well. Indeed, the film's opening number is a 1950s-style rock homage to 1950s-style science fiction, including references to such classics as *The Day the Earth Stood Still* and *Forbidden Planet*, but treating the genre as the stuff of late night double features. The film's central figure, transvestite Frankensteinian mad scientist

Frank-N-Furter (Tim Curry, in an inimitable performance) turns out to be an alien emissary from the planet Transsexual in the galaxy Transylvania.

In the 1980s, films such as Lamont Johnson's *Spacehunter: Adventures in the Forbidden Zone* (1983) and John Carpenter's *They Live* (1988) employed campiness to beef up weak plots and low-budget looks, though the latter also uses its cheesy feel to cloak an extremely serious—and unusually radical—critique of consumer capitalist society. It was, however, in the 1990s that the addition of campy elements to basic science fiction plots became a major strategy of SF film. For example, the Sylvester Stallone vehicle *Demolition Man* (1993) is essentially an action film (with a futuristic setting) in which unconventional cop John Spartan (Stallone) battles against arch-criminal Simon Phoenix (Wesley Snipes). It is also a dystopian critique of conformism in its future society, though not a very inventive one. Most of its ideas are mere clichés, though it is an entertaining film, not only for its spectacular action scenes but also for its humor and for its clear understanding that it belongs to a genre that is always in danger of plunging into silliness. Snipes's campy performance as Phoenix is particularly effective, though Stallone has some good comic moments as well, especially in the (potentially prophetic) scene where Spartan, having been transported into the future from 1996, is stunned to learn that Arnold Schwarzenegger (in whose shadow Stallone remained as a SF action star in the 1990s) has served a term as President of the United States.

In a similar way, Stuart Gordon's *Space Truckers* (1996) seems awful on the surface, but is actually a perfectly effective medium-budget space opera that scores a number of satirical points about the excesses and abuses of capitalism. It also substitutes campiness for big-time special effects and draws considerable energy from the over-the-top performances of Dennis Hopper (as a working-class space pilot battling against his exploitative corporate bosses) and Charles Dance (as a former corporate scientist turned rapacious—but hilariously dysfunctional—cyborg). Rachel Talalay's *Tank Girl* (1995) lacks the satirical punch of *Space Truckers*, though its vision of an evil corporate entity that controls the water and power supply of a post-apocalyptic future world has some possibilities. The film proudly displays its origins in a British cult comic-strip, and what could have been a truly awful film has a number of highly entertaining moments thanks to the sheer excess of Lori Petty's performance as the ass-kicking title character and the very zaniness of concepts such as an underground guerrilla band of half-man, half-kangaroo freedom fighters.

In other cases, relatively high-quality, high-budget films used campy, comic elements to good effect, mixing farce with genuine drama in a highly postmodern fashion. Terry Gilliam's *Twelve Monkeys* (1995), for example, is a superb time-travel thriller in which scientists from a dystopian, post-apocalyptic future send agents back to the past to help them learn more about a deadly plague that wiped out most of the Earth's population in 1996 and 1997. In a twist on the usual time-travel plot, the film stipulates that the past cannot be changed, so that there is no question of averting the plague. Instead, the future scientists hope simply to gain information to help the human race to fight the plague in the future. The film features some of the same weirdly old-fashioned "steampunk" future technology that had marked the distinctive visual style of Gilliam's *Brazil*, supplemented by excellent lead performances from A-list actors such as Bruce Willis and Madeleine Stowe. However, some of its most memorable moments come from Brad Pitt's (Oscar-nominated) over-the-top performance as a mental patient and would-be terrorist—not to mention the whacked-out future scientists, who in many ways recall the strange hospital doctors of Dennis Potter's classic BBC miniseries *The Singing Detective* (1986).

In *Twelve Monkeys*, Willis plays a genuinely vulnerable man on the verge of complete mental collapse. In Luc Besson's *The Fifth Element* (1997), he returns to his more usual role of action hero (much in the vein of his portrayal of troubled cop John McClane in the *Die Hard* films). This time, Willis plays a retired military operative who returns to duty from his job as a cab driver (in a futuristic hovercraft cab) in order to save Earth from total destruction. Little else about this film is predictable, however, as it plays with a number of SF clichés. To save Earth, Willis's Korben Dallas must locate and retrieve the five "elements" of an ancient high-tech weapon, the fifth of which is one Leeloo (Milla Jovovich), a sort of goddess whose physical perfection becomes a running joke throughout the film. In fact, though the action plot is perfectly functional and though Willis and Jovovich perform well in the lead roles, the slightly excessive visuals and the outrageous performances of Gary Oldman as a key villain and Chris Tucker as a glitzy media personality lend the entire film a campy air. *The Fifth Element* is a virtual compendium of SF film elements, all of which seem just a bit out of kilter, making the film both a successful space opera and a running commentary on the entire genre of SF film.

Other SF film parodies have addressed specific individual predecessors in the genre. *Death Machine* (1995) is largely an extended riff on *Alien*, with clear echoes of *Robocop* and *The Terminator* tossed in for good measure. Actually, *Death Machine*, directed by Stephen Norrington (who would go on to direct the 1998 vampire action flick *Blade* and who had worked on the creature effects crew for *Aliens*), is a fairly effective (and rather dark) SF thriller. However, the performance by Brad Dourif as a crazed sex-maniac mad scientist adds a strong dose of campiness to the mix, as do the often light-hearted allusions to other films—including the use of character names such as "John Carpenter" and "Sam Raimi," nodding toward the well-known horror-film directors, as well as "Scott Ridley," "Weyland" and "Yutani," which wink at the director of *Alien*, as well as the evil Weyland-Yutani Corporation that figures so prominently in the *Alien* films. In a lighter vein, Mel Brooks's *Spaceballs* (1987) is a hilarious spoof of the *Star Wars* franchise (with side nods to a variety of other SF films), employing an unending stream of sight gags and puns that work only because Brooks can assume that his audience has extensive familiarity with the works being parodied. Dean Parisot's *Galaxy Quest* (1999) similarly relies largely on references to *Star Trek* (and the phenomenon of *Star Trek* fandom), though it also gains energy from the presence of SF superstar Sigourney Weaver as the actress who plays busty blonde space babe Lt. Tawny Madison (the antithesis of Weaver's Ripley in the *Alien* films) in a television series that bears a remarkable resemblance to the original *Star Trek*.

The frequent excesses of the alien-invasion genre have made it a prime target of SF films spoofs. For example, in Ivan Reitman's *Evolution* (2001), David Duchovny virtually resurrects his wise-cracking Fox Mulder character from television's alien-invasion drama *The X-Files*, complete with an evolving romantic tension between himself and a red-haired government scientist (played by Julianne Moore) who looks a bit like Gillian Anderson's Dana Sculley. Orlando Jones adds comic energy as well, and this tale of alien microbes that arrive on Earth inside a meteorite then evolve at breakneck pace into more complex (and more dangerous) alien invaders definitely has its moments. However, Duchovny and Moore's characters lack the on-screen chemistry of Mulder and Sculley, while Reitman's obvious attempts to draw upon his own *Ghost Busters* (1984) formula are unable to keep the film from going flat about halfway through.

Sometimes, as in the notorious case of Ed Wood's *Plan 9 from Outer Space* (1959), alien-invasion films had been so awful as to be unintentionally self-parodic. Tim Burton's *Ed Wood* (1994) drew upon Wood's campy reputation in a fine non-SF film, then Burton himself, in *Mars Attacks!* (1996) made what may be the finest—or at least funniest—comic science fiction film ever made. Like *Ed Wood*, *Mars Attacks!* plays on nostalgia for the notorious science fiction films of the 1950s and even earlier. The title, for example, looks back to the 1938 Flash Gordon serial *Mars Attacks the World*. Burton's film draws much of its plot and imagery from classic alien-invasion films such as *The Day the Earth Stood Still*, *War of the Worlds*, *Invaders from Mars*, and *Earth vs. the Flying Saucers*, though it functions particularly directly (and effectively) as a parody of *Independence Day*, a huge blockbuster that had been released only five months earlier. *Mars Attacks!* is one of Burton's campiest films and, as such, it tends to make the films on which it is based seem a bit ridiculous. At the same time, it remembers those films almost tenderly, seeming wistfully to wish for a time when it was possible to make such simple films in a (mostly) serious way. *Mars Attacks!* itself is anything but simple. A relatively big-budget production, it features an impressive all-star cast (headed by Jack Nicholson) and an array of expensive high-tech special effects, thus differing dramatically from the 1950s films to which it centrally refers. At the same time, the film also includes a number of cheap, old-fashioned effects, as when the Martians zap Earthlings with hokey ray guns that look like children's toys or when they approach Earth in an armada of 1950s-style flying saucers that one character describes as looking suspiciously like hub caps. In the end, the Earthlings triumph in a way that comments on the unlikely nature of such triumphs in many earlier films: it turns out that the Martians have no resistance to the music of Slim Whitman, the sound of which tends to make their brains explode.

Mars Attacks! may have a great deal of fun at the expense of science fiction, but it also draws much of its energy from the same phenomenon. The same might be said for another alien-invasion comedy, Barry Sonnenfeld's *Men in Black* (1997) and its sequel, *Men in Black II* (2002). The films have a great deal of fun with the whole tradition of UFO lore, positing the presence on Earth of a wide array of bizarre alien invaders and the existence of an extensive secret organization that battles against the invaders. Both films star Will Smith and Tommy Lee Jones as the titular men in black, agents of this secret organization. Partly building on Smith's momentum as a central figure in *Independence Day*, the *Men in Black* films together grossed more than a billion dollars worldwide, making them easily the most commercially successful comic SF films ever.

If comedies such as *Men in Black* and *Mars Attacks!* gained ironic energy from a certain nostalgia for earlier SF films, it is also the case that turn-of-the-century SF film seemed in general to look backward more than forward. For example, not only was the the second *Star Wars* trilogy (released in the years 1999–2005) a prequel to the first trilogy, but it clearly built on nostalgic memories of that first trilogy, which had appeared almost a generation earlier. The years 2000 and 2001, meanwhile, were marked by a series of Mars-exploration films, which clearly looked back to such predecessors as *Rocketship X–M, Conquest of Space* (1955), and *Robinson Crusoe on Mars* (1964), while renewing a fascination with the planet Mars that had marked science fiction since the time of Wells. Some of these films were quite ambitious. In *Mission to Mars* (2000) renowned director Brian de Palma produces a film that contains some genuine moments of wonder, while working hard to place itself within the tradition of SF film. Visually and thematically reminiscent of *2001: A Space Odyssey*, the film focuses on the first manned mission to Mars, and particularly on a rescue mission mounted when a strange phenomenon kills off most of the members of the first expedition. This second mission leads to the discovery of a repository left behind by an ancient, highly-advanced race that once lived on Mars. The virtual-reality archive left in this repository reveals that Mars had been rendered unlivable by a sudden catastrophe, apparently a strike by a large asteroid. The inhabitants of the planet were thus forced to evacuate to the stars, though they also sent a ship to Earth, seeding it with DNA and leading to the evolution of life on Earth. Humans are thus in a very real sense the cousins of the ancient inhabitants of Mars. In fact, one of the human astronauts, Jim McConnell (Gary Sinise), rather than return to Earth, decides to stay on the alien ship that is in the repository and that is about to take off, presumably to follow its makers to their new home in the stars.

In the somewhat confused *Red Planet* (Antony Hoffman, 2000), over-population and environmental degradation on Earth have forced humanity to look to Mars for a new home. However, a project to terraform the planet by sending algae there to grow and produce oxygen has gone awry and oxygen levels have started inexplicably to drop. The film begins as an American crew travels to Mars to investigate the situation. A solar flare damages their ship severely just as they reach Martian orbit, triggering a series of misfortunes (including the by-now-obligatory damaged robot that turns on the crew) in which three of the original five crew members are killed. However, they also find that oxygen levels on Mars have now risen dramatically, so much so that humans can breathe on the surface. Mission Commander Kate Bowman (Carrie-Anne Moss) and mechanical systems analyst Robby Gallagher (Val Kilmer) survive to return to Earth and report that the surface of Mars is now swarming with "nematodes" (of unknown origin and looking more like insects than nematodes) and that these creatures have eaten the original algae but are now themselves producing oxygen in large quantities. The implication is that the human project to colonize Mars has been saved, though it is not at all clear that the nematodes (who had already almost completely depleted their algae-food supply) can survive long-term (and co-exist with humans, whom they also find appetizing) on Mars. Meanwhile, there are vague attempts at quasi-religious hints that the nematodes may have a supernatural, even divine origin.

John Carpenter's *Ghosts of Mars* (2001) is more of a pure action flick. Here, a mining operation on a colonized and partly terraformed Mars uncovers the ghosts of an ancient Martian civilization. In an attempt to defend their planet from human occupation, the ghosts then possess the miners, turning them into crazed killers who then attack every human in sight. After a terrific, high-action battle, the ghosts seem to have been defeated by a contingent of Martian police, led by Melanie Ballard (Natasha Henstridge) and joined by notorious criminal James "Desolation" Williams (Ice Cube). Unfortunately, the ghosts reappear, attacking the major human settlement at Chryse. Ballard and Williams prepare to rush back into battle as the film ends.

One of the most obvious signs of a turn to nostalgia was the number of remakes of earlier SF films that appeared at the beginning of the new century, starting with John Harrison's Sci Fi Channel miniseries remake of *Dune* (2000), which sticks more closely to the original novel in plot but falls far short of the original Lynch film as a work of cinematic art. Tim Burton's 2001 remake of *Planet of the Apes*, on the other hand, is vastly superior to the original as a work of visual art, but falls far short of the original's intelligent social and political commentary. Simon Wells's *The Time Machine* (2002) lacks Burton's special visual flair but still makes good use in advances in special effects technology to spice up its look, though somehow lacking the energy and impact of the original. Big-time action director John McTiernan remade *Rollerball* in 2002 with even worse results, turning a film that at least attempted to critique our culture's fascination with violence into one that simply celebrated violence as spectacle.

Finally, in 2005, Spielberg directed a remake of *War of the Worlds* (2005), updating that classic with state-of-the-art big-budget special effects, while in many ways remaining more faithful to the original Wells novel than had the 1953 film adaptation.

With the notable exception of Spielberg's *War of the Worlds*, almost all of these remakes fall far short of the originals, suggesting that it takes more than impressive special effects to make an effective SF film. It also suggests that SF film may be at its best not when it looks back to the past (including its own past) but when it looks toward the future. Thus, while the new century does not appear to be off to a good start in the production of interesting science fiction cinema, recent examples such as the *Matrix* trilogy and Spielberg's excellent *Minority Report* suggest that SF film has far from exhausted itself and that we can probably anticipate a number of new breakthroughs in the coming years.

1

The Day the Earth Stood Still

Released 1951; Director Robert Wise

The Day the Earth Stood Still, a statement in favor of international peace and cooperation at the height of the Cold War, was a courageous film that can rightly claim to be the first truly important work of American science fiction cinema. A thoughtful, well-made, relatively high-budget film that was also a box-office success, *The Day the Earth Stood Still* demonstrated that science fiction on the screen need not be limited to low-budget B-films or films for children. In so doing, it paved the way for future developments in the genre, setting the stage for the explosion in SF films that marked the decade of the 1950s. At the same time, it also exerted a powerful influence on the look and sound of the SF films that followed it.

THE STORY: ALIENS, ROBOTS, AND THE COLD WAR

From the basic, and rather simple, short story on which it was based, screenwriter Edmund North and producer Julian Blaustein, eventually joined by director Robert Wise, crafted a sophisticated, message-laden film, keeping only a few basic elements of the original. In the film, an alien flying saucer lands on the mall in Washington, D.C. The Christ-like alien Klaatu (British actor Michael Rennie) and the giant robot Gort (portrayed by 7' 7" giant Lock Martin, inside an aluminum-painted rubber suit that makes him appear even taller) emerge from within, bearing a message of peace. They are, however, greeted with violence, triggering a chain of events through which the film broadcasts a stern warning against automatic hatred of anyone who appears to be different. The film also condemns the rapidly accelerating Cold War arms race and applauds the notion of international cooperation, with the recently formed United Nations looming in the background as the ultimate hero of the piece.

As the film opens, news of the approaching spacecraft is broadcast around the world. Police and military react swiftly, mobilizing to surround the ship (a classic flying saucer) as it lands amid several baseball diamonds near the Washington Monument. They train their weapons on the ship as Klaatu emerges to walk down a long ramp onto the grassy surface. Klaatu immediately announces that "We come to visit you in peace and with good will." However, when he attempts to offer a gift for the President of the United States, it is thought that he is pulling a weapon, and a trigger-happy soldier shoots him down. Gort responds by vaporizing the weapons in the vicinity (including tanks and artillery) with a ray that emanates from his visor. Luckily, Klaatu calls him off before any humans are harmed, but his demonstration of power adds a note of suspense to the film, a note that will be dramatically reinforced later when it becomes obvious that Gort has the power to destroy the entire planet if he so chooses.

Klaatu finally gets a chance to explain his peaceful intentions and is taken away to Walter Reed Army Hospital, where his wound heals overnight thanks to the use of a powerful salve that he happens to have in his possession. Examinations in the hospital show that he has an entirely normal human physiology, though he claims to be seventy-eight years old, yet looks thirty-five. He explains that, due to advanced medicine, life expectancy on his planet is one hundred thirty years. The unspoken implication is that the knowledge of Klaatu's people might be of great benefit to Earth, though the xenophobic Earthlings are so concerned with defending themselves that they never really pursue this possibility.

The identity of Klaatu's home planet is never revealed. "Let's just say we're neighbors," he says when asked, though he does say that he has come from 250,000,000 miles away, a distance that would place Klaatu's planet well within the solar system, but that does not correspond well to any given planet. (Media speculation on Klaatu's origins predictably focuses on Mars, which is generally much closer than the cited distance.) When the U.S. government sends a high-level envoy to invite Klaatu to an audience with the President, the alien visitor refuses, insisting that he wants to speak simultaneously to representatives from all of the nations of the

Earth. Told that the tense geopolitical situation makes such a meeting impossible, Klaatu announces that he is "impatient with stupidity," then slips out of the hospital to go among Earth's people in pursuit of his mission. Having stolen a suit from the hospital that still carries a laundry tag identifying it as the property of a Major Carpenter, Klaatu adopts the name "Carpenter," in one of the many motifs in the film that identify him as a sort of Christ figure. He then takes up residence in a boarding house, apparently so that he can live among the people of Earth and learn more about them and their ways.

The lodgers at the boarding house include Helen Benson (Patricia Neal) and her young son Bobby (Billy Gray), as well as a Mrs. Barley (played by Frances Bavier well before she became the beloved Aunt Bea of *The Andy Griffith Show*), who stands as a marker of Cold War anti-Soviet bigotry with her theory that the spacecraft and its inhabitants come not from outer space but from right here on Earth: "and you know where I mean," she archly explains. Carpenter/Klaatu strikes up a friendship with Helen and (especially) Bobby, who serves as his guide around Washington and eventually takes him to see Professor Jacob Barnhardt (Sam Jaffe), a renowned physicist. Klaatu convinces Barnhardt to convene an international meeting of the world's leading intellectuals, hoping to find in them a more receptive audience than he had found among politicians. As these luminaries gather in Washington, Klaatu gets their attention with a show of force, immobilizing all the Earth's electrical/mechanical devices for half an hour—and giving the film its title. However, hospitals, planes in flight, and similar critical cases are spared this demonstration, thus presumably assuring that the electrical stoppage will not lead to loss of human life—and confirming that Klaatu is a benign visitor.

Unfortunately, before the meeting of intellectuals can begin, Klaatu is hunted down by the authorities using information supplied by Helen's self-serving insurance salesman boyfriend, Tom Stevens (Hugh Marlowe). He is shot down and killed, his body locked in a cell. Before he dies, however, he gives Helen a message to take to Gort, knowing that Gort will otherwise automatically retaliate with mass destruction. Helen then averts this destruction with the now famous message: "Klaatu barada nicto," quoted in numerous science fiction works in the subsequent half century. In response to the message, Gort retrieves Klaatu's body and takes it back to the ship, where he uses advanced technology to resurrect his fallen leader, again echoing the story of the execution and resurrection of Christ.

The risen Klaatu, however, explains that his resuscitation is a matter of science, not miracles, and that he will now remain alive only for a limited time, absolute power over life and death being reserved to the "almighty Spirit."

The film reaches its didactic climax as Klaatu emerges from the spacecraft to issue his stern final warning to Barnhardt's gathered dignitaries. He explains that he represents an organization charged with keeping interplanetary peace, something it has managed to do by inventing a race of invincible robot supercops (of whom Gort is one), programming those robots to enforce peace by any means necessary. "It is no concern of ours how you run your own planet," he tells the gathering. "But if you threaten to extend your violence, this Earth of yours will be reduced to a burned-out cinder. Your choice is simple: join us and live in peace, or pursue your present course and face obliteration." He and Gort then reenter the ship and fly away into space, ending the film with this ultimatum hanging in the air.

THE SOURCES OF THE MOVIE

The Day the Earth Stood Still is very loosely based on a story by Harry Bates entitled "Farewell to the Master." In the story, a strange craft (apparently traveling through both space and time) suddenly materializes just outside the Smithsonian Museum in Washington, D.C. When the humanoid (but somehow god-like) alien Klaatu emerges from the craft accompanied by Gnut, a giant metallic robot, he is shot and killed by a sniper. Fearing retribution, the authorities order Klaatu buried in a hero's monument, then build a special new wing of the Smithsonian around the craft, which remains on the ground with Gnut standing motionless outside it. Most of the plot involves the efforts of protagonist Cliff Sutherland, a reporter-photographer, to get a scoop by hiding inside the museum at night to try to catch Gnut engaged in some sort of secret activity. He finds that Gnut does indeed move during the night, becoming involved in strange goings-on such as a battle with a large gorilla that emerges from the craft in the night. Eventually, it turns out that all of the activities are part of an effort to find a way to resurrect (or, actually, re-create) the fallen Klaatu, an effort that seems headed for success after a suggestion made by Cliff himself. Armed with the necessary information to make a perfect duplicate of Klaatu, Gnut prepares to leave. Just before his ship dematerializes, he reveals a final plot twist: he is not Klaatu's loyal servant, as Cliff has assumed all along. Instead, it is Gnut who is the master and Klaatu the servant.

SCIENCE FICTION WITH A MESSAGE: ALIENS AND THE ARMS RACE IN *THE DAY THE EARTH STOOD STILL*

The Day the Earth Stood Still was a landmark of American science fiction cinema. Unlike most of its immediate predecessors (and, for that matter, successors) it was a well-crafted A-list film, with strong support from a major studio (20th Century-Fox) and a top-notch director and cast. Moreover, in opposition to the notion that science fiction films were intended for pure entertainment (oriented especially toward children), *The Day the Earth Stood Still* was a film for thinking adults; serious and cerebral, it addressed crucial contemporary political issues in a mature and courageous way. At the same time, the film is highly entertaining, even to children, especially because of the important role played by young Bobby.

Due to the controversial antimilitaristic stance of *The Day the Earth Stood Still*, the U.S. Department of Defense refused to cooperate when asked to loan some equipment and soldiers from the army for use in the film. Instead, the makers of the film had to borrow equipment and manpower from the Virginia National Guard, which was reportedly happy to cooperate. Nevertheless, its message of international peace caused *The Day the Earth Stood Still* to be awarded a Golden Globe Award for "Best Film Promoting International Understanding." Then again, the Golden Globes are given out by the members of the Hollywood Foreign Press Association, an organization that might have been expected to support international peace and oppose American militarism. Meanwhile, the film's political stance may also have contributed to the fact that the film received no Academy Award nominations, though the science fiction genre of *The Day the Earth Stood Still* might have precluded it from extensive consideration by the Academy in any case. Granted, the politically orthodox *Destination Moon* had won an Oscar for Special Effects and had been nominated for another for Best Art Direction a year earlier. However, *The Day the Earth Stood Still* is an elegantly simple black-and-white film that actually includes very little in the way of razzle-dazzle special effects or space-age stage settings. The most impressive demonstration of superior alien technology occurs in the scene in which the earth's machinery is brought to a halt, a phenomenon that requires no special effects at all—just a few shots of stalled machines. Similarly, Klaatu, the principal alien, appears entirely human, so that his representation does not involve special effects. Gort, portrayed by a man in a rubber suit, requires little in the way of special effects either, though the scenes in which a ray emanates from his eyes (created simply by adding animation to the filmed sequences), destroying Earthly weaponry (and, in one case, two Earthling soldiers) are, in fact, the most obvious examples of special effects in the film. The other instance of special effects concerns the ship itself, though those effects are minimized by the fact that the ship spends most of its time sitting motionless on the ground. While in that position it is primarily represented by a full-scale model made mostly of wood, though some scenes (especially those shot from above the ship) employed a smaller scale model. The design of the ship is rather minimalist, a simple, smooth flying saucer with no lights, bells, or whistles, though the hatch that opens to extend a long entry ramp, then completely disappears when closed, is a good touch. The simple, clean design of the interior of the ship was quite effective as well, providing a model for any number of future cinematic alien interiors. Finally, the most impressive special effect in the film may be the initial landing of this craft (also achieved via animation), which shows it flying past various Washington landmarks, then coming to rest among the baseball diamonds, complete with the shadow that it seems to cast on the ground as it lands.

Director Robert Wise had been the film editor on such illustrious works as Orson Welles's *Citizen Kane* (1941) and *The Magnificent Ambersons* (1942). Wise had also started his career as a director on the latter film, though with a somewhat inauspicious debut: at the behest of RKO Radio Pictures and with Welles away in South America on another project, Wise directed a new ending sequence for *Ambersons* (the one that was ultimately released in theaters) that many critics have felt undermines the entire film. Nevertheless, by the time of *The Day the Earth Stood Still*, Wise had already begun to show genuine talents as the director of a number of competent Westerns and as the director of at least one film, *The Set-Up* (1949), that is now considered a film noir classic and one of the best boxing dramas ever made. He had also directed *The Body Snatcher* (1945), a now much-admired horror film that featured legends Boris Karloff and Bela Lugosi. Wise would go on to direct a number of classics, including *West Side Story* (1961) and *The Sound of Music* (1965). He would also later expand his science fiction credentials as the director of *The Andromeda Strain* (1971) and *Star Trek: The Motion Picture* (1979).

The Day the Earth Stood Still clearly shows the mark of its director's hand. For one thing, it is extremely competently made: well photographed and well edited. Stock shots, process shots, and location shots of Washington, D.C. (shot by a second unit directed by Bert Leeds) are seamlessly merged with the rest of the film (shot in the 20th Century-Fox studios) to create an effective sense that the action occurs in the U.S. capitol, even though the cast members and the main crew never left California during the seven weeks of shooting. The entire film is shot in black and white (Wise at that time had yet to make a color film), and that medium is used to good atmospheric effect. In particular, low-key lighting and dramatic shadows are used to build tension and to create a sense of suspense, much in the mode of the German expressionist predecessors of American science fiction film but also in the manner of American film noir, a genre to which Wise made important contributions in such films as *The Set-Up*, *The House on Telegraph Hill* (1951), and *Somebody Up There Likes Me* (1956). For example, when Carpenter/Klaatu first appears at the boarding house, the boarders sit in a dimly lit room watching television reports concerning the alien visitor that urge citizens to be on the lookout, though they acknowledge that available photographs are of little help for identification purposes because they are mostly silhouettes that do not show Klaatu's face. When the boarders look up upon Carpenter's entrance, already jittery from the news reports, they see only a dark, ominous-looking, back-lit silhouette that immediately links the newcomer to the television reports. As Carpenter steps into the light, the boarders are ironically reassured, concluding that his calm human visage could not be that of an invader from outer space.

One of the most striking technical aspects of *The Day the Earth Stood Still* is the music, based on Bernard Herrmann's outstanding score, which smoothly merges with the noirish look of the film to further enhance the atmosphere of strangeness and potential peril. Herrmann's impressive screen credentials include classics such as *Citizen Kane* and many of the films of Alfred Hitchcock and Brian De Palma. He also worked extensively in science fiction, supplying the scores for such films as *Journey to the Center of the Earth* (1959), *Mysterious Island* (1961), and *Fahrenheit 451* (1966), as well as several episodes of *The Twilight Zone*. The music of *The Day the Earth Stood Still* has been so widely imitated that it now sounds almost clichéd. It is important to realize, however, that, at the time, the music marked a genuine breakthrough in science fiction cinema. Herrmann himself stated that this score was the most innovative and experimental film music he ever wrote. It features a number of electronic-sounding effects produced through the creative use of instruments such as harps, electric violins, and a mixed brass section.★ However, the most important instruments in this regard were probably the two theremins that were used to produce particularly eerie and otherworldly background music for the opening titles and for key sequences during the film, especially those involving Gort. The theremin, then very seldom used, is an electronic instrument (invented by the Russian engineer Léon Theremin, subject of the 1994 documentary film *Theremin: An Electronic Odyssey*) that produces a tone with two high-frequency oscillators, the pitch of which is produced by the movement of the player's hands over the instrument's electronic circuits—much in the way the controls of the spaceship in *The Day the Earth Stood Still* are operated by the movement of Klaatu's hands over them. The theremin would go on to be used in popular music such as the Beach Boys' 1967 hit "Good Vibrations," though its greatest importance to popular music probably came from the inspirational effect it had on Robert Moog in the development of his synthesizer, which dramatically changed popular music. The theremin itself had been used earlier to create an eerie atmosphere in such noir films as Hitchcock's *Spellbound* and Billy Wilder's *The Lost Weekend* (both 1945, both with music by Miklós Rózsa), but it has seen its widest use in science fiction film, where it quickly became a staple.

However, despite its highly influential look and sound, *The Day the Earth Stood Still* is probably best remembered today not for its technical accomplishments but for its advocacy of peace and international cooperation, an advocacy made all the more striking by the fact that the film appeared during the Korean War and thus at the very height of international Cold War tensions. Of course, the film also appeared in the midst of a rising tide of UFO sightings and popular concern over the possibility that alien spacecraft, generally in the form of "flying saucers," were visiting earth, possibly with hostile intentions. This concern had been particularly spurred by the widely publicized rumors of the crash of a UFO near Roswell, New Mexico, in 1947.

★ Herrmann's comments are contained in an interview with Ted Gilling printed in the journal *Sight and Sound* (vol. 41, Winter 1971/72).

The Day the Earth Stood Still, with its vision of benevolent aliens who have come to Earth on a mission of peace (only to be greeted with suspicion and violence), thus went against the grain of both anti-Soviet and anti-alien hysteria. Of course, these two forms of hysteria are informed by a similar xenophobia, and it is no accident that the height of fears over invasion by extraterrestrials occurred precisely when the American public had been primed by official propaganda to expect an unprovoked attack by the sinister forces of communism. Indeed, the numerous alien invasion films and novels produced during the 1950s are quite widely regarded as allegorical responses to the fear of Soviet invasion on the part of American audiences during that period.★

Thus, if the paranoid treatment of the possibility of alien invasion in many SF films of the 1950s can be taken as an allegorical representation (and sometimes even endorsement) of the fear of communist invasion or subversion, the critique of xenophobia in *The Day the Earth Stood Still* can be taken as a sort of counter-allegory—as a critical commentary on the anti-communist hysteria that was then sweeping the United States. This aspect of the film includes an extensive interrogation of the role of the media in producing and stimulating mass hysteria by sensationalizing accounts of the dangers posed to Earth by the alien visitors. Indeed, from its very opening scenes, in which radio commentators in India, France, Britain, and the United States are seen announcing the approach of the spacecraft even before it lands, the film acknowledges the crucial role played by the media in determining the popular perception of events in the world.

The then-new medium of television is prominent among the media represented in *The Day the Earth Stood Still*, marking still another way in which the film was a landmark in American cultural history. Indeed, film historian Vivian Sobchack has argued in her book *Screening Space: The American Science Fiction Film* that the depiction of television broadcasts in the film may have "set the standard for all traditional film telecasts and news montages to follow." Radio, however, remains the dominant medium in *The Day the Earth Stood Still*—and the one most given to lurid accounts of the alien threat. In one scene, a radio interviewer questions the crowd gathered on the mall around the spacecraft, clearly leading those

---

★ See, for example, my discussion of this phenomenon in my book *Monsters, Mushroom Clouds, and the Cold War* (Greenwood Press, 2001)

interviewed to express fear and anxiety. When Klaatu (in the guise of Carpenter) is himself questioned, he begins to make a statement against fear and in favor of understanding; the interviewer abruptly cuts him off and moves on, hoping for more interesting responses. The most sensational account of all occurs in a radio broadcast made by nationally-known radio commentator Gabriel Heatter, who appeared as himself in the film despite the fact that it portrays him and similar commentators in a very negative light. Heatter, urging his audiences to aid in the hunt for Klaatu, announces in a mood of near hysteria that "the monster must be found. He must be tracked down like a wild animal; he must be destroyed."

Given what we already know about Klaatu, Heatter's frenzied entreaty comes off as particularly wrongheaded, and the similarity between his rhetoric and the rhetoric that was being used daily to whip up anti-communist hysteria among the American populace gives this scene a much broader significance. *The Day the Earth Stood Still* clearly suggests that Earth's violent response to the appearance of aliens on the planet is immature and reprehensible, and it is certainly the case that the construction of the film invites audiences to identify with Klaatu and to side against the military forces that are mobilized against him. Audience sympathy with Klaatu is reinforced by the numerous parallels between the alien visitor and Christ, which also serve to suggest that the wave of militarism sweeping Cold War America at the time of the film was inconsistent with America's claim to be a nation informed by Christian principles.

Of course, the antimilitaristic message of *The Day the Earth Stood Still* is quite clear even without these Christian parallels. Indeed, Wise himself has stated that he was entirely unaware of these parallels until they were brought to his attention after the film had been completed. On the other hand, these parallels are so obvious that Wise's claim seems a bit difficult to believe; the film even film ran afoul of 20th Century-Fox's censors over the scene in which Klaatu arises from the dead, a scene that the censors felt made the parallel between Klaatu and Christ all too clear, causing them to insist on the insertion of the line concerning the limited nature of Klaatu's resurrection.

In any case, the most important message of the film concerns its plea for international cooperation rather than nationalist competition, accompanied by its rejection of the kind of xenophobic hysteria that informed contemporary American anti-communism. In his book *Seeing Is Believing: How Hollywood Taught Us to Stop Worrying and Love the Fifties*, film critic Peter Biskind thus describes *The Day the Earth Stood Still* as "left-wing sci-fi" (150). Moreover, he suggests that the film was able to make its left-wing statements precisely because it was science fiction, a genre that provided "freedom for uncompromising left-wing statement" because it was "so thoroughly removed from reality" (159). Then again, one might also argue that the film was able to get away with its controversial political stance partly because it was made by 20th Century-Fox (one of the more conservative of the major studios) and endorsed by studio head Zanuck, a Republican who had attained the rank of lieutenant colonel as the head of a documentary film unit in World War II.

The Day the Earth Stood Still is certainly critical of the anti-communist fervor that was so widespread in the United States at the beginning of the 1950s, and there is no doubt that the film's politics are further to the left than those of many alien-invasion films of the decade. On the other hand, the political stance of the film is probably not nearly as far to the left as Biskind seems to indicate. The film is in no way pro-Soviet or pro-communist but is simply an anti-militarist denunciation of the folly of the Cold War arms race. More accurate as an assessment of the film's politics is James Shaw's description of it (published in the journal *Creative Screenwriting* in 1998 and based on interviews with several of the film's principals, including Wise, North, and Blaustein), as a "rational response to the McCarthy era," arising from the politics of the New Deal. More than anything, the film is an endorsement of the then relatively new United Nations and a plea to give the United Nations more power to enforce international peace. The interplanetary organization represented by Klaatu is clearly a sort of galactic United Nations, and the film's endorsement of the power granted this organization to keep peace by any means necessary can be taken as a powerful statement in favor of such intervention on earth by our own United Nations.

In his book *Rational Fears: American Horror in the 1950s*, Mark Jancovich argues that *The Day the Earth Stood Still* is not left-wing at all. Instead, he believes the film's positive figuration of Klaatu's interventionism makes it an intensely authoritarian work that supports and defends "the scientific-technical rationality of the American state" (42). This reading probably goes too far in the context of 1951. However, from the perspective of the early twenty-first century, when the United States openly accepted the role of global policeman, the film's acceptance of interventionism seems almost prescient. There is very little difference between Klaatu's warning that Earth will face dire consequences if it develops weapons of mass destruction that pose a threat to other planets and the 2003 U.S. invasion of Iraq precisely on the premise that Iraqi aggression was a threat to America and other nations.

In any case, *The Day the Earth Stood Still* is politically charged in ways that go beyond its obvious opposition to the Cold War arms race. For one thing, the film takes a number of passing satirical swipes at various aspects of American society. For example, the boarder Mr. Barley (John Brown) is not only just as thick-skulled as his wife, but he is also apparently a Republican, thus linking the narrow-mindedness of both Barleys to that party. Told that the people in government (then the Truman administration) will handle the crisis caused by the arrival of the alien visitors, Barley scoffs, "They're not people—they're Democrats." In addition, it is no accident that the Judas figure, Tom Stevens, is an insurance salesman; his negative depiction as a venal, opportunistic cad takes a jab not only at that particular profession but at American business in general. Stevens is more than willing to sell out Klaatu, even though he has been assured of the alien's good intentions. After all, he reasons, if he can become known as the man responsible for the capture of the alien invader, it might open up all sorts of opportunities for him. Warned by Helen that his intervention might lead to dire consequences for the rest of the world, he simply announces, "I don't care about the rest of the world."

One of the most important political statements in *The Day the Earth Stood Still* involves its extremely positive representation of Professor Barnhardt as a figure of courage, wisdom, and compassion. Barnhardt serves as a transparent stand-in for Albert Einstein, a controversial figure during the Cold War: not only was he both a foreigner and a Jew (World War II had discredited, but had not eliminated, American anti-Semitism), but he was also an international celebrity who openly used his prominence to agitate for peace. Meanwhile, the casting of Jaffe in the role made Barnhardt even more controversial as a character. The anti-communist purges that swept Hollywood in the late 1940s and early 1950s were at their very height, and many actors, directors, and screenwriters had been blacklisted for suspected communist sympathies. Jaffe was among those who were suspected of having such sympathies, causing the film's casting director to ask that he be replaced in the role of Barnhardt for that reason. Backed by Zanuck, producer Blaustein insisted on keeping Jaffe in the role, though it would be his last appearance in an American film for seven years.

Science in general had a complex and contradictory reputation in 1950s America. On the one hand, science was widely endorsed as a key to progress and prosperity and to continuing improvements in a variety of technologies, including communication, transportation, and even household appliances. On the other hand, science had also led to the development of atomic weapons that threatened to destroy human civilization. Further, science (especially atomic physics) had become so complex that ordinary people increasingly saw it as beyond their understanding. Scientists seemed engaged in unknown and mysterious activities, a fact that immediately made them objects of suspicion in the paranoid 1950s. To make matters worse, many of the leading scientists who had been involved in the Manhattan Project and who remained crucially involved in key American research projects were foreigners, which again made them objects of xenophobic scrutiny.

In addition to the specific link between Barnhardt and Einstein, *The Day the Earth Stood Still* represents intellectuals in general as positive figures who can potentially provide better leadership toward global peace than can the world's political leaders. Klaatu himself is clearly an intellectual of sorts. Thoughtful and wise, he is well enough versed in mathematics and science to be able to help Barnhardt complete a thorny calculation that had previously proved intractable.

Of course, the fact that Klaatu's facility with mathematics goes beyond even that of Barnhardt (portrayed as Earth's greatest scientist) is one of the film's many reminders of the superiority of his civilization to that of Earth. The vast superiority of the medical knowledge of Klaatu's people (which makes the doctors at Walter Reed feel like primitive witch doctors) is another such example. Thus, the final lesson of the film is one of humility, suggesting that the people of Earth have a long way to go before they are sufficiently advanced to be able to deal with Klaatu's people on equal terms. Indeed, from the lofty perspective of Klaatu, the various political and other disagreements that seemed of such cosmic importance to humans in 1951 are downright silly, the squabbles of ill-behaved children.

SERIOUS SCIENCE FICTION: THE LEGACY OF *THE DAY THE EARTH STOOD STILL*

The Day the Earth Stood Still is an effective counterweight to any number of paranoid alien invasion films of the 1950s. It also influenced several other films that represented aliens in a positive light. One of the most effective of these is Jack Arnold's *It Came From Outer Space* (1953), in which an alien craft crashes on Earth due to mechanical difficulties, but in which the aliens otherwise have no interest in Earth or Earthlings (who, of course, greet them with suspicion and violence). Also worth a look is *The Man from Planet X* (1951), directed by the semi-legendary Edgar G. Ulmer, famous for his ability to turn ultra-low-budget films—such as *The Black Cat* (1934) and *Detour* (1945)—into minor classics. Here, a perfectly harmless alien is greeted with hostility by paranoid Earthlings and eventually blown to bits by the British military. Ultimately, of course, the suggestion in *The Day the Earth Stood Still* that the Cold War is just plain silly leads directly to Stanley Kubrick's *Dr. Strangelove, or, How I Learned to Stop Worrying and Love the Bomb* (1964), the film that virtually finished off Cold War paranoia as a film motif by demonstrating the utter folly and absurdity of the arms race. However, in Kubrick's film a nuclear holocaust occurs precisely because the most deadly of Earth's weaponry has been handed over to the control of machines, a move that *The Day the Earth Stood Still* seems to believe might be a good idea.

The Day the Earth Stood Still suggests that we might be better off were we to allow superior robots like Gort to have dominion over us. This suggestion in turn echoes the one made in Isaac Asimov's story collection *I, Robot* (1950) that the Earth might be well served if vastly sophisticated thinking machines ruled the planet. However, a very different take on this kind of suggestion can be found in Joseph Sargent's *Colossus: The Forbin Project* (1970). Perhaps building on the antiauthoritarian 1960s, this film views planetary rule by an advanced computer as a horrifying tyranny, despite the fact that the computer seems devoted to the overall good of humanity and to solving various problems (such as wars, famines, and plagues) that humans have proved unable to solve for themselves. Paul Verhoeven's later *Robocop* (1987) splits the difference. Automated law enforcement is depicted in the film as an unscrupulous ploy on the part of a giant corporation, which cares very much about profit and not at all about people. However, the title "robot" (actually a cyborg) is a positive figure, if only because he is part human and retains many of his human characteristics, thus setting him apart from other automated products of the corporation. Similarly, the cyborg played by Arnold Schwarzenegger in the later *Terminator* films is a positive figure because he sides with humanity against machines, though his character in James Cameron's original *Terminator* film (1984) exemplified the vision in that series of computerized machines with no use for human beings at all.

The Day the Earth Stood Still also anticipates a spate of films in the late 1970s and early 1980s that presented aliens in a positive light, including Steven Spielberg's *Close Encounters of the Third Kind* (1977), *E.T. the Extra-Terrestrial* (1982), and John Carpenter's *Starman* (1984). These films then lead directly to James Cameron's *The Abyss* (1989), in which vastly superior aliens once again issue an ultimatum that forces the opposed forces of the Cold War to bring their rivalry to an end.

2

Forbidden Planet

Released 1956; Director Fred McLeod Wilcox

Forbidden Planet is a virtual compendium of pulp science fiction themes from the 1950s. It features space travel, an alien planet, a mad scientist, numerous high-tech devices (including a remarkable robot), and an advanced (but extinct) alien race. Filmed in brilliant color and widescreen Cinemascope, it provides some of the most memorable science fiction images of the decade, from the dazzling green sky of the planet Altair IV; to the marvelous high-tech residence of the mad scientist Morbius; to the lovable, but formidable, Robby the Robot. In addition, the film's ambivalence about technology nicely captures the combination of fascination and anxiety with which American society regarded the scientific and technological advances of the time. However, based partly on William Shakespeare's *The Tempest*, the film has literary aspirations that set it apart from most of the run-of-the-mill SF films of its era.

THE STORY: SHAKESPEARE IN SPACE

Forbidden Planet begins with a brief future history of space exploration, informing us that the conquest of space has begun with the first manned mission to the moon in the last decade of the twenty-first century. This history places the action of the film in the twenty-third century, when the discovery of "hyper-drive" technology has allowed interstellar travel, which has clearly by the time of the action of the film become routine. In this case, the United Planets cruiser C57D (a basic flying saucer design), commanded by Commander John J. Adams (Leslie Nielsen), is on a relief mission to the planet Altair IV, where another expedition (aboard the spaceship Bellerophon) landed twenty years earlier, never to be heard from again. As the new ship approaches the planet, Dr. Edward Morbius (Walter Pidgeon), a philologist attached to the earlier expedition, greets them by radio and urges them to turn back, assuring them that he needs no relief and that he cannot answer for their safety if they land on the planet.

Their curiosity piqued, they land anyway, and are immediately greeted by the remarkable Robby the Robot, who turns out to have the principal responsibility for carrying out the bidding of Morbius, his creator—just as Ariel does Prospero's bidding in *The Tempest*. The robot takes Adams, Lt. "Doc" Ostrow (the ship's doctor, played by Warren Stevens), and Lt. Jerry Farman (the ship's first officer, played by Jack Kelly) aboard his high-speed vehicle to Morbius's residence. Morbius then introduces the visitors to the considerable capabilities of Robby (a creation he nevertheless dismisses as "child's play") and the other accoutrements of his high-tech home. He describes these technological wonders as "parlor magic," providing one of many links between himself and Shakespeare's Prospero. Though he is by training a specialist in languages, not science, he also links himself to the SF tradition of the mad scientist when he assures his visitors that, because of safeguards built into the robot's programming, he could not convince Robby to harm them even if he were "the mad scientist of the taped thrillers."

Morbius explains that, within the first year of their arrival on the planet, all members of the Bellerophon expedition except himself and his wife were killed by some sort of strange "force" indigenous to the planet. Many of them were torn limb from limb, though the last three of them were killed when the Bellerophon was vaporized when it attempted to lift off to return to Earth. Soon afterward, Morbius's wife died of "natural causes." However, Morbius is now accompanied by his beautiful nineteen-year-old daughter, Altaira (generally referred to in the film as Alta, played by Anne Francis), who is most impressed when she meets the visitors, the only men other than her father she has ever seen. In this, she echoes Prospero's daughter Miranda, who is much impressed by the new arrivals on their island. Morbius, on the other hand, seems anxious to get rid of the newcomers, presumably because he fears that they will meet the same sad fate as the other members of the crew of the Bellerophon. Adams, however, decides that he must contact Earth (not an easy matter at these interstellar distances) for instructions on how to proceed.

Robby helps the visitors as they construct a transmitter with which to contact Earth, meanwhile meeting up with the ship's cook (Earl Holliman), a comic character for whom he fabricates a large supply of bourbon in the kind of comic subplot often found in science fiction films (and World War II films, for that matter). In this case, however, the subplot inevitably recalls the comic subplot of *The Tempest*, in which the lowly Trinculo and Stephano are also much given to drink. Over Morbius's objections, Alta continues to fraternize with the newcomers, her scanty costumes stirring the hormones of the young all-male crew, who haven't seen a woman for over a year while in space. Farman, a notorious womanizer, undertakes to teach the totally naïve girl the joys of sex, but is interrupted by an angry Adams, who orders him to stay away from her.

As work proceeds on the transmitter, something or someone sneaks into the compound set up around cruiser C57D and sabotages some crucial components. Informed of the sabotage, Morbius explains that strange things happen on this planet. He tells Adams and Ostrow about the mysterious Krel, an ancient advanced race that had formerly inhabited the planet but that was suddenly wiped out 200,000 years earlier. It is, in fact, leftover Krel technology that has allowed Morbius to build Robby and the other devices in his futuristic house. He takes Adams and Ostrow into a secret laboratory, where he works to decipher Krel texts and thus recover their astounding knowledge.

Morbius shows the visitors some of the leftover Krel devices. He also explains that, in the final days before their annihilation, the Krel were devoting all of their resources to a new project designed to boost their already considerable brain power to the point of freeing them from dependence on other physical technology by enabling them to produce all they needed by the sheer power of their minds. He takes Adams and Ostrow for a tour of the vast underground complex of machinery that the Krels had developed in conjunction with this final project, though Morbius himself remains unaware of the exact function of this complex.

Meanwhile, back at the compound, an invisible creature breaks through the electronic barriers that have been set up to prevent further sabotage. Chief Engineer Quinn (Richard Anderson) is killed in this second attack, after which Morbius again warns the visitors that if they remain on the planet, they will all be killed, recapitulating the fate of the crew of the

Bellerophon. Adams takes this warning as a threat and begins to suspect that Morbius is involved in the attacks on his compound. Adams and his men beef up security and manage to repel a third attack, though not before three more crewmen, including Farman, are killed.

Still suspicious that Morbius is involved, Adams and Ostrow go back to Morbius's lab to investigate. Ostrow hooks himself up to the Krel mind boosting device and thereby learns that, in addition to materializing conscious mental projections, it can also project subconscious desires, thus unleashing "monsters from the id." Ostrow dies as a result of mental overload from using the machine but is able to relay his discovery to Adams before he dies. Soon Adams realizes that the creature attacking the visitors is precisely one of these id monsters, a product of Morbius's subconscious mind brought into physical being by Krel technology, though Morbius himself had been unaware of this fact. The Krel, he now realizes, must have been destroyed by the monstrous power unleashed from the savage forces at work in their own subconscious minds. "The beast," muses Morbius in a moment of sudden understanding, "the mindless primitive—even the Krel must have evolved from that beginning."

At this point, the monster that had been attacking the compound approaches Morbius's house and begins to break through the nearly impenetrable barriers that surround it. Morbius realizes that Alta, having pledged her love to Adams and decided to return to Earth with him (just as Miranda decides to marry Prince Ferdinand in *The Tempest*), is no longer immune to the monster. "We're all part monsters in our subconscious," says Adams, explaining that Morbius unconsciously sent his id-monster out to kill the crew members of the Bellerophon after they had voted to return to Earth. As the monster breaks through the barrier guarding the secret laboratory, where they have taken refuge, Morbius confronts it and manages to make it go away. He then dies, but not before activating an unstoppable chain reaction that will destroy the Krel machinery and the entire planet.

Adams and his remaining crew, along with Alta and Robby, take off in their ship and watch the destruction of the planet from outer space. Robby, a quick learner, now serves as the ship's pilot, replacing the dead Farman. Attempting to comfort Alta, Adams muses that humans, in a million years or so, will have reached the point earlier reached by the Krel, when her father's experience will serve as a warning that "we are not God," thus preventing a repetition of the Krel disaster.

THE SOURCES OF THE MOVIE

Forbidden Planet is based on an original story for the screen by Irving Block and Allen Adler, developed into a screenplay by Cyril Hume. However, the story itself has an important source in *The Tempest*, in which a group of Europeans are shipwrecked on a remote island inhabited by the magician Prospero, his innocent daughter Miranda, and his two servants, Ariel (an obedient but mischievous spirit with considerable powers of his own) and Caliban (a recalcitrant, primitive brute, enslaved against his will). This link gives the film (which otherwise seems to have its sources in the kinds of stories found in pulp science fiction magazines in the 1940s and 1950s) a certain literary respectability. Still, the background of *Forbidden Planet* in the popular science fiction that came before it is important as well, perhaps most obviously in the way Robby the Robot's fundamental programming forbids him from harming a human being, much as in the famed "First Law of Robotics" that informs Isaac Asimov's robot stories and novels of the late 1940s and early 1950s.

Forbidden Planet also builds on a number of SF films that came before it. Robby had important sources in previous film robots such as the title figure in *Tobor the Great* (1954). Indeed, the sources of Robby and the film's other high-tech devices clearly go back at least as far as *Metropolis* (1927). The film also mixes in elements from other genres, most obviously in the way the interactions among the film's spaceship crew echo such interactions among GIs in any number of World War II films. One could, in fact, argue that one of the major limitations of *Forbidden Planet* as science fiction is the way its depiction of human relationships (especially between men and women) is so firmly rooted in the pop cultural images of the time; the film fails to imagine that, after hundreds of years of technological progress, human beings and their relationships would surely have changed as well.

FUTURE TECHNOLOGY AND MONSTERS FROM THE ID: *FORBIDDEN PLANET* AND AMERICAN CULTURE IN THE 1950s

Forbidden Planet was the only science fiction film by director Fred McLeod Wilcox, who is best known for the series of "Lassie" films (beginning with the 1943 classic *Lassie Come Home*) that he directed in the 1940s. Indeed, he directed relatively few films overall—and only one more (the 1960 B-picture *I Passed for White*) after *Forbidden Planet*. Most of Wilcox's films are routine B-pictures, yet several, including *Lassie Come Home*, the children's film *The Secret Garden* (1949), and the noir thriller *Shadow in the Sky* (1952) are gems of their kind. *Forbidden Planet* is certainly in this category, and its combination of style and technique made it one of the standout films of its era, often considered the Golden Age of science fiction cinema.

Buoyed by the largest budget of any science fiction film that had yet been made, *Forbidden Planet* is itself a demonstration of advanced technology of precisely the kind that makes film in general an especially interesting medium for science fiction: such films not only tell stories about the technological future but push film technology itself beyond the bounds of the present. Thus, even though the film is centrally concerned with the danger posed by technologies so advanced that they get out of human control, this technological anxiety is tempered by an almost loving fascination with the marvelous possibilities offered by advanced technology harnessed in the service of humanity.

The futuristic look of *Forbidden Planet* is enhanced by its high-tech sound, produced according to a groundbreaking all-electronic soundtrack. Created by Bebe and Louis Barron, this soundtrack does a great deal to create an otherworldly aura for the film, somewhat in the manner of the theremin music from *The Day the Earth Stood Still*. The electronic music of *Forbidden Planet* is much more extensive, however, providing background atmospherics for the entire film. The music was produced on an advanced homemade synthesizer that the Barrons built themselves (employing insights from the new science of cybernetics), which had a range of expressive capabilities well beyond that of the theremin. The soundtrack to the film (still available on CD) is considered an historic landmark in the development of electronic music, especially for use in film.

Forbidden Planet won no Academy Awards, but did get an Oscar nomination for best special effects. The special effects of the film are indeed impressive for the time, partly because MGM Studios provided an unusually large budget that allowed for the construction of large, elaborate sets and complex devices such as Robby the Robot. For example, space cruiser C57D is a significantly more complex effect than the flying saucer of *The Day the Earth Stood Still*, using animation and a miniature model to produce lights and moving parts as the ship swoops in over Altair IV for its landing. This model was effective enough to be repeatedly used in later MGM productions, particularly in several episodes of *The Twilight Zone*.

Robby the Robot, though, is surely the most memorable effect in *Forbidden Planet*. Designed by Robert Kinoshita, Robby was, at the time, one of the most complex and expensive (he reportedly cost $125,000 to make) devices ever created for the movies. Actually, the "robot" was played by an actor (officially Frankie Darrow, though prop-man Frankie Carpenter stood in for Darrow in many of the scenes) inside a costume made of vacuum-formed plastic. However, this plastic was itself an advanced material, and the costume included a number of high-tech flourishes, including the spinning antennae outside and the whirling mechanisms inside the robot's see-through head, as well as a system of electrical motors that allowed various parts of the body to be manipulated from an exterior control panel, independent of the actor inside.

Robby was also given a genuine personality of its own and, as voiced by announcer Marvin Miller, had some of the funniest lines in the entire film. For example, when the newly arrived astronauts marvel at the high oxygen content of the atmosphere of Altair IV, Robby replies, "I rarely use it myself, sir. It promotes rust." Robby's convincing high-tech look and winning personality combined to make him an immediate hit with audiences, so much so that MGM brought him back the following year to play a leading role in *The Invisible Boy*. Indeed, the Robby character (though played by different actors and, ultimately, replaced by a facsimile of the original) became something of a star in its own right, appearing in such later films as *Gremlins* (1984), *Cherry 2000* (1987), and *Earth Girls Are Easy* (1989). It also made numerous appearances on television, including guests roles on *The Twilight Zone, Wonder Woman, Mork and Mindy*, and *Lost in Space*. In the latter case, it even demonstrated its range as an actor, playing a villainous robot that does battle against the lovable robot of that series (a robot that was, incidentally, also designed by Kinoshita—and was basically just a low-budget version of Robby). Finally, in one of the first examples of successful movie-related merchandising, Robby has also, over the years, been the model for a variety of children's toys and even expensive full-scale replicas on sale to collectors.

Other important visual effects in *Forbidden Planet* include the various planetscapes (created via large scale studio sets) that help to provide a reasonably believable sense of being on an alien world. The scene in which the invisible monster from the id tries to break though the security field around space cruiser C57D, allowing us to see its electronic outline (produced by the animators at Disney Studios), is also impressive. A particularly important visual aspect of the film is Morbius's residence and the elaborate Krel facility that lies beneath it. Along with Robby, it is this residence that contains the film's central positive images of advanced technology. These images seem rather positive, despite the film's overall anxiety about the dangers of technological progress.

The vast Krel facility seems intended primarily to give viewers a visual suggestion of the incredibly advanced nature of Krel technology. However, from the perspective of our later digital age, this technology (which still includes a number of analog devices such as dials and switches) seems oddly clunky. The huge size of the complex is clearly meant to indicate its vast power, but it also indicates that the film was made before the use of miniaturization tended to make *smaller* devices seem more advanced. Even the amazing Robby seems unimpressive compared to the human-like androids of later science fiction films. Indeed, it seems rather surprising that the crew of the C57D find Robby so astonishing: one would think that a twenty-third-century Earth so technologically advanced as to have made interstellar travel routine should have developed robots at least as capable as Robby. Then again, *Forbidden Planet* is often rather conservative in its estimation of the capabilities of Earth technology, as in its assumption that travel to the moon would not be accomplished until the last decade of the twenty-first century.

Similarly, while Morbius's residence is a marvel from the perspective of the 1950s, it seems odd that the twenty-third-century Earthlings of the film are so impressed by it. But then, the film is appropriately viewed from the perspective of the 1950s, not the 2200s, and the house is best seen as an example of the kind of future home that was the object of much fascination in the American 1950s. With household technology in the form of appliances and other conveniences advancing at an unprecedented pace in the decade, Americans in general looked to a future when their homes would become more and more streamlined and automated. When the Disneyland theme park opened in 1955 (the year before the release of *Forbidden Planet*), one of its four main thematic areas was "Tomorrowland," which featured visions of future space technology, future cities, and (perhaps most importantly) future homes. A central display was the Monsanto House of the Future, though this display did not open until 1957. Surrounded by a lush garden, the house, inspired by the abstract, futuristic contemporary architecture known as "Googie," looked something like a flying saucer in its own right.★ The house and its furnishings were made largely of plastic (a crucial product of its sponsor, the Monsanto corporation), and in this the house was typical of the 1950s celebration of plastic as the material of the future. Tupperware figured prominently in the kitchen, which was, in fact, the focal point of the entire house. Special emphasis was placed on kitchen appliances (supplied by the General Electric Corporation), a key interest of American consumers at the time. The high-tech, largely push-button kitchen included such items as ultrasonic dishwashers, microwave ovens, atomic food preservation, high-tech garbage disposal, and plastic sinks with adjustable heights. Other innovations included an advanced climate control system, sophisticated lighting, insulated glass walls, picture telephones, plastic chairs, speaker phones, and electric toothbrushes.

Morbius's home in *Forbidden Planet* clearly embodies many of the same future expectations as the Monsanto House of the Future, which to a viewer in the twenty-first century gives it a retro, 1950s feel. Though we see only a brief view of the green exterior, the home is round, surrounded by gardens. The interior is elaborately decorated (as opposed to the minimalist views of the future seen in many SF films of the 1950s), though not necessarily with high-tech devices. Most of the décor is provided by scattered art objects and flowers, as well as a variety of modernistic pieces of furniture. Given the mild climate of Altair IV, much of the house is open to the out of doors, though it can be quickly enclosed by steel security shutters. There is also a special emphasis on advanced kitchen technology. On their first visit to the house, the newcomers are treated to lunch at a futuristic semi-circular counter; the food, produced by Robby, is a synthetic copy of Earth food, using a process that seems similar to that employed by the replicators of television's *Star Trek*. Cleanup is then achieved by zapping the leftovers in a household disintegrator.

Among other things, the technology in Morbius's Krel laboratory contains a "plastic educator" that allows one to exercise one's mental abilities and that can, apparently, lead to vast improvements in intellectual power. On the other hand, this device is extremely dangerous to mere

---

★ On the Googie style, popular in bowling alleys and coffeeshops of the 1950s, see Alan Hess's book *Googie: Fifties Coffee Shop Architecture* (Chronicle Books, 1986).

humans, who lack, by and large, the brainpower to handle this machine. Morbius, with an IQ of 183, barely survived his own first exposure to the machine, but that exposure has also lead to a doubling of his intellectual capacity, giving him the intelligence to be able to understand some of the Krel technology, though his intelligence quotient remains, by Krel standards, that of a "low-grade moron." This technological boost to Morbius's intellect enacts a typical science fiction fantasy. Unfortunately, it also gives Morbius the mind power to tap into the vast underground Krel power grid, causing the monster from the id to materialize as a projection of his own subconscious desires.

In this double vision of technology as both wondrous and dangerous, *Forbidden Planet* has predecessors that go back at least as far as Mary Shelley's *Frankenstein*, first published in 1818. Indeed, Adams's final reminder that human beings are not gods links *Forbidden Planet* to warnings against human hubris that go back as far as the Old Testament story of the tower of Babel or to any number of stories from Greek mythology, that of Prometheus being the most obvious and direct predecessor to the story of the film. (*Frankenstein*, after all, was subtitled, *The Modern Prometheus*.)

Despite such predecessors, *Forbidden Planet* is very much a work of its time. If Americans of the 1950s were fascinated by the prospects of a better future through technology, they were also all too painfully aware that some of the most important technological advances of the decade were in nuclear weaponry, to the point that humanity for the first time literally had the power to wipe itself off the face of the planet, just as the Krel of *Forbidden Planet* had done on Altair IV. The warning seems clear: if the Krel, described as a million years more advanced than humans, "ethically, as well as technologically," can be destroyed by extending their technology into realms better left alone, then primitive humans—of the 1950s or even the 2200s—are surely in danger of a similar fate.

Then again, in *Forbidden Planet*, humans of the 2200s seem to have advanced very little socially or "ethically" over humans of the 1950s. We learn essentially nothing about the political organization of the future, though the fact that the crew of the cruiser C57D represents the "United Planets" suggests an interplanetary political organization perhaps somewhat along the lines of the United Federation of Planets in *Star Trek*. On the other hand, the crew of the cruiser in *Forbidden Planet* is decidedly all-white, all-male, and (for that matter) all-American, with absolutely no suggestion of the diversity that marks the crew of *Star Trek*'s starship *Enterprise*. *Forbidden Planet*, in its failure to imagine advanced social, political, and economic structures that might overcome the present-day problems of the society in which it was produced, thus lacks an important utopian dimension of *Star Trek* and of much of the best science fiction.

In this sense, *Forbidden Planet* is again a representative work of 1950s science fiction, which, especially in film, tends to be short on utopian imagery, partly because the film industry was under intense pressure in the midst of an anti-communist political climate in which Hollywood was often suspected of left-leaning tendencies. In this climate, the film industry had to tread rather cautiously, though it is also the case that science fiction film (because it was considered unrealistic and not regarded as "serious") could sometimes get away with more extensive political commentary than could more mainstream films. Indeed, even the veiled and indirect warning in *Forbidden Planet* against the unrestrained development of more and more advanced nuclear weapons went well beyond most American films of its time as a political statement.

In addition to the fear that any criticism of American society might be taken as an indication of pro-Soviet sympathies, American science fiction filmmakers were a bit hesitant to project dramatically different futures because 1950s American society, in the throes of burgeoning social changes that would erupt in the sometimes violent protests of the 1960s, was in the grip of such rapid changes that it had a kind of social vertigo. Long standing social attitudes and practices, particularly with regard to race and gender relations, were under intense pressure, leading to widespread insecurity. American audiences turned to films not for indications that change was possible but for reassurances that some things might, after all, remain the same.

Forbidden Planet does not address the issue of race at all, other than to suggest, via the makeup of the crew of the C57D, that whites would maintain their elite status in American society well into the twenty-third century. Gender, however, is treated more directly, if equally unimaginatively. Alta, the only female character in the film, is represented as young, blonde, beautiful, and sexually pliant. Importantly, though, her obvious sexual accessibility arises not from any arrant erotic desires on her own part; it comes from her total innocence and ignorance of sexuality, which not only makes her easily impressed by virtually any man who comes along but also leaves that man in a position of complete mastery, able to tutor his innocent young conquest and to mold her to fit his own sexual style. Alta is, in short, the quintessential 1950s-style sexual object—and a far cry from the intelligent, sophisticated, and independent Helen Benson of *The Day the Earth Stood Still*.

When Alta makes her first entrance as Morbius is entertaining Adams, Farman, and Ostrow, the wolfish Farman immediately identifies her as an easy mark, quickly seeking to ingratiate himself with her—and meanwhile warning her that the commander is a danger to any woman who lets herself be caught alone with him. The next day, when Alta visits the compound where the crew of the C57D is building their transmitter to contact Earth, Farman takes her aside to a private spot. Attempting to introduce her to the practice of kissing, he explains to her that the activity is an indispensable part of the social practices of all advanced civilizations and that it is also extremely good for one's basic health. He then "selflessly" volunteers to show her how it is done, for which she seems entirely grateful, though he is a bit perturbed to discover that she does not find his initial kisses particularly stimulating. Nevertheless, he keeps at it, and it is quite clear that, despite her lack of response, the innocent Alta would be perfectly willing to try whatever other activities he might recommend as salubrious.

Luckily, Adams arrives at this point and sends Farman packing, at the same time making it clear both that he wants Alta for himself and that, as a responsible commander, he is far too principled to take advantage of the girl's innocence in the way Farman had been more than happy to do. He thus berates Alta for her behavior with Farman and for running around in such skimpy costumes, a practice that he warns her might lead to dire consequences given that he is in command of eighteen sex-starved "super-perfect physical specimens with an average age of 24.6." Alta rushes away, hurt by his attitude, which she clearly doesn't understand.

On the other hand, the young woman is obviously smitten with Adams and immediately sets about attempting to construct (with Robby's help) a new wardrobe that will better meet with his approval: she tells the robot to construct something that will cover her completely, yet still "fit in all the right places." In her next tantalizing appearance in the film, Alta swims nude in a pool and innocently asks Adams to join her when he approaches. When he declines (and demurely turns his back), she emerges from the water and puts on the fetching new long dress that Robby has made for her. Adams says she looks lovely, to which she responds, "Then why don't you kiss me like everybody else does?" After a quick conversation in which

Adams attempts to discern the level of her education in "biology," they finally do kiss. This time she responds passionately—at which point her normally docile pet tiger appears and attempts to attack them, only to be blown out of existence by Adams's handy blaster.

By the end of the film, it becomes clear that the tiger is itself a projection of Morbius's subconscious mind, harmless to Alta as long as she does nothing that would conflict with her father's basic desires. In other words, this is the moment in the film when her basic allegiance switches from her father to Adams, enacting the ideal 1950s narrative of the loyal virgin daughter who nevertheless gives herself without reservation to her husband once the right man comes along. Granted, she displays the appropriate hesitation, arguing that she can't leave her father alone on the planet when Adams first asks her to leave with him. Yet when Morbius appears soon afterward (in the wake of Ostrow's final discovery and death), she announces to her father that she has chosen to go with Adams. Soon afterward, the id monster appears and attacks the residence, leading to Morbius's death. Alta is then free to go with Adams without conflict, melting into his arms for comfort after they watch from space as Altair IV is destroyed in a fiery planetary explosion.

If there is something vaguely Freudian about the Morbius–Alta–Adams triangle, the basic monsters-from-the-id premise of the film is even more so. Of course, Freudian psychoanalysis was an object of widespread fascination in America in the 1950s, so much so that Freud became a key element of the popular culture of the decade. Any number of works of the decade incorporated elements from the popular conception of Freudianism. *Forbidden Planet*, while suggesting that Freudian terminology will be obsolete by the twenty-third century (Morbius has to explain the archaic term "id" to Adams at one point), nevertheless adopts Freud's vision of the id as a subconscious realm of dark, seething, savage desires. While Freud has often been accused of excessive universalism in believing that the basic structure of the human psyche is the same across cultures and historical periods, the film goes even further, attributing a basically Freudian psychic structure even to the alien (and immensely advanced) Krel.

Perhaps even more tellingly, *Forbidden Planet* employs an evolutionary version of Freudianism in which the id is seen as the site of primitive desires dating back to the dawn of mankind, as opposed to the conscious mind, which is the site of more "civilized" thoughts. In its anxiety that the primitive forces of the id might somehow be reactivated, the film shows a concern that thousands of years of evolution have not eradicated humanity's most primitive tendencies but have merely coated them with a thin and fragile veneer of civilization and refinement. In short, the film shows a concern that all those centuries of evolution might suddenly be reversed, causing a reversion to the primitive. This fear of "degeneration" to a primitive state was particularly widespread in the United States in the 1950s, indicating only one of many ways in which the characteristic concerns of an America faced with stepping into the shoes of the British Empire as a global standard-bearer of Western values resembled those of America's European imperial predecessors.

Degeneration was, in fact, one of the central anxieties that occupied the European popular imagination in the late nineteenth century, fueled by a popular fascination with the then-new Darwinian theory of evolution and by fears of the dark forces that might be encountered as Europeans went about the rapid colonization of Africa in the last decades of the century. Perhaps the central expression of this anxiety was Max Nordau's 1895 book *Degeneration*, an enormously popular work that helped to fuel the widespread fascination with the concept of degeneration. Late Victorian British literature is filled with tales of degeneration, of which Robert Louis Stevenson's *Dr. Jekyll and Mr. Hyde* (1886) is perhaps the classic example. The same can be said for American science fiction in the 1950s, especially in film. Vaguely aware that evolution was driven by mutation and that mutation could be caused by radiation, Americans in the 1950s put two and two together and concluded that radiation could cause evolution, or (more probably, given the negative connotations of radiation in the decade) degeneration. Thus, in its concern with the possibility of degeneration (as with its concern about the dangers of runaway technology and its fascination with the Freudian subconscious) *Forbidden Planet* is a classic case of the way in which science fiction often looks to the future but in ways that are thoroughly embedded in the concerns of the present.

ICONS OF OUTER SPACE: THE LEGACY OF *FORBIDDEN PLANET*

Charles Matthews, in his book *Oscar A to Z*, notes the influential status of the film, concluding that "every subsequent sci-fi movie and TV show is indebted to *Forbidden Planet*." The many appearances of Robby the Robot on television are a good indicator of the influence of *Forbidden Planet* on SF television, as is the similarity between Robby and the sometimes histrionic, arm-waving robot of *Lost in Space*. On the other hand, far more films and television series have been influenced by the overall style and message of *Forbidden Planet* than have overtly attempted to reproduce its effects. For example, *Forbidden Planet* resembles an especially good episode of television's *Star Trek*, and for good reason: Gene Roddenberry acknowledged the film as an important general influence in his conception of the television series. Yet there are no specific episodes of *Star Trek* that might be considered "remakes" of *Forbidden Planet*.

Among films, *Forbidden Planet* may be most important for the standard of quality it set with its settings, costumes, and special effects, standards that would not be surpassed until Stanley Kubrick's *2001: A Space Odyssey* in 1968. Meanwhile, its robot, its flying saucer, and its high-tech house and machinery are important icons of science fiction film. Films about the exploration of space have been particularly influenced by *Forbidden Planet*, though *Forbidden Planet* sometimes echoes earlier films as well, as when the expedition to Mars in *Rocketship X-M* (1950) discovers a once-mighty Martian civilization, now destroyed by a long-ago nuclear war, with the only survivors having degenerated to a primitive state thanks to the effects of radiation. Finally, the ambivalence shown toward technology in *Forbidden Planet* is echoed in any number of later science fiction films, including *2001: A Space Odyssey*, *Colossus: The Forbin Project*, *Blade Runner* (1982), *Robocop* (1987), the various *Terminator* films, and *The Matrix* (1999).

3

Invasion of the Body Snatchers

Released 1956; Director Don Siegel

Invasion of the Body Snatchers was a relatively low budget black-and-white film featuring a little-known cast and minimal special effects. Nevertheless, it went on to become one of the signature films of the 1950s—and one of the most important alien invasion films of all time. Its paranoid theme of alien invaders who replace individual humans, becoming virtually indistinguishable from the original, resonated in a powerful way with any number of widespread anxieties in the America of the time. Most obviously, the film functions as an allegory of fears about communist invasion and subversion. However, the film can also be read as a commentary on concerns about the dehumanizing effects of a rapidly expanding capitalist system that was increasingly becoming a dominant factor in every aspect of human life in America.

THE STORY: SEEDS OF DESTRUCTION

Invasion of the Body Snatchers begins like a classic film noir, as a police car rushes through dark streets to a hospital emergency room. There, a frantic Miles Bennell, having been picked up on the busy highway where he was trying to flag down traffic to warn of an alien invasion, is being held on suspicion that he is a madman. A Dr. Hill (Whit Bissell) arrives from the State Mental Hospital to interview Bennell, who begins to tell him his story. This hospital scene, to which we return at the end of the film, thus becomes a frame narrative around the main part of the film, which relates the story that Bennell tells to Hill.

As this story begins, Bennell is returning from a medical convention to Santa Mira, the quiet small town where he was born and raised and where he now practices family medicine. He immediately senses something strange about the familiar town, but is unable to find any concrete reason for the feeling of apprehension he experiences on his arrival. His nurse, Sally Withers (Jean Willes), picks him up at the train station, warning him that he has a waiting room full of patients anticipating his arrival at the office. As they drive to the office, they nearly hit young Jimmy Grimaldi (Bobby Clark), who runs out into the street fleeing his mother. Bennell notices that the once-thriving Grimaldi fruit stand seems to have closed down. When he gets to his office, he finds that most of his patients have canceled their appointments. Then old flame Becky Driscoll (Dana Wynter)—who has been married and away in England—arrives with news that she, like Bennell, is recently divorced. Meanwhile, she seeks his advice concerning her cousin Wilma Lentz (Virginia Christine), who swears that her Uncle Ira (Tom Fadden) has been replaced by some sort of impostor. Soon afterward, Jimmy Grimaldi comes to the office in near hysteria, claiming that his mother has been similarly replaced.

Bennell goes to see Wilma, who reports that the man purporting to be her Uncle Ira resembles Ira exactly and even has all of his memories, but seems oddly lacking in all feeling and emotion, very unlike her real uncle. Bennell concludes that Wilma is suffering from some sort of delusion and suggests that she go to see psychiatrist Dan Kaufman (Larry Gates). Meanwhile, Bennell and Becky make a date for dinner, realizing that much of their old mutual attraction is still there. Outside the Sky Terrace Playroom, where they plan to have dinner, they run into Kaufman, who reports that there have been several recent cases in the area of people swearing that relatives or close friends are not the people they claim to be. He interprets the phenomenon as a psychological reaction to "worry about what's going on in the world"—leaving it up to Bennell and Becky (and the audience) to interpret that phrase, and also providing a key to the success of the film. After Kaufman agrees to talk with Jimmy and Wilma, Bennell and Becky go in for dinner and find the once-popular club nearly deserted. Then, just as they start a pre-dinner dance, a phone call comes in for Bennell from local mystery writer Jack Belicec (King Donovan), who urgently asks the doctor to come see him.

Bennell and Becky drive to the Belicec home where Jack and wife Theodora (Carolyn Jones) show them a body lying on their pool table. Bennell examines the body and finds the face vague, unfinished, somehow lacking in features. They try to take the fingerprints of the corpse, but find that it has none. Theodora is convinced that the body is a blank waiting to take on the stamp of its final features—those of her husband. Bennell asks them to sit up to observe the body during the night and to call the police if anything happens.

Bennell takes Becky home, where they find her father emerging from the basement, which seems odd at this late hour. Meanwhile, back at the Belicec residence, Jack falls asleep, and Theodora sees the body on the table beginning to take on Jack's features and to stir into life. She becomes hysterical and awakes her husband, who takes her to see Bennell. In turn, Bennell calls Kaufman and asks him to come over, even though it is the middle of the night.

Realizing that something very out of the ordinary is going on in Santa Mira, Bennell suddenly has a feeling that Becky is in danger. He drives hurriedly over to her home, where he sneaks into the house by breaking a basement window. Inside, he finds another of the blank bodies, this one resembling Becky. He rushes upstairs, grabs the sleeping Becky out of bed and carries her down the stairs and out to his car. Back at his house, he greets Kaufman. He and Belicec leave Becky with Theodora and take Kaufman back to see the body at the Belicec house, but the body has now disappeared. Kaufman argues that Bennell probably just hallucinated the body in the Driscoll basement. The three men go to the Driscoll home and indeed find no body there. Police Chief Nick Grivett (Ralph Dumke), having been called by Becky's father, arrives with news that the missing body, that of a man with his fingerprints burned off with acid, has recently been found in a burning haystack and is now in the morgue.

Becky and the Belicecs stay the night at Bennell's house. The next morning, Bennell and Becky seem well on the way to a romantic involvement as she cooks his breakfast. Later that day Wilma flags Bennell down to tell him that she now realizes she was wrong about Uncle Ira. The doctor then arrives at his office to find Jimmy Grimaldi in the waiting room, now perfectly comfortable with his mother. When Bennell returns home for dinner, he finds Jack preparing dinner on the outside grill. Soon afterward, Bennell notices a strange, oozing seed pod inside his greenhouse. Jack immediately concludes (somehow) that such a pod was also the source of the blank bodies. The others agree and conclude (in a rather sudden deductive leap) that all of the strange cases of suspicious identity in the town have arisen from replacements coming from such pods.

Realizing that Kaufman and Grivett may have already been replaced, Bennell attempts to call the FBI office in Los Angeles to report the strange events in Santa Mira, explaining to Becky that the pods may arise from a radiation-induced mutation, or perhaps a weird alien organism. The telephone operator reports to Bennell that the FBI is not answering, then that all circuits to Los Angeles or Sacramento are busy, making it clear that the pod people are now in charge of the local phone system, cutting off communication with the outside world. Meanwhile, the pods in the greenhouse are gradually growing into replacement bodies for all four of the occupants of the house.

Bennell sends the Belicecs away in their car so they can seek help from another town. He himself insists on staying in case the operator calls back so that she will not know anyone has gone. Becky insists on staying in Santa Mira with Bennell, who goes into the greenhouse and destroys the newly forming bodies with a pitchfork. He and Becky then decide to drive off to seek help. When they stop for gas, the attendant puts more seed pods in the trunk while Bennell is attempting to get help via the pay phone. Realizing what has happened, Bennell drives away, then stops and destroys the pods in the trunk. They drive to Sally's house, hoping she can still be trusted. Unfortunately, they find a group of the pod people meeting there. Bennell and Becky barely escape, while the police put out an all-points bulletin emphasizing that the two must not be allowed to leave town. They nevertheless manage to make it to Bennell's office, seeking a place to hide. Bennell deduces that the final stage of the replacement process change occurs while the original human sleeps, so he insists that they stay awake at all costs. Musing on the situation, he tells Becky, "In my practice I've seen how people have allowed their humanity to drain away, only it happened slowly instead of all at once. They didn't seem to mind. . . . All of us a little bit. We harden our hearts, grow callous. Only when we have to fight to stay human do we realize how precious it is to us."

The next morning, a Saturday, Bennell looks out his office window onto the town square, finding it oddly busy. He watches as three truckloads of seed pods arrive, distributing them for transport to neighboring towns. Then Belicec and Kaufman arrive at the office, both having been replaced. In a speech that fills in many of the questions raised in the film, Kaufman explains that the pods grew from seeds that drifted in from space and that they can produce exact duplicates of any form of life. He urges Bennell and Becky to give in to the change, which he assures them will be to their benefit, though neither he nor the film as a whole explains what happens to the original bodies once the replacement bodies take over. He assures Becky and Bennell that the replacement process will be entirely painless, occurring while they sleep. They will then be "reborn into an untroubled world." Bennell retorts, "Where everyone's the same?" "Exactly," agrees Kaufman, though he obviously disagrees with Bennell's implication that such sameness would be a nightmare. He goes on to explain that the new life, free of emotion and competition, will be much easier. "Love, desire, ambition, faith—without them life's so simple."

However, Bennell and Becky, having rediscovered each other, would rather opt for love, despite its pitfalls. They manage to inject Kaufman, Belicec, and Grivett with sleeping drugs, then dash out of the building, hoping to make it to the highway by pretending to have been changed. Unfortunately, they blow their emotionless cover when Becky cries out as a dog is nearly hit by a truck. They flee cross-country in rough terrain, with the other townspeople in hot pursuit. Still struggling to stay awake, they take refuge inside an old mine tunnel. While they rest, they hear angelic, ethereal singing, and conclude that, being so beautiful, it must be produced by genuine humans. Bennell leaves Becky in the tunnel as he goes to seek out the singers. Unfortunately, he discovers that the music is simply coming from a radio in a truck being loaded with seed pods at a large greenhouse facility growing thousands of pods. He returns to the tunnel to find Becky, seemingly near sleep. He lifts her in his arms and starts to carry her, but trips and falls. He kisses her and then realizes from her emotionless response that she has been replaced.

Becky calls for help from the other pod people as Bennell rushes out into the night. He manages to make it to a busy highway, where he rushes out into the traffic, crying for help. The passing cars ignore him as a madman or drunk. To make matters worse, he jumps onto the back of a truck, which he finds is loaded with seed pods, which are apparently now being shipped out of Santa Mira. Eventually, Bennell is picked up and taken to the hospital, taking us back to the beginning of the film. Then, just as Dr. Hill is about to conclude that Bennell is a lunatic, an accident victim is brought into the emergency room, having been hit by a truckload of giant seed pods from Santa Mira. Hill frantically orders the police to sound the alarm to all law enforcement agencies in the state and to block all roads out of Santa Mira. He himself calls the FBI, seemingly setting into motion forces that might be able to resist the alien pods. On the other hand, it is not at all certain that these forces will succeed, and this ending even leaves open the possibility that the FBI, police, and military may themselves already be controlled by the pod people.

THE SOURCES OF THE MOVIE

Invasion of the Body Snatchers is a relatively faithful adaptation of a novel of the same title by Jack Finney, first published in serialized form in *Collier's* magazine in 1954. The film's plot and characters are taken almost directly from the novel. The setting in a small California town is also essentially unchanged, though the Mill Valley of the novel is renamed Santa Mira in the film. The major change has to do with the ending. In the novel, protagonist Dr. Miles Bennell heroically battles against the alien invaders, inflicting so much damage that, in the end, the alien invaders decide to leave Earth to seek out a planet that will be less resistant to colonization. The film also ends on a relatively positive note as Bennell (played by Kevin McCarthy) finally manages to get the authorities to listen to his incredible story of alien seed pods growing into human replacements, and to begin to mobilize against the invasion. The ending, however, is left open: it is not entirely clear that this mobilization will succeed or that the invasion can, at this point, be stopped. This ambiguous ending was imposed at the insistence of Allied Artists, the small studio that produced the film. Initially, director Siegel had envisioned a much more pessimistic ending in which a near-hysterical Bennell would be left standing in the midst of a busy highway, screaming out warnings that go unheeded by the passing drivers, many of whom may already be aliens.

INVASION OF THE BODY SNATCHERS AND THE COMPLEXITY OF FEAR IN THE AMERICAN 1950s: TERROR FROM WITHOUT, CONFORMITY FROM WITHIN

Invasion of the Body Snatchers was shot in 3–4 weeks with a total budget of approximately $400,000, perhaps one-tenth that of the roughly contemporaneous *Forbidden Planet*. It employs very little in the way of special effects or other fancy visual techniques. Nevertheless, it is a skillfully made film that does an excellent job of creating an atmosphere of forboding and suspense, largely by tapping into numerous basic anxieties that informed American society in the 1950s.

Director Don Siegel had directed a number of competent, but unremarkable, B pictures before *Invasion of the Body Snatchers*. His work on this film indicated considerably greater promise as a director of commercial features, promise that would ultimately come to fruition in a number of later classic genre films, including crime thrillers such as *The Killers* (1964), *Coogan's Bluff* (1968), *Dirty Harry* (1971), and Westerns such as *Two Mules for Sister Sara* (1970) and *The Shootist* (1976). Indeed, *Invasion of the Body Snatchers* already shows some of the same deft handling of action and suspense that made those later films so successful. Siegel did not return to the science fiction genre after *Invasion of the Body Snatchers*, but then that film, in many ways, has more the texture of a thriller than of science fiction, given that it depends largely on suspense for its effects and that it features essentially nothing in the way of scientific or technological speculation.

The lack of the usual science fiction hardware made it possible to produce *Invasion of the Body Snatchers* with virtually no special effects. Similarly, the fact that the alien replacements look exactly like humans meant that the film required nothing in the way of alien makeup or prosthetics. Probably the most striking effect that does occur in the film involves the partly formed replicants that are shown vaguely to resemble Bennell, Becky, and the Belicecs in Bennell's greenhouse. This effect works well, but it is a very simple one, achieved by the straightforward expedient of dipping the actual actors in plaster of Paris to make molds from which the plastic replicates could be made.

What *Invasion of the Body Snatchers* lacks in the way of eye-catching visuals is more than made up for by its mind-catching theme. The notion of stealthy invaders who essentially take over the minds of normal Americans, converting them to an alien ideology, resonates in an obvious way with the Cold War fear of communist subversion. Indeed, the film has come to be widely regarded as an iconic cultural representation of its contemporary climate of anti-communist paranoia. It is certainly the case that the replacements, who look the same as everyone else, but feel no emotion and have no individuality, directly echo the era's most prevalent stereotypes about communists. Thus, the assurances given Bennell by the replacements that his life will be far more pleasant if he simply goes along with the crowd and learns to live without emotion can be taken as echoes of the supposed seductions offered by communist utopianism.

On the other hand, the makers of the film (and, for that matter, the author of the original novel) have stated that they intended no such allegorical commentary on the threat of communism. Meanwhile, even if one does choose to see communism as the indirect topic of the film, it is also quite possible to read the paranoid vision of the film as a subtle critique of anti-communist hysteria. By this reading, the film suggests that the notion of communists secretly taking over various aspects of American life (as envisioned by anti-communist alarmists like Senator Joseph McCarthy) is about as likely as tiny seeds blowing in from outer space, then developing into large pods that grow perfect replicas of specific human beings, whom they then do away with and replace. In this view, the film suggests that the communist conspiracy warned against by McCarthy and others is incredibly far-fetched, the stuff of B-grade science fiction.

Of course, there were many much more overtly anti-communist films of the 1950s, including such science fiction fare as *Red Planet Mars* (1952) and *Invasion U.S.A.* (1952), in addition to more mainstream films such as *I Was a Communist for the FBI* (1951) and the John Wayne vehicle *Big Jim McLain* (1952). But even these films, in retrospect, can be read as critiques of anti-communist hysteria, simply because they are so extreme that they make anti-communism look ridiculous. In the case of *Invasion of the Body Snatchers*, meanwhile, the allegorical significance of the film is complicated by the fact that many of its elements can be taken as direct criticisms of the emergent consumer capitalism of the 1950s.

Star Kevin McCarthy (whose shared surname with Senator McCarthy provides an additional irony) has stated in an interview that he himself felt that the pod people were reminiscent of the heartless capitalists who work on Madison Avenue. Indeed, if communism was perceived by many Americans of the 1950s as a threat to their cherished individuality, capitalism itself was often perceived in much the same way. While the burgeoning capitalist system of the 1950s produced unprecedented opportunities for upward mobility in America, this highly complex system also required, for its operation, an unprecedented level of efficiency and standardization. Thus, if the 1950s represented a sort of Golden Age of science fiction film, the decade was also the Golden Age of American homogenization, as efficiency-oriented mass production techniques pioneered by industrialists such as Henry Ford reached new heights of sophistication and new levels of penetration into every aspect of American life. While television helped to homogenize the thoughts and dreams of the rapidly expanding American population, General Motors, the great industrial power of the decade, achieved unprecedented success in the business in which Ford's techniques had originally been developed. At the same time, Bill Levitt's Long Island suburb of Levittown brought mass production to the housing industry, ushering in the great age of suburbanization, perhaps the single most important step in the commodification of the American dream. The 1950s were also the Golden Age of branding and franchising, as standard brands, aided by television advertising, installed themselves in the collective American consciousness, while chain franchises spread across the nation, informed by the central driving idea of homogeneity—selling identical products in identical ways at thousands of identical franchises across the country. Thus, if Levitt's vision helped to homogenize the American home, Kemmons Wilson's Holiday Inn chain made identical lodgings available to Americans wherever they drove on the nation's rapidly expanding (and more and more homogeneous) highway system in their increasingly powerful, standardized automobiles. Similarly, Ray Kroc made homogeneous food available on the road when he took the fast-food production techniques pioneered by Ray Kroc and the McDonald brothers and made standardized hamburgers an indispensable part of everyday cuisine in America.

And so on. It is thus not for nothing that the 1950s developed such a reputation for homogenization, not only of material life, but of thought itself. Critiques of capitalism-driven conformism were central to the cultural criticism of the decade, as witnessed by the prominence of such works as David Riesman's *The Lonely Crowd* (1950), C. Wright Mills's *White Collar* (1951) and *The Power Elite*, and William Whyte's *The Organization Man* (the latter two both published in 1956, the same year *Invasion of the Body Snatchers* was released). Whyte's book was probably the most important single critique of conformity in the 1950s. In his book, Whyte argued that the growing regimentation of corporate culture in the 1950s was producing a population of corporate clones, virtually bereft of any genuine individual identity. For Whyte, the enforced corporate conformism of the 1950s represented a betrayal of American individualism.

If *The Organization Man* thus expresses some of the same anxieties that are central to *Invasion of the Body Snatchers*, McCarthy's evocation of Madison Avenue, heart of the advertising industry, directly recalls Sloan Wilson's best-selling 1955 novel *The Man in the Gray Flannel Suit*, another iconic work of American culture in the 1950s. Wilson's title image suggests the organization man struggling to make his way up the corporate ladder in competition with fellow young executives dressed in identical clothing while pursuing identical dreams of wealth and success. In so doing, *The Man in the Gray Flannel Suit* comes as close as anything we have to being the decade's signature novel, despite having received relatively little critical attention and even less critical respect as a work of literature.

Wilson's title image became an emblem of the 1950s drive for conformism, a drive that threatened individual identity but that also offered a certain comfort level for those (mostly male WASPs) who were able to fit in. Indeed, *The Man in the Gray Flannel Suit*, despite some criticism of the era's corporate culture, with its emphasis on the drive for success at the expense of all else, is ultimately an affirmative work that assures Americans that they can succeed and still be themselves. Granted, the flannel-clad protagonist, Tom Rath, is faced with considerable difficulties. Freshly arrived from a World War II tour of duty chock full of military and sexual adventures, Rath finds his new routine of job and family a considerable challenge. Yet he meets the challenge and is, in the end, able to adjust to marriage, fatherhood, and the demands of corporate life while keeping his individuality intact.

The Man in the Gray Flannel Suit thus soothes us with a demonstration that it is possible to be a happy and distinct individual without making any fundamental changes to our system or its institutions. *Invasion of the Body Snatchers* is much more anxious in its vision of conformism as a deadly threat to one's individualism or even humanity. Surrounded by an army of emotionless and essentially interchangeable replacements, Miles and Becky become images of remarkable individuals who fight to maintain their own distinctive identities and their ability to experience human emotion. Scenes in which masses of townspeople pursue the two lone surviving individuals seem to make the film's privileging of the individual over the community quite clear.

On the other hand, if the film's anxiety over conformism can be taken as a critique of either capitalism or communism, it is also possible to see in the film an opposed anxiety over difference. After all, by the end of the film, Bennell is the only citizen of Santa Mira who has not been replaced by an alien replicant. He is a one-of-a-kind outcast from a community in which everyone else gets along perfectly. From this point of view, *Invasion of the Body Snatchers* is a film not about conformism but about alienation, the seemingly opposed phenomenon that was also so crucial to the American experience in the 1950s. The particular form of alienation that was prevalent in America in the 1950s can be described as a fear of exclusion, as a fear of not fitting in. Surrounded by a pressure to conform, individuals feared the loss of their distinct individual identities. Yet they also feared their own inability to fit in; they feared being identified as different, as being, in fact, the Other. In short, Americans in the 1950s suffered from two principal fears: the fear of being different from everyone else and the fear of being the same as everyone else.

Alienation was a central concern of American culture in the 1950s. It was a great theme of the Beats and of the decade's literature as a whole: Ralph Ellison's *Invisible Man* and J. D. Salinger's Holden Caulfield are nothing if not alienated. American film of the 1950s also responded to the decade's alienation anxieties. Central film icons of the decade, such as Marlon Brando and James Dean, owed much of their popularity to their ability to radiate alienation on the screen, thus making their alienated audiences identify with them. Given the pervasive concern with alienation in the culture of the 1950s, it should come as no surprise that the science fiction of the decade was often concerned with this issue. For example, Mark Jancovich notes in his book *Rational Fears: American Horror in the 1950s* that the fiction of writers such as Ray Bradbury and Richard Matheson and the films of Jack Arnold are centrally concerned with the phenomenon of alienation. But *Invasion of the Body Snatchers* is virtually unique among American films of the 1950s in the extent to which it is able to address contemporary concerns over both alienation and conformism.

This double focus no doubt accounts for much of the film's status as one of the most remembered products of 1950s American culture, though the more obvious reason for this status has to do with the way in which the film has been seen as a marker of the communism anti-communism confrontation of the decade. The film addresses other contemporary concerns as well. For example, the fact that both Miles Bennell and Becky Driscoll are recently divorced (a situation taken directly from the novel) is something of a landmark in American film, indicating the way in which divorce was becoming more socially acceptable amid a general climate of changing gender roles. On the other hand, the gender roles occuped by these two central characters are still rather traditional. As the film begins, Bennell is a successful professional, while Becky seems to have no occupation other than keeping house for her father, with whom she lives. There is one scene in which Bennell expresses doubt in his ability to take on a group of replicants, causing Becky to remind him that there are two of them and that she can help in the battle, despite being female. Mostly, though, Becky plays the weak, endangered female who must turn to a strong male for protection and support, though the fact that Bennell ultimately fails to provide this protection can be taken as a sign of anxieties over masculinity in the decade.

If the film thus at least touches on contemporary concerns over changing gender roles, it engages even more extensively with the 1950s American fascination with Freud and psychoanalysis. This fascination, like the twinned concern over alienation and conformism, was double-edged. On the one hand, in an era terrified of abnormality, mental illness came to be a central marker of the abnormal—thus Bennell's horror at being considered insane when he attempts to warn others of the alien invasion. On the other hand, while an awareness of Freud and psychoanalysis became part of American popular culture in the 1950s, there was an increasing concern that the mental health establishment was acting to suppress individual difference in the interest of psychological conformism. It may thus be no accident that the psychiatrist Kaufman is perhaps the most important leader of the pod people, while the film's vision of an enforced placidity, in which the emotional aberrations of individuals have been suppressed, can be taken as a warning against the potential negative effects of the decade's drive for "mental health." It might be noted, in this regard, that the central advertising campaign with which Tom Rath becomes involved in *The Man in the Gray Flannel Suit* is in support of a national mental health committee headed by the president of his firm (who had formerly been in analysis in an unsuccessful attempt to cure himself of his workaholism).

Finally, the opposition between Kaufman and Bennell can be seen as a comment on the 1950s concerns over professionalism and specialization. As Mills pointed out in *The Power Elite*, American society was coming increasingly to be dominated by technical specialists whose work the general population could not understand. The psychiatrist Kaufman can be seen as a representative of this elite group of specialists, while the general practitioner Bennell can be taken as a representative of an older, more generalized form of knowledge that relies on a direct and personal understanding of people rather than mere technical expertise. In short, *Invasion of the Body Snatchers*, though a seemingly simple genre film, has a rare ability to address any number of issues in its contemporary historical context, making it one of the central cultural products of its time and putting to rest any notion that science fiction needs to disengage itself from contemporary reality in order to be imaginatively powerful.

ALIEN PARANOIA: THE LEGACY OF *INVASION OF THE BODY SNATCHERS*

Invasion of the Body Snatchers is perhaps *the* classic alien invasion film, especially of the 1950s, when Cold War anxieties made that genre particularly prominent. Among the numerous alien invasion films of the decade, several closely resemble *Invasion of the Body Snatchers* in their focus on alien invaders who are able to take on the appearance of humans, though none of them are quite as successful at evoking the terror of this possibility. For example, in *Invaders from Mars* (1953), a young boy, David Maclean (Jimmy Hunt), is initially the only one who realizes that a series of authority figures (including his own parents) are turning into robot-like zombies, controlled by the Martian invaders. Gene Fowler's *I Married a Monster from Outer Space* (1958), described by Cyndy Hendershot in her book *Paranoia, the Bomb, and 1950s Science Fiction Films* as a "feminine analogue" of *Invasion of the Body Snatchers*, gives the theme still another twist. In this film, aliens from the "Andromeda constellation" are scouring the universe trying to find females with whom they can mate in order to preserve their species, all of their own females (presumably being weaker than males) having been killed when their sun became unstable. The alien males come to earth, inpersonating Earth men and replacing most of the male inhabitants of a small American town in order to mate with their women.

Despite its obvious embeddedness in the 1950s, *Invasion of the Body Snatchers* has also exerted a powerful influence on a number of subsequent films in the alien-invasion genre. In particular, it has spawned two remakes:

Philip Kaufman's *Invasion of the Body Snatchers* (1978) and Abel Ferrara's *Body Snatchers* (1993). The former, featuring Donald Sutherland as the central character (now named Dr. Matthew Bennell) is relatively faithful to the original, except that it updates the setting to the late 1970s and moves the action to San Francisco. It even features Kevin McCarthy in a cameo role, running into traffic and screaming warnings about the alien invaders, much as he did near the end of the original film. However, this film ends on a pessimistic note: surrounded by aliens, Nancy Bellicec (Veronica Cartwright), still human, is thrilled to spot her friend Bennell, but when she runs up to him she realizes that he, too, has been replaced by an alien replicant. The second remake drifts much farther from the original. It is set in a small Southern military town and features an EPA agent who has brought his family with him on a trip to inspect a toxic chemical storage facility on the army base that dominates the town. This film actually has the best special effects of the three, but lacks much of the drama of the others, substituting effects for substance. It is also the most pessimistic of the three, ending with the suggestion that the alien replicants have virtually completed their takeover of the entire planet.

Of other alien invasion films that can count *Invasion of the Body Snatchers* as an important predecessor, the most obvious is Stuart Orme's *The Puppet Masters* (1994), also starring Sutherland and based on the 1951 novel by Robert A. Heinlein of that title. This film follows the book fairly closely, except that it is set in the 1990s and drops Heinlein's transparent anti-communist allegory. It features essentially the same story as *Invasion of the Body Snatchers*: an army of alien parasites invades Earth and begins taking over the bodies and minds of humans toward the eventual goal of world domination. In this case, however, the aliens are opposed (and ultimately defeated) by powerful forces, including a top-secret government intelligence organization headed by Andrew Nivens, Sutherland's character. Actually, the parasites are killed when Nivens and his group infect them with encephalitis, recalling H. G. Wells's classic novel *The War of the Worlds* (1898, also made into an excellent film of the same title in 1953), in which Martian invaders die off because they have no resistance to the common microbes in the Earth's atmosphere.

The paranoid atmosphere of *Invasion of the Body Snatchers* also links it to films outside the science fiction genre. It is related in a particularly direct way to Cold War espionage thrillers such as John Frankenheimer's

The Manchurian Candidate (1962), in which the takeover of individual humans by alien invaders is replaced by the takeover of individual American minds by communist brainwashing. *Invasion of the Body Snatchers* also bears a clear family resemblance to paranoid conspiracy thrillers like Alan J. Pakula's *The Parallax View* (1974).

4

2001: A Space Odyssey

Released 1968; Director Stanley Kubrick

One of the most successful and widely-discussed films of the late 1960s, Stanley Kubrick's *2001: A Space Odyssey* resurrected science fiction film at a time when the genre had largely faded from view during the four years after Kubrick's own *Dr. Strangelove* had essentially made the Cold War paranoia SF film obsolete. Brilliant, thought-provoking, and visually stunning, *2001* brought new credibility to the science fiction film as an art form, demonstrating the ability of film as a medium to produce precisely the kind of mind-expanding images that readers of science fiction literature had long imagined but had never before seen on the screen.

THE STORY: HUMAN EVOLUTION
AND ALIEN INTERVENTION

2001 relies far less on plot than most other science fiction films. Indeed, it largely leaves it up to viewers to construct a coherent story that connects a sequence of narrative fragments. Moreover, plot is almost beside the point. This is a film that stretches the resources of the medium to their limit, creating some of the most striking sights and sounds ever experienced by film audiences. Nevertheless, it is possible (and helpful) to discern a story beneath all of the film's dazzling images.

As if to announce its self-consciously artistic nature (an announcement already made, in fact, in the film's titular allusion to the Homeric epic),

2001 begins more like an actual opera than a space opera, with a long (nearly three minutes) musical overture (György Ligeti's "Atmospheres"), during which the screen is entirely blank. Then, to the dramatic music of Richard Strauss's *Also Sprach Zarathustra*, the opening credits flash over a shot of a sun rising over a planet. After a fade to black, we are presented with a sequence, introduced by the on-screen title "THE DAWN OF MAN," in which the sun rises over a primeval landscape, followed by a series of scenes involving primitive man-apes, the ancestors of modern man. In the first sequence, a group of man-apes scrounges for food until one of them is attacked and killed by a leopard. In the second sequence, two groups of man-apes battle over a water hole, until one group retreats without any actual blows being struck. In the third sequence, the man-apes huddle together at night as ominous animal noises fill the air. A glowing streak is seen in the sky. As the fourth sequence begins, the man-apes awake to eerie, cacophonous musical sounds (Ligeti's "Requiem for Soprano, Mezzo-Soprano, Two Mixed Choirs, and Orchestra") to find a strange rectangular black monolith that has appeared nearby during the night. The sun is shown rising over the top of the monolith. In the next sequence, one of the man-apes (apparently having received an intelligence boost from exposure to the monolith) hits on the idea of using a bone as a club—again to the accompaniment of the *Also Sprach Zarathustra* theme. This advance marks a breakthrough in the ability of the man-apes to kill large animals for food—and to kill their fellow man-apes in the competition for resources, as we see when the newly-armed group of man-apes uses its bone-clubs to drive the rival group from the watering hole, killing one of them. A man-ape triumphantly tosses his club into the air, which then fades into a shot of a similarly-shaped orbiting spacecraft, which is thus identified as the ultimate result of the technological advances that began with the bone-clubs.

Accompanied by Johann Strauss's *Blue Danube* waltz, the second major sequence of the film begins with shots of the Earth as seen from space and a wheel-like space station to which another spacecraft is traveling, carrying a single passenger, Dr. Heywood Floyd (William Sylvester) of the National Council of Astronautics. Extensive shots of the weightless interior of the spacecraft (still accompanied by *The Blue Danube*) are followed by the waltz-like approach of the craft to the space station. Floyd is shown arriving in an elevator-like compartment at the "main level" of the station, as announced by an attendant who accompanies him—and who speaks the first words of the film, after more than twenty-five minutes without dialogue.

Floyd checks in with station security, then calls home on a picture-phone, speaking with his small daughter, whose birthday party he will be missing because of his trip to the moon. He runs into a group of Russian scientists, professional acquaintances of his, who suggest that strange things are going on at the American Clavius Base on the moon, to which Floyd is headed. He explains to them that he is not at liberty to discuss his trip or the rumors that some sort of epidemic has broken out at the base.

When Floyd arrives at the base after another flight on which he is the only passenger (and during which we again get an extensive view of the trappings of future technology), he is briefed on the recent shocking discovery that has prompted his trip: a monolith (like the one shown in the first segment) has been found buried beneath the surface of the moon, apprently left there by an advanced intelligence four million years earlier. Concerned about the "social shock and cultural disorientation" that this evidence of alien intelligence might cause on Earth, the authorities have carefully suppressed news of the discovery in favor of the cover story about the epidemic.

Floyd travels out to the site of the mysterious monolith in a shuttle craft. While he is there, he and the others in the party hear a piercing, high-pitched noise, apparently coming from the monolith. They cover their ears in pain, followed by a fade to black and an on-screen announcement bearing the title of the next segment of the film, "JUPITER MISSION, 18 MONTHS LATER." (Significantly, all of the action on the moon is still a part of the "Dawn of Man" segment, suggesting that, until the location of the second monolith, humanity was still in its initial stage of development as an intelligent species.)

We will eventually learn that the discovery of the monolith on the moon triggered a signal that seems to be aimed at Jupiter, causing the authorities on Earth to mount a mission to Jupiter in an attempt to discover the nature and origin of the monolith. This new segment of the film begins with a long, slow external pan of spaceship *Discovery*, followed by a long shot of the exterior of the ship, then a cut to the interior, in which a man (at this point unidentified) jogs along a rotating circular path that uses centrifugal force to simulate gravity. We then see a variety of views of everyday life on the craft, which is manned by Dr. David Bowman (Keir Dullea), the commander of the mission, and Dr. Frank Poole (the jogger, played by Gary Lockwood), his deputy, in addition to three other crew members who were placed in hibernation before departure in order to save life-support resources. The day-to-day operations of the ship are controlled by an advanced HAL 9000 computer, an intelligent machine designed to think much like a human, except more quickly and more efficiently. Indeed, HAL is supposedly incapable of error.

We see the crew members exercising, eating, watching the BBC, playing chess with HAL, and receiving videophone messages from their families back on earth. All is very routine, especially with the infallible HAL ensuring that the ship operates smoothly. Still, HAL's soothing-but-creepy voice (provided by Shakespearean actor Douglas Rains) suggests an air of menace, especially when the computer begins to shows signs of condescension toward the human crew. This voice, in fact, becomes one of the most memorable features of the film and is now one of the signature sounds of modern American popular culture.

HAL suddenly announces that the ship's AE–35 unit is about to fail; Poole must then go outside the ship in a space pod to replace the unit, which is crucial to maintaining communications with Earth. The replacement goes smoothly, but when Bowman and Poole examine the replaced unit they can find nothing wrong with it. HAL, seeming puzzled, recommends that they put it back in operation until it fails, so that they can better diagnose the problem. Mission control endorses the plan, especially as their own analysis shows that HAL was in error when it predicted the fault, indicating a potentially serious problem with the computer. HAL responds that no 9000 series computer has ever made a mistake and that the only possible explanation is some sort of human error, again signaling its growing sense of superiority to humans.

Bowman and Poole go inside one of the pods so that they can discuss the situation without HAL overhearing. They agree that, if the computer is indeed malfunctioning, they will have to disconnect it and continue the mission under Earth-based computer control. However, just as the film goes into intermission, it becomes clear that HAL is reading their lips through a window in the pod, which sets the stage for a sinister turn in the computer's behavior in the latter part of the film.

After the intermission (during which the screen then goes blank, with Ligeti's "Atmospheres" providing a musical backdrop), Poole goes back out to replace the original AE-35 unit, exiting the space pod in order to do so. HAL then takes control of the pod and kills the astronaut by ripping loose his air hose and sending his body hurtling off into space. Bowman goes out in another pod and retrieves the body, though he knows it is too late to save Poole. In the meantime, HAL cuts off the life support to the three sleeping crewmen, killing them as well. HAL refuses to open the pod bay doors to let Bowman back in the ship, claiming that the mission is too important to allow humans to jeopardize it by disconnecting the computer.

Bowman manages to use the mechanical arms of the pod to open an emergency hatch and get back into the ship. He then sets about the daunting task of disconnecting HAL, which is made difficult by the complexity of the computer and by the fact that no HAL 9000 computer has ever been disconnected. All the while, HAL pleads with him to stop, but he finally succeeds, sending the computer into a reversion to its infancy as it begins to sing a song ("Daisy") taught it by its first programmer nine years earlier, then drifts off into oblivion.

The disconnection of HAL triggers a recording designed to explain the full parameters of the mission upon arrival at Jupiter. The recording explains the discovery of the monolith on the moon and notes that the monolith has done nothing since but emit a single, very powerful radio signal aimed at Jupiter. The screen then cuts to the title of the next segment, "JUPITER AND BEYOND THE INFINITE."

In this segment, *Discovery* approaches Jupiter, again to the sound of the Ligeti requiem that usually announces the appearance of a monolith. Indeed, when Bowman leaves the ship in a pod, he approaches what seems to be one of the monoliths slowly spinning in space. Suddenly, he seems to enter another dimension (hyper-space), goes through a Stargate that is something like a psychedelic tunnel, then emerges in a field of stars. He then moves through a series of strange, incomprehensible sights and shapes, taking him out of the solar system and into a different part of the galaxy. At the same time, the film shifts from a relatively comprehensible SF narrative and into a mode of avant-garde art cinema. The pod seems to be flying over a sort of canyon (in a variety of weird changing colors), then an ocean and more planetary surface. Finally, as the cacophonous music builds to a crescendo, then falls to near silence, Bowman realizes that the pod has somehow come to rest. He discovers that he is now in a simulated period hotel suite, decorated with bits and pieces of Earth furnishings, apparently designed to provide comforting surroundings for someone from Earth, though the overdone decor of the room suggests that it may have been an alien's idea of what an Earth hotel room would look like. Bowman, now an old man, emerges from the pod and begins to explore the suite. He approaches an old man eating at a table.

The man turns around and looks at him, then slowly rises and approaches him. It is an even older version of Bowman himself, and the space-suited Bowman now disappears from the film. After the other Bowman drops and breaks a glass on the floor, he looks over onto the bed and sees an even older version of himself. A monolith appears at the foot of the bed, and the aged Bowman in the bed is suddenly replaced by a gestating fetus (apparently as a signal that he dies and is reborn), the Star Child. *Also Sprach Zarathustra* again plays, announcing another step in human evolution. As the film closes, the fetus is seen approaching Earth from space, inside a sort of embryonic bubble.

THE SOURCES OF THE MOVIE

2001 is based (very loosely) on a short story entitled "The Sentinel," by Arthur C. Clarke. In the story, a strange alien artifact is discovered buried beneath the surface of the moon, left there long ago by an advanced alien race as a means of detecting when the human race had become advanced enough to travel to the moon. From this seed, Clarke and Kubrick constructed the screenplay of the film. Meanwhile, Clarke expanded his short story into a novel with the same title as the film. The film is thus not literally based on this novel, though some of the novel was written before the script and helped provide a basis for it. The novel fills in numerous details on which viewers of the film are left to speculate. In particular, the novel provides an ending that is less vague than that of the film, making it clear that the Star Child, representing the next step in human evolution, has returned to Earth to become master of the planet (he destroys an orbiting weapons station as he approaches the atmosphere), even though he is as yet unsure what he will do with this power. Otherwise, the plots of the film and book are similar, though there are a few differences in details, as when the pivotal space mission in the book is actually aimed at Saturn, rather than Jupiter, as in the film.

IMAGES, SOUNDS, AND IDEAS: SCIENCE FICTION AS ART IN *2001: A SPACE ODYSSEY*

The science fiction ideas that inform *2001: A Space Odyssey* are relatively conventional. For example, the notion of an advanced alien race guiding human evolution can be found in any number of science fiction novels, such as Clarke's own *Childhood's End* (1953) and Octavia Butler's more recent *Xenogenesis* trilogy (1987–1989). More recently, David Brin's popular series of "Uplift" novels makes such evolutionary guidance a central feature of intergalactic civilization. The notion of a runaway computer that turns on its programmers is by now a virtual cliché (Jean-Luc Godard's 1965 *Alphaville* is perhaps the locus classicus of the motif in film), though it was not quite as familiar in 1968 as it is now. In fact, in many ways, the story of HAL in *2001* is simply a high-tech retelling of the Frankenstein story. Nevertheless, *2001* is an extremely innovative film that broke important new ground in the history of science fiction cinema. Its use of sound and visuals to create a compelling SF vision of a fictional universe represented a genuine breakthrough. The film won an Oscar for its special visual effects and was nominated for best set direction, best director, and best original screenplay. It was ranked twenty-second on the 1998 American Film Institute's list of the all-time great films, making it the second highest-ranked science-fiction film on that list (*Star Wars* was ranked fifteenth).

Initially, *2001* was greeted by audiences with a combination of astonishment and bewilderment. Many complained that the film was simply boring and incomprehensible, but the film did well at the box office, partly because its unconventional nature (especially the psychedelic light show near the end) helped it to appeal to the countercultural sensibilities of the late 1960s. Critics were even more strongly divided than audiences. Pauline Kael, in a remarkably unperceptive review published in *Harper's,* called *2001* "monumentally unimaginative" and concluded that it was "the biggest amateur movie of them all." Charles Champlin of the *Los Angeles Times,* on the other hand, called it a milestone in the art of film that surpassed anything he had ever seen in terms of technical achievement.

If it appears that Kael and Champlin were seeing different films, then perhaps they were. Such disagreements came about because *2001* is such a complex film and because it cedes so much of its work to the imagination of viewers, allowing different viewers literally to construct different films from the material at hand. Because of its combination of excellence and complexity, *2001* has spawned a great deal of academic criticism as well as a number of book-length guides intended for the general viewer—several of them proclaiming *2001* the greatest science fiction film ever made. Other commentators go even further, as when Leonard Wheat, in *Kubrick's*

2001: A Triple Allegory (London: Scarecrow Press, 2000, p. 160) calls *2001* "the grandest motion picture ever filmed." Book-length works from Jerome Agel's early *The Making of Kubrick's 2001* (1970) to Piers Bizony's recent *2001: Filming the Future* (2000) have detailed the intricate three-year-plus process of making the film, while one recent work, *The Making of 2001: A Space Odyssey* (2000, edited by Stephanie Schwam), compiles testimonies on the making of the film by those involved in the process, as well as a number of reviews of the film.

All of this available commentary is highly useful given the intricacies of the film itself, while the continuing critical interest in the film testifies to its ongoing importance. The special effects, made in the days before computer-generated imagery revolutionized the entire field, continue to impress; the way in which Kubrick's camera seems almost lovingly to caress the technological artifacts it films represents a powerful pro-technology statement, even as the malfunction of HAL sounds an ominous warning. The glorious music that accompanies many of the film's images of high-tech devices makes these devices seem to be works of art as much as technology.

Indeed, the much-discussed music of *2001* is, as a whole, one of the key ingredients that makes this film so special. For one thing, the choice of classical music for the soundtrack announces that this film takes itself very seriously as a work of art (complete with overture and intermission), as opposed to the often cheesy and campy SF productions that had preceded it. The music certainly makes a substantial contribution to the grandeur that many viewers note when they watch the film, and in some cases even makes thematic contributions. For example, the title of Strauss's *Also Sprach Zarathustra*, strategically placed at points in the film when the monoliths are about to initiate a new stage in human evolution, is taken from a book by nineteenth-century German philosopher Friedrich Nietzsche, whose best-known concept is the notion of the coming of a new variety of superior human, or "Übermensch," who could lead humanity into a new era.

Nevertheless, despite the film's impressive score, it is the visual imagery for which *2001* is ultimately most important. Kubrick himself was heavily involved in designing the special effects for the film, though it also had several "special photographic effects supervisors," including Douglas Trumbull, who went on to become something of a legend in the special effects world, designing special photographic effects for a number of the most important SF films ever made, including *The Andromeda Strain* (1971),

Close Encounters of the Third Kind (1977), *Star Trek: The Motion Picture* (1979), and *Blade Runner* (1982). He also directed such excellent SF films as *Silent Running* (1972) and *Brainstorm* (1983) and developed the special "Showscan" process which has been used to provide the visual effects for a variety of automated theme-park rides.

The ballet-like presentation of the various space vessels in *2001* is particularly effective, but for two seemingly contradictory reasons. On the one hand, the various spacecraft and space stations in *2001* look entirely realistic and convincing, far more so than in any previous science fiction film. That audiences are entirely aware that the technology of *2001* is *not* real, that it is merely the product of movie magic, only serves to make the film's special effects all the more impressive. Indeed, the real technological marvel of the film is not the *Discovery* spacecraft or the HAL computer but the ability of Kubrick and his special effects team to create such vivid and believable images of what the technology of the future *might* be like.

In 1968, one year before the first manned landing on the moon would occur, and only eight years after the first manned spaceflight of Yuri Gagarin, it was easy to believe that technology would advance to the state depicted in the film by the year 2001. Interestingly enough, however, the film's images of future technology remain just as effective in our own post–2001 era, when we *know* that the level of spaceflight technology represented in the film has not been reached and is not likely to be reached in the near future. Again, that is because the real object of representation in *2001* is not spaceflight technology at all but special effects technology—and the special effects of the film are all the more impressive because we know that the available technology for the production of special effects has now moved vastly beyond that which was available to Kubrick and his team, yet no subsequent film has been able to produce images that were more aesthetically stunning or technologically convincing than those produced in *2001*.

The dazzling images of the film clearly outweigh its plot and themes in importance. In fact, at first glance, one of the most noticeable things about *2001* is its almost total absence of any sort of social or political commentary, especially for a film released in 1968, the peak year of the global political unrest that marked the 1960s. When there are themes, they seem more metaphysical than political. However, the film is actually thematically richer than might first appear, sometimes in ways that have distinctly social and political implications. For example, one of the most striking things about the representation of spaceflight in the film—at least as regards flight between Earth and the moon—is how utterly routine it has become, as when Heywood Floyd's flight to the moon is carefully constructed to look very much like contemporary airline travel. In fact, the flight is not only routine, but boring; when we first see Floyd, in fact, he has fallen asleep while watching television on the flight.

This routinization of space travel seems at first to be simply an indication of the technological advancement. On the other hand, a closer look at the film suggests that this sort of routinization of technology is part of a far broader tendency toward routine that afflicts Kubrick's future society. Meanwhile, the film's lack of dialogue (usually interpreted as a sign of the primacy of its images) can also be taken as a sign of the general linguistic poverty of the denizens of the year 2001. One perceptive early reviewer, F. A. Macklin, noted in *Film Comment* that the film revealed "the wretched decline in language" in Kubrick's future world, a motif common to dystopian fictions such as George Orwell's *Nineteen Eighty-Four* and that can be taken as a hint at the dystopian nature of the future society of the film. When the first human voice is finally heard in the film, it belongs to the uniformed attendant of the high-tech elevator that delivers Floyd to his destination on the space station, giving him what is basically a prepared script: "Here you are, sir. Main level, please." Floyd responds with meaningless small talk, then walks into the lobby where he is greeted by a similarly-uniformed receptionist with whom he exchanges similarly empty chatter. She asks him, "Did you have a pleasant flight, sir?" to which he responds, "Yes, very nice, thanks." Mr. Miller of station security then greets him with an equally banal exchange, then takes him to a video screen on which a recording asks him to identify himself and the nature of his journey for security purposes.

What is striking at this point is that the language of the video recording is no more mechanical than that of the humans we have encountered thus far in the film. Indeed, as the film goes forward, we discover that all of the characters in the film tend to speak and act mechanically, almost as if they have been programmed to speak and act in this way. In some cases, this manner of speech seems motivated by the situation, as when various characters speak in purely official capacities or when Floyd speaks with the Russian scientists on the station, each side (especially Floyd) tiptoeing verbally through the conversation in ways that indicate the ongoing distance between the two sides in a Cold War that continues in the 2001 of the film. Meanwhile, most of the communication in the film is purely impersonal, as in Floyd's speech upon arrival at the moon base (a masterpiece of trite bureaucratese). Later he receives clichéd congratulations from colleagues on the quality of the speech, followed by his own formulaic reply that they themselves have done a "hell of a job" in handling the matter of the monolith. However, even personal (and potentially touching) moments, such as Floyd's call home to his daughter, consist of nothing more than an exchange of clichés, bereft of emotion. Floyd's cute-but-fidgety daughter seems bored by the entire conversation; she seems neither disappointed nor surprised that he will miss her upcoming birthday party, while the fact that her first choice of a birthday present is a telephone suggests her total lack of imagination, a telephone being the first thing at hand. It also emphasizes the mediated nature of most communication in this future society, in which technology allows for the exchange of messages across great distances, including those of outer space. In fact, the only other personal "conversation" that occurs in the film is even more mediated; Poole's parents wish him a happy birthday via a recorded message sent to the *Discovery* and to which he is not even able to respond.

It is also significant that Floyd's video display shows us the cost of his call home ($1.70) immediately after the end of the conversation with his daughter, suggesting the way in which even the most personal of relationships in this future society have been reduced to the status of mere economic commodities. Similarly, in their birthday greeting to their son, Poole's parents speak largely of economic matters, assuring him that he will soon be receiving his promised pay raise and asking how much they should spend on a gift he has asked them to buy for some friends.

Of course, this "hell of a job" consists of little more than suppressing information about the monolith on the moon, a tactic that might be understandable but that also gives this future society a subtly dystopian flavor. Indeed, Floyd comes to the moon as a representative of the National Council of Astronautics, which seems to have political authority on Earth that goes well beyond that of NASA, its real-world counterpart. For example, the Council has requested, among other things, that formal security oaths be obtained in writing from everyone who has any knowledge of the monolith. The requirement of such oaths (reminiscent of those associated with the era of McCarthy-ite anti-communist repression in the United States in the 1950s), like the official suppression of information about the monolith itself, suggests anything but a utopian future.

Of course, this suppression is consistent with the general lack of real communication among the characters in the film. The mediated and mechanical conversations that fill the film suggest the alienation that separates one person from another in this dystopian future, where the phenomenon of the "waning of affect" that cultural critic Fredric Jameson sees as a crucial aspect of experience in the postmodern world has reached an extreme. Indeed, the question posed of HAL midway through the film about whether he actually has feelings and emotions might just as well have been posed of any of the human characters in the film. Thus, when Poole (speaking in the typically banal language of the film) suggests of HAL that "you think of him really just as another person," it is not clear whether that is because HAL is so human-like or because the humans in the film are so robotic and computer-like.

Humans in the film not only act and speak alike, but they also look alike. Most of them dress in uniforms, of course, but even the civilian clothing in the film has a uniform-like quality. The fact that Kubrick chose two nearly identical looking and sounding actors to play the parts of Poole and Bowman was surely no accident but can be taken as another marker of the suppression of individuality in his society of the future. Meanwhile, the citizens of this society are limited by an almost total lack of genuine sensual experience. There is no hint of sexuality in the film; the only food we ever see consumed is the unappetizing, characterless blocks and puddles of prepackaged food served aboard spaceships; and the only culture available is canned elevator music and banal television programming.

In fact, it has been frequently observed that HAL may well be the most "human" of all of the characters in the film. While most of the humans in the film seem to be operating in an almost trance-like state, HAL remains alert, engaged, and alarmed. He is also capable of taking radical action on his own, while the humans seem to need instructions from the home office (or HAL) before undertaking even the simplest of tasks. Probably the most poignant moment in the film occurs as Bowman begins to shut down HAL's memory circuits, causing a reversion to "childhood" in which the computer first begs for its "life," then announces its growing sense of fear as its "mind" goes. "I can feel it," it repeatedly says, which sets it apart from the many humans in the film who seem to feel nothing at all. It then regresses through the nine years of its programming, a time period chosen by Kubrick in order to endow the computer with additional humanity by giving it a personal history (even though it now seems absurd to imagine that a nine-year-old computer would not be obsolete, a fact Clarke apparently understood by making HAL only four years old in the novel version).

Indeed, as Carl Freedman notes in an extremely useful essay on *2001* that appears in his book *The Incomplete Projects: Marxism, Modernity, and the Politics of Culture* (Middletown, CT: Wesleyan University Press, 2002), HAL's relatively lively intellect and personality highlight the "vacuity of humanity in the human crew members" (109). However, whereas Freedman sees the banality of the film's plot and characters as a sort of metafictional commentary on the difficulties of science fiction film as an art form (and thus sees *2001* as essentially apolitical, if in an interesting way), I would argue that there is a great deal of implicit political commentary in Kubrick's presentation of a future in which forces of conformism and routinization have battered humanity into a collection of lifeless and essentially interchangeable near-robots. Granted, Kubrick does not overtly diagnosis the malaise of humanity in the year 2001 as specifically political, though it does have clear political dimensions via the vague mentions of the shadowy "Council." Humanity seems to have reached a sort of impasse, a dead end; the stage of development labeled in the film as "The Dawn of Man" has gone as far as it can go. The revolt of HAL, meanwhile, signals the fact that humans have now been outstripped by their own technology, which again means that the first stage of human evolution has reached its limit. The evolutionary "boost" provided by the film's mysterious aliens (or gods, or whatever they might be) is thus not only desirable but necessary for the continued survival of the species—if, in fact, the Star Child is still the same species at all.

There is, of course, a certain optimism in the film's suggestion that, just as humanity has been all but exhausted, something will come along to inject new life into the human endeavor. Indeed, Freedman concludes that *2001* "conveys genuine utopian energy in its glimpse of a spiritual richness that may rescue humanity from the bureaucratic pettiness of Heywood Floyd or his Russian counterparts" (110). One might argue, however, that the film's requirement of supernatural, or at least superhuman, intervention for this rescue to take place makes it a rather weak utopian gesture that signals the inability of human beings to achieve a better future of their own accord. From this point of view, the film is profoundly pessimistic, suggesting that we are already inescapably on the downward historical slope toward the film's dehumanized future. There is, however, a powerful utopian proclamation in *2001* and that is the film itself, the sensuousness of which contrasts dramatically with the sensually deprived society it depicts. The film, with its dazzling sights and sounds, announces its own ability to transcend its banal plot, characters, and dialogue—just as the film's impressive inventiveness stands as concrete proof that there are still human beings in the year 1968 who can think beyond banality and who are not quite as bereft of imagination as the film warns us we are beginning to be. The film thus stands not as a pessimistic prediction of an empty, routine, and banal future but as a suggestion of directions we might take to avoid that future.

SCIENCE FICTION AS CINEMA: THE LEGACY OF *2001: A SPACE ODYSSEY*

2001 has no peers or direct successors in SF film. However, elements of it resemble a number of other films, partly because it has been so influential on subsequent SF films. It inspired a sequel in the form of Peter Hyams's *2010: The Year We Make Contact* (1984), which directly continues the narrative of the original film but is otherwise unremarkable, never quite reaching the grandeur of its predecessor, though it does at times attempt to reproduce the look of *2001*. Virtually every other SF film made since 1968 draws upon the imagery and themes of *2001* as well, including dozens of films that visually or verbally refer to the film and a number of others (such as Mel Brooks's 1985 *Spaceballs*) that include spoofs of it. Meanwhile, Kubrick's own slightly later *A Clockwork Orange* (1971) is not only occasionally visually reminiscent of *2001* but also, in its depiction of a future society that employs psychological conditioning to enforce conformity, echoes the earlier film's concern with a social tendency toward the banal and the routine.

Films that involve journeys into outer space have been particularly influenced by *2001*, as when the famous special effects of *Star Wars* (a film otherwise distinctly different from its illustrious predecessor) sometimes recall Kubrick's film in their attention to detail in the representation of space-travel technology. *Star Wars* also seeks to achieve some of the grandeur of *2001*, though in a sort of pop cultural way quite different from the classicism of *2001*. Other space-travel films, such as Paul W. S.

Anderson's *Event Horizon* (1997), contain plot elements that are reminiscent of *2001*, while SF films such as *The Abyss* (1989) frequently attempt to announce their importance by projecting a sense of magnitude and grandeur, especially through the use of music, again suggesting the influence of Kubrick's film.

5

Planet of the Apes

Released 1968; Director Franklin J. Schaffner

Planet of the Apes joined Stanley Kubrick's *2001: A Space Odyssey*, released in the same year, as a landmark film in the history of American science fiction cinema. Though perhaps not as artful as Kubrick's film, *Planet of the Apes*, distinguished particularly by the makeup that transformed human actors into believable ape characters, was nevertheless an impressive bit of filmmaking. Even more, it was a highly successful venture in storytelling and mythbuilding that captured the imaginations of audiences in 1968 not only with its basic scenario and plot, but also in the way the film commented on the political concerns of that volatile year. Ultimately, the film spurred one of the most important phenomena in SF film history, leading to four successful film sequels, two not-so-successful television series, and one of the most profitable merchandising campaigns produced in conjunction with any film franchise up to that time.

THE STORY: THE INVOLUTION OF SPECIES

Planet of the Apes begins as astronaut George Taylor (Charlton Heston) records his final log entry before touchdown after a planned six-month flight at near-light speed, during which time nearly 700 years have passed on Earth. Taylor indicates early on the disgust with his contemporary humanity that is central to his character: "You who are reading me now are a different breed—I hope a better one. I leave the twentieth century with no regrets." He then wonders if the hundreds of years that have passed have brought about changes on Earth, announcing the political concerns that have helped to make the film such an important monument of American popular culture: "Does man still make war against his brother? Keep his neighbor's children starving?"

Taylor then joins the other three crew members of the spacecraft in hibernation, in preparation for the automated landing. We are then treated to a disorienting, spinning sequence that attempts to show the landing as it would look from within the cabin. The ship lands in water, surrounded by a wasted, craggy planetary surface. Taylor, now bearded (to his obvious surprise), awakes as do two other crew members, Landon (Robert Gunner) and Dodge (Jeff Burton). However, the only female crew member, Lt. Stewart (Dianne Stanley), is found dead within her cracked hibernation chamber, apparently of old age, though it is not clear why that would be if they have indeed been traveling at near-light speed.

Water begins to leak into the cabin, and they have to abandon ship. Taylor discovers that, according to the ship's chronometer, they have been propelled forward to the Earth year 3978; approximately eighteen months (rather than the scheduled six) have passed for them during the flight. They paddle ashore in an inflatable life raft, watching the ship sink behind them, leaving them stranded permanently on the planet. They believe they are 320 light years from Earth, in orbit around a star in the constellation Orion, though something has obviously gone wrong and they are not really sure where (or when) they are. They have a few supplies and food and water enough for three days, and survival on the planet will not be easy. The atmosphere is similar to Earth's, so the air is breathable, but a test shows that the soil is dead, unable to support any vegetation.

They set out on foot, hoping to find a source of food and fresh water on the apparently barren planet, encountering along the way thunder and lightning, but no rain. Taylor (who will, ironically emerge as mankind's champion in the film) continues to make misanthropic remarks. Eventually, they come upon a waterfall feeding a pool of clear, fresh water. They all strip and dive in, celebrating. Soon afterward, they discover a group of primitive-looking people, causing Taylor to remark, "If this is the best they've got around here," he remarks, "in six months we'll be running this planet." If this remark reveals the impulse toward imperialistic domination that the astronauts have brought to the planet from our own world, they very quickly discover that they will have formidable opposition if they plan to try to "run" this planet when a party of intelligent gun-bearing apes appears, some on horseback. The apes chase the people into preset nets and ditches, capturing many. Dodge is shot and killed; Landon is knocked unconscious, his ultimate fate unknown; Taylor is shot in the throat and captured, placed in a cage with several other humans, including a beautiful woman (Linda Harrison) he had noticed earlier, whom he will subsequently name "Nova."

The captives are taken to a town, where Taylor is given medical treatment. The apes, surprisingly, speak English. Taylor hears two ape doctors talking. One, Zira (Kim Hunter), an animal psychologist, notes that the humans are being used for medical research in their efforts to develop effective techniques of brain surgery. Unable to talk because of his wound, Taylor repeatedly attempts to communicate with his captors, but they think he is just mimicking them. "Human see, human do," one of them concludes, in one of the film's many humorous (but telling) reversals of clichés from our own world. Zira does not understand Taylor's attempts at communication, but she recognizes that he seems to be special. She dubs him "Bright Eyes" and is so impressed that she shows him to her superior, the orangutan Dr. Zaius (Maurice Evans), whose title is "Minister of Science and Chief Defender of the Faith," indicating the way in which scientific research on this planet seems limited by religious bigotry. Interestingly, Zaius's disparaging attitude toward humans (he thinks they are a nuisance and should be exterminated) is not so far from Taylor's own, though Taylor will ultimately defend humans against Zaius's prejudices.

Taylor continues to try to communicate with his captors, eventually managing to scribble a message to Zira: "MY NAME IS TAYLOR." Zira immediately orders a collar and leash and takes Taylor out of the cage. Taylor writes more messages for Zira and Cornelius, attempting to explain where he came from. Cornelius, who is working in his research to demonstrate that apes evolved from men (having discovered evidence of an ancient culture that predates the Sacred Scrolls, founding texts of the ape culture), realizes that Taylor could provide important support for his theory, but he also realizes that he is treading on dangerous ground because his work might prove the Sacred Scrolls wrong and thus be condemned as heresy. Zaius arrives with Dr. Maximus (Woodrow Parfrey), the Commissioner for Animal Affairs, then orders Taylor sent back to his cage and gelded. Taylor, however, overcomes his guard and escapes out into the dusty streets of the town. After a furious chase scene, he is finally recaptured. Once again caught in a net, Taylor cries out, regaining his voice and shocking the apes around him, who believe humans incapable of speech: "Take your stinking paws off me, you damn dirty ape!"

Back in captivity, Taylor attempts to teach Nova to speak, but without success. His captors remove her from the cage, holding him at bay with a fire hose (in an image that could not fail to resonate with audiences of the late 1960s, who had often seen the forces of authority holding demonstrators at bay with fire hoses in the streets of American cities). "It's a madhouse! A madhouse!" Taylor screams in one of the film's landmark moments—commenting both on the craziness of an ape planet and (at least for contemporary audiences) on the madness of the official repression of dissent in American streets. Watching Nova in the cage across from him, Taylor realizes that he misses her. "Imagine *me* needing someone," he mutters as much to himself as to Nova. "Back on Earth I never did. Oh, there were women. Lots of women. Lots of lovemaking, but no love. That was the kind of world we'd made." He explains to an uncomprehending Nova that they had brought Stewart along to be the new Eve (apparently they had planned to found a colony, though it would make little sense to bring three men and only one woman for that purpose). Then he bitterly adds, "with our hot and eager help, of course."

Weeks after his near escape, Zaius has Taylor brought to a meeting room for a hearing before a high-level tribunal of the National Academy of Science, chaired by the President of the Academy (James Whitmore), who is joined by Maximus and Zaius, with the Deputy Minister of Justice, Dr. Honorius (James Daly), as prosecutor. Zira and Cornelius are to act as Taylor's advocates, but the tribunal is shocked when he speaks up for himself. Zaius immediately orders him silenced. Honorius (adapting Alexander Pope's dictum that the proper study of mankind is man) proclaims that "the proper study of apes is apes," and denounces Zira for studying humans instead. In particular, he charges that Zira and her surgeon-associate Dr. Galen (Wright King) have surgically tampered with Taylor to produce a "speaking monster," noting that their work is intended to support a heretical theory of evolution.

Soon afterward, we learn that, in a reversal of the procedure described by Honorius, Landon has been lobotomized to efface signs of his intelligence, though Zaius claims that Landon suffered a skull fracture in the course of his capture and had to undergo surgery to save his life. As the hearing proceeds, Cornelius and Zira grant that Taylor surely did not come from another planet, but that he clearly must have come from somewhere, perhaps within the Forbidden Zone. Zira and Cornelius are promptly charged with contempt of the tribunal, malicious mischief, and scientific heresy, and the hearing is adjourned. Taylor is dragged away, while Zira and Cornelius walk slowly away as if in shock. Taylor is taken to Zaius's office, where Zaius tells him that Zira and Cornelius will soon be tried and that Taylor himself will be emasculated, then subjected to experimental brain surgery, leaving him in a state of living death. But Zaius tells him he will be spared if he tells the truth about his origins. In particular, Zaius believes Taylor is a mutant and that he comes from a community of such mutants, which Zaius wants to locate and destroy. When Taylor sticks to his original story, Zaius sends him back to his cage.

Zira and Cornelius engineer an escape with the help of Zira's nephew, Lucius (Lou Wagner). The four travel to a seashore in the Forbidden Zone, where Cornelius had earlier discovered the ruins of an ancient civilization. When Zaius arrives with a group of armed guards, Taylor aims his rifle at Zaius and orders him to send the guards away. Zaius does so but warns Cornelius and Zira that they will be hanged for treason if they do not desist. When Zaius announces that "There is no contradiction between faith and science. *True* science," Taylor gets him to agree to drop his charges against Cornelius and Zira if they can find evidence in the diggings that the Sacred Scrolls do not tell the whole story of ape history. Taylor orders Lucius to stand guard outside while they all go inside what seems to be a large cave. Lucius, whose attitudes humorously resemble those of human teenagers, complains, "Always giving orders, just like every other adult."

Inside, Cornelius uncovers evidence of an ancient (possibly human) culture of perhaps 2000 years earlier that is more advanced than the current ape culture. Taylor then uses Zaius as a hostage to force the apes to give him and Nova horses, food, water, and ammunition. Based on the evidence in the diggings, Taylor speculates that civilized humans predated the apes on this planet but were wiped out by some sort of plague or natural catastrophe. He charges that Zaius knew of this all along. Zaius, in response, has Cornelius read from the Sacred Scrolls, 29th scroll, 6th verse: "Beware the beast man, for he is the devil's pawn. Alone among God's primates, he kills for sport or lust or greed. Yea, he will murder his brother to possess his brother's land. Let him not breed in great numbers, for he will make a desert of his home and yours. Shun him, drive him back into his jungle lair, for he is the harbinger of death."

Taylor prepares to ride off with Nova, following the shoreline, though Cornelius and Zira opt to stay behind. Taylor leaves Lucius with the injunction to keep the flags of discontent flying and not to trust anyone over thirty. He kisses Zira goodbye, though she is appalled that he is so "damned ugly." Zaius, asked by the departing Taylor why he has always feared and hated him so, replies simply, "Because you're a man." He admits that he has always dreaded Taylor's coming because he has indeed known about man all along: "From the evidence, I believe his wisdom must walk hand in hand with his idiocy." Asked by Taylor what evidence he means, he cryptically says, "The Forbidden Zone was once a paradise. Your greed made a desert of it ages ago." He also warns Taylor that he may not like what he finds if he continues to investigate the history of the planet. After Taylor leaves, Zaius orders the cave sealed with explosives and Zira and Cornelius tried for scientific heresy in spite of the evidence that their theories are correct. Zira asks him, referring to Taylor, "What will he find out there, doctor?" Zaius simply replies, "His destiny."

Riding along the shoreline, Taylor and Nova come upon an outcropping protruding from the sand. Taylor looks up and stares at it in shock. He drops to his knees, screaming at his discovery: "Oh, my God! I'm back. I'm home. All the time it was . . . We finally really did it! You maniacs! You blew it up! Ah, damn you! Goddamn you all to hell!" The camera pans back to show us that the outcropping is the top half of the Statue of Liberty, apparently half buried in the holocaust (presumably nuclear) that destroyed the original civilization of this planet, which is, of course, Earth.

THE SOURCES OF THE MOVIE

Planet of the Apes is based on Pierre Boulle's 1963 French novel *La planéte des singes* (literal translation "Planet of the Monkeys," but published in English as *Planet of the Apes* the same year). As adapted for the screen by the legendary Rod Serling, then reworked by veteran screenwriter Michael Wilson, the film is reasonably faithful to the original novel, including the direct transcription of most of the character names. Many of the changes are incidental and simply involve "Americanizing" the work by making the human protagonists American astronauts rather than French explorers, as they are in the novel. Other changes were made simply as matters of convenience for the film medium, as when the apes of the film speak English, while those of the book speak their own ape language. One major difference between the film and the book is that the ape society of the book has reached roughly the same level of technological advancement as Earth in the 1960s, while the society in the book is in most ways extremely backward and primitive. This choice was made primarily for budgetary reasons because it allowed the filmmakers to avoid the expense of creating a credible-looking advanced ape culture, and it was primarily in order to implement this change that Wilson was brought in to rework Serling's original script. Perhaps the biggest difference between the two works is that, in the novel, the explorers really do go to another planet (in the Betelgeuse system), while protagonist Ulysse Mérou returns to Earth in the end only to discover that apes have displaced humans there as well. In the film, on the other hand, protagonist George Taylor discovers that he has been on Earth all along. In this sense, the film is probably more powerful than the book, while also providing a clearer explanation (in its suggestion of a nuclear holocaust) for the downfall of human civilization in the first place.

SCIENCE FICTION AS POLITICAL SATIRE IN *PLANET OF THE APES*: RACISM, NUCLEAR DESTRUCTION, AND THE 1960s

Planet of the Apes was a major box-office success on its initial release. It was also recognized with Academy Award nominations for Best Costume Design and Best Original Score. In addition, John Chambers, who designed the ape makeup for the film, was given a special Oscar for his "outstanding achievement" in the film. Chambers came to the film mostly with experience in doing makeup for television programs such as *The Munsters, The Outer Limits*, and *Lost in Space*; perhaps his most important achievement prior to *Planet of the Apes* was the design of Spock's ears for *Star Trek*. But his achievement in designing the ape makeup for the film was indeed outstanding, overcoming the initial fears on the part of Fox Studio executives that audiences would be unable to take the film seriously because actors in ape costumes would inherently look ridiculous. Perhaps the best evidence of the quality of the makeup in the film comes from comparison to the later Tim Burton "reimagining" of the film in 2001, where the makeup is far more sophisticated, realistic, and expensive, but not one bit more effective. (Indeed, Burton's version is a gorgeous film that looks much better than the original in all sorts of ways—but that is almost entirely lacking in the emotional power and political commentary of the original.) Clearly, audiences who watched McDowall, Hunter, and the other actors in the film in 1968 were perfectly well aware that they were watching humans in ape makeup, but were willing to accept them as ape characters nevertheless; in this and other ways, *Planet of the Apes* thus stands as a lasting testament to the ability of film as a medium to convince audiences to suspend their disbelief and to accept the premises on which individual films are based.

Much attention has been devoted to the ape makeup in *Planet of the Apes*, and discussions of its development can be found in numerous places, such as the recent guide *Planet of the Apes Revisited*, by Joe Russo and Larry Landsman, with Edward Gross (New York: Thomas Dunne Books, 2001). But *Planet of the Apes* is far more than an exercise in creative makeup and costuming, as can be seen by the fact that the film and the franchise it spawned have become one of the crucial phenomena of American popular culture in the last four decades. For example, it is clear that the great emotional impact of the film owes a great deal to Jerry Goldsmith's musical score, while aspects of the film other than the makeup are similarly effective without being truly realistic. For example, art director William Creber's design of the ape city, with architecture that looks as if it were carved out of stone, is very effective in producing the desired atmosphere, despite the fact that there seems to be no logical way the apes could have built such architecture with the technology available to them, while the buildings actually look much too primitive for a society that is in the process of developing sophisticated technologies such as brain surgery. Indeed, the carved-stone buildings make the ape city look very much like something out of *The Flintstones* (which had, by the way, just completed its initial run on ABC in 1966), but the architecture somehow still seems appropriate and effective in its contribution to the overall impression of an ape-dominated society.

However, most of the serious critical attention given the film and its sequels has focused not on their technical achievements but on their political implications, and especially on the ways in which the various films, in their depiction of relations between apes and humans, can be read as allegories of interracial relations in our own world, especially in the United States. Eric Greene has argued particularly well, in his book-length study *Planet of the Apes as American Myth: Race, Politics, and Popular Culture* (Middletown, CT: Wesleyan University Press, 1996), for the importance of these racial allegories and other political aspects of the films. For Greene, "the makers of the *Apes* films created fictional spaces whose social tensions resembled those then dominating the United States. They inserted characters into those spaces whose ideologies, passions, and fears duplicated the ideologies, passions, and fears of generations of Americans. And they placed those characters in conflicts that replicated crucial conflicts from the United States; past and present" (9).

As Greene also notes, the racial allegories that are for him the central political issue dealt with in the *Apes* series become even clearer in the sequels than in the original. Still, even in the original film it is clear that the relationship between apes and humans on the Ape Planet can be read as a commentary on the relationship between whites and African Americans in our own world. For example, the roundup in which Taylor is initially captured carries resonances of the nightmarish hunts of our own history in which Africans were captured and then shipped to the Americas to be sold as slaves. And many of the stereotypes spouted by the apes about humans as irrational, lazy, lascivious, and violent clearly echo stereotypes that have, in our own world, been applied to African Americans and other nonwhite peoples. The sudden shift in perspective that makes humans the object of race hatred on the part of animals (and, by extension, whites the despised Others of blacks) provides precisely the sort of cognitive jolt that provides all the best science fiction with its principal power. This jolt asks audiences to see racism with fresh eyes, and the effect is only enhanced by the fact that the rhetoric of modern racism, as first developed in the nineteenth century, has long employed the strategy of suggesting that supposedly inferior races are in fact more similar to apes than to genuine human beings.

In the sequels *Escape from the Planet of the Apes* (1971) and *Conquest of the Planet of the Apes* (1972) the terms of the allegory are reversed, as intelligent apes encounter suspicion, fear, and hatred in our own world—and in ways that make the comment on racism much more overt. For example, a rebellion of oppressed apes in the latter of these two films was specifically based on the Watts "riots" of 1965 in Los Angeles. On the other hand, the allegory of the original film, perhaps because it is the least overt, is probably the most complex of that in any of the *Apes* films, leaving room for a variety of simultaneous meanings. For example, the treatment of humans by the intelligent apes serves in *Planet of the Apes* not only as a commentary on the racist treatment of some humans by others but also on the often cruel treatment of nonhuman species (including our close cousins, the apes) by human beings.

One of the central motifs in the original Boulle novel is the apes' use of human specimens for medical research, especially in their attempts to develop more advanced forms of brain surgery. The ghoulish medical experiments observed by Ulysse Mérou are made all the more so by the realization that human researchers in our own world quite routinely perform equally grisly procedures on laboratory animals—and have historically performed them even on other human beings, as in the Nazi experiments on Jewish prisoners of war. This aspect of the novel is considerably toned down in the film, but there are still suggestions that clearly derive from this aspect of the novel, including the lobotomization of Landon and the threatened castration and lobotomization of Taylor. Indeed, the very fact that the film includes the brain surgery motif at all (despite the fact that brain surgery seems well beyond other aspects of the technology of the ape society) seems a bit forced, suggesting that the filmmakers found the implications of this motif important to the power of the story they were trying to tell, even if it didn't quite fit in with the rest of the film.

Planet of the Apes is a film that depends on the impact of shocking images rather than always making sense, and surgical images do carry a visceral power, a fact that would be demonstrated a few years later via the lobotomies of Milos Forman's *One Flew Over the Cuckoo's Nest* (1975). These images warn particularly of the potential horrors that can be produced by unchecked technological progress, making *Planet of the Apes* typical of much of the most powerful science fiction. At the same time, they pave the way for the film's final (and most shocking) image of technological destruction, the half-buried Statue of Liberty, with its implication of nuclear holocaust.

These technological themes of the dangers of unscrupulous medical research and the nuclear arms race make it clear that *Planet of the Apes* is a complex film that addresses a number of issues other than racism. Even the treatment of racism may be more complex than it might first appear. For example, the first film, more than any of the sequels (though in less detail than the original novel), deals not only with ape-human discrimination but with discrimination among the different species of apes. As indicated (and explored in much more detail) in Boulle's novel, the ape population consists of three distinct groups—orangutans, chimpanzees, and gorillas—each of which tends to occupy a different position in the ape society, essentially arranged hierarchically. Orangutans occupy the positions of highest political authority, chimpanzees are the scientists and intellectuals, and gorillas are soldiers and manual laborers.

The specific conflicts that we see within the ape society, however, are strictly between the conservative, officious orangutans and the more liberal, open-minded chimpanzees. Thus, in our first introductions to the scissions in ape society, the chimpanzee scientist who is treating the injured Taylor complains to Zira of having to work with dirty animals like humans, thus functioning as little more than a veterinarian. He then reminds her that she had promised to speak with Zaius about a different position for him. "I did," she replies. "You know how he looks down his nose at chimpanzees." He responds that the quota system has been abolished, suggesting that the ape society had once been much more formally stratified than it now is. He also points out that Zira herself seems to be doing quite well in getting space and resources for her research, though she is also a chimpanzee, but she responds that her success is due simply to the fact that Zaius recognizes the importance of her work, which is helping to lay the foundations for "scientific brain surgery."

In the Boulle novel, Mérou's demonstrated intelligence causes Zaius to lose his position as head of the research institute where humans are being studied, to be replaced by Cornelius, who in the book is already a prominent scientist, rather than the aspiring junior scientist that he appears to be in the film. However, it is also clear in the film that Zaius's authority over Cornelius is not merely a case of seniority but also has to do with the racial hierarchy between orangutans and chimps. On the other hand, that Zaius is clearly older also contributes to the generation-gap theme of the film, though this theme resides primarily in the treatment of the character of Lucius and is treated more as a joke (aimed at contemporary audiences in 1968) than as serious social commentary.

Still, the generation gap theme highlights the way in which the film addresses social hierarchies that go beyond the central one of race. Perhaps most importantly, the distinction between different species of apes is really a question more of class than of race, and the fact that class boundaries tend to run along the boundaries between species potentially calls attention to the fact that, in the United States, racial differences have historically tended to disguise class differences and therefore to reinforce the myth that American society is classless, refusing to privilege one economic class over another.

It is significant that the struggle for power in the ape society appears to exclude gorillas altogether. Indeed, no gorilla characters are represented in the film as having distinct points of view—or even as having distinguishable personalities. They simply do their jobs, carrying out orders that are given to them, primarily by orangutans but also by chimpanzees. This absence provides a potentially significant political commentary, echoing (though perhaps unintentionally) the relative lack of power on the part of working-class individuals in our own society. Meanwhile, the fact that "liberal" chimps like Cornelius and Zira are highly concerned about human rights but seem little concerned about the oppression of gorillas provides a potential reminder of the relative lack of attention to working-class concerns on the part of our own intellectuals. Indeed, the fact that the subservient position of gorillas goes unchallenged and unremarked throughout the film may also suggest that the filmmakers themselves, clearly concerned about racial oppression, were blind to the class-based commentary in their own film.

The central political moment of *Planet of the Apes* is Taylor's hearing before the tribunal at the Academy of Science. It is here that the orangutans most clearly express—with institutional support—their racial hatred of humans and their condescending attitude toward chimpanzees (and gorillas, who serve as guards in the hearing but do not actively participate in it). Among other things, the fact that such attitudes are central to an official procedure provides reminders of the way in which our own institutions sometimes facilitate and validate racial and other forms of discrimination.

As a comment on our own institutions, particularly the legal system, the tribunal scene can be seen to derive, if indirectly, from a scene in the original novel in which Mérou, having witnessed several official proceedings in the ape society, suddenly thinks back to a trial he once covered as a journalist and suddenly concludes that the seemingly adept legal professionals he observed at the trial were performing entirely scripted roles, like so many trained apes. Of course, the fact that the "heresy" of evolution is a central point brought before the tribunal unavoidably makes the hearing function as a commentary on the infamous Scopes "Monkey Trial" of 1925, in which Tennessee small-town schoolteacher John T. Scopes was prosecuted for teaching evolution, an act that was then against state law. Indeed, any number of commentators have noted the connection between the tribunal in *Planet of the Apes* and the Scopes trial, which seemed to be informed by the same kind of ignorance and religious intolerance as those that drive the "prosecution" of Taylor in the film. Moreover, this connection proved to be more timely than it might first appear: the kind of anti-evolution laws on which the prosecution of Scopes was based were not outlawed by the U.S. Supreme Court until November of 1968 (nine months *after* the release of *Planet of the Apes*), when the Court declared a similar Arkansas statute unconstitutional.

The hidebound refusal of the tribunal to recognize the truth when it is presented to them is symbolized in the film in a classic shot in which the three members of the tribunal respectively cover their eyes, mouth, and ears, enacting the famous stereotype of monkeys who see no evil, speak no evil, and hear no evil. This scene is a bit over the top, of course, injecting a humorous note that seems inconsistent with the serious nature of the proceedings. On the other hand, it also serves to make the members of the tribunal look ridiculous and in that sense reinforces the rest of the scene. Meanwhile, this humorous jab at the members of the tribunal cannot help but suggest a parodic glance at the members of the House Un-American Activities Committee (HUAC), who had called screenwriter Wilson to testify before them in September of 1951, as part of its paranoid investigation of "communist" activity in Hollywood. Wilson took the Fifth Amendment, refusing to answer any questions because he judged the entire proceeding inappropriate and illegal.

Wilson was subsequently blacklisted, unable to work for any Hollywood studios until he co-scripted the 1965 film *The Sandpiper*. *Planet of the Apes* was his second credited Hollywood feature script since the blacklist. However, Wilson, who won a Best Screenplay Oscar for *A Place in the Sun* (1952), his last film before the blacklist, remained active. He went on to write the script for the near-legendary independent leftist film *Salt of the Earth* (1954), a film whose makers were hounded by HUAC, the FBI, and the CIA during filming and that was subsequently kept from wide distribution by government pressure until the 1960s, when it became a cult favorite of the counterculture. He also worked secretly (without credit) on the scripts of several films, including such classics as *The Bridge on the River Kwai* (1957, also based on a novel by Boulle, for which Wilson received a posthumous Best Screenplay Oscar in 1995) and *Lawrence of Arabia* (1962, for which Wilson received a posthumous Best Screenplay Oscar nomination in 1995).

Wilson thus had good reason to treat the tribunal negatively, and it is certainly the case that the apes come off as ignorant bigots, uninterested in the truth. Meanwhile, the religious nature of the tribunal's proceedings also recalls medieval inquisitions in which the Catholic Church sought to block the progress of the new science that was beginning to challenge religion as a discourse of authority in Europe. Of particular relevance here is the 1633 trial (and conviction) of Galileo for the "heresy" of continuing to hold that the earth revolved around the sun rather than the opposite, even after the Church had ordered him to desist. The fact that Galileo's inquisitors refused even to examine any of the scientific evidence that he hoped to present in his defense clearly resembles the refusal of Zaius and the other members of the tribunal to accept evidence of Taylor's intelligence, leading to Zaius's ultimate destruction of conclusive evidence of a human civilization that predated that of the apes.

In the film, religious zealotry stands firmly in the way of scientific progress, placing science and religion in direct opposition, as they often are in science fiction. Through most of the film science occupies the positive pole of this opposition, with Zaius and his religious attitudes appearing to be markers of ignorance and superstition that lead to intolerance and cruelty. Here again, *Planet of the Apes* is typical of science fiction, which tends to take a dim view of religion, especially if it impedes the scientific quest for "truth." One might recall here Mark Rose's argument, in his book *Alien Encounters* (Cambridge, MA: Harvard University Press, 1981) that "it is because the content of the genre is a displacement of religion that science-fiction stories are often concerned to disassociate themselves from religion by characterizing it as the ignorant or feeble opposite of science" (41). That is, for Rose, science fiction and religion are competing for the same territory as discourses of authority. In particular, using terms that are strikingly relevant to *Planet of the Apes*, Rose notes that "like science fiction, religion is concerned with the relationship between the human and the nonhuman" (40).

Then again, some of the best known science fiction films (*Star Wars, Close Encounters of the Third Kind*, and *The Matrix* would be the most obvious examples) draw energy *from* religious imagery rather than in opposition to it. At any rate, among its many twists and shocks, *Planet of the Apes* itself has one more surprise in store for those who have comfortably accepted the fact that Zaius and his ilk are religious bigots inhibiting progress in the ape society. In the end, we realize that Zaius actually has good reason for suppressing the truth, because he fears that it will lead to a resurgence of humankind and its violent impulses, a resurgence that could prove deadly and destructive. (In fact, Taylor himself triggers the doomsday device that destroys all life on the planet in the first sequel.) Zaius thus may simply be a wise ape acting in the interests of his civilization. Young Lucius asks him, after he has ordered the destruction of the evidence of an ancient human civilization, "Why must knowledge stand still? What about the future?" Zaius simply replies, "I may just have saved it for you." This final complication is entirely appropriate in a film that treats so many complex issues in nuanced ways, even though a casual viewer could easily mistake the film for a lightweight adventure film intended to appeal to children. Indeed, it may well be because of its appearance as an "unserious" film that *Planet of the Apes* was able to get away with so much trenchant social and political commentary.

PLANET OF THE SEQUELS: THE LEGACY OF *PLANET OF THE APES*

Perhaps the most important impact of *Planet of the Apes* on subsequent science fiction films resides in the success of its numerous sequels, which continued to draw profitable audiences even as the budgets and (by most accounts) the quality of the films steadily deteriorated. The *Apes* sequence was thus the first successful SF multifilm series, leading to such later series as the *Star Trek*, *Star Wars*, and *Alien* films. It also ushered in Heston as a science fiction action star, something like the Arnold Schwarzenegger of his day. He quickly followed *Planet of the Apes* with starring roles in such SF classics as *The Omega Man* (1971) and *Soylent Green* (1973), in addition to his appearance in the first sequel.

All in all, the films most directly related to *Planet of the Apes* are the sequels themselves, plus Burton's 2001 version of the original story. Of these, *Beneath the Planet of the Apes* (Ted Post, 1970) follows directly on the story of the original; it even features a leader actor, James Franciscus, who looks something like Heston and seems to go through the entire film doing a running imitation of Heston's acting style. In the film, an astronaut named Brent (Franciscus) is sent on a mission to find Taylor and his crew by retracing their flight trajectory. The plan works, and Brent arrives on the planet shortly after the events of the first film. By now, however, Taylor has disappeared, leaving Nova (still played by Linda Harrison) alone, searching for him. Instead, she finds the newly arrived Brent, whom she joins in the search for Taylor. Ultimately, they find him (still played by Heston) imprisoned by an advanced (but decadent) group of humans living beneath the ruins of New York City. These humans have telepathic powers but are all horribly disfigured (presumably by radiation), though for some reason they wear masks that make them appear normal except when they are revealing their "true selves" to their god. This god, as it turns out, is a doomsday bomb left over from the human nuclear war that had earlier destroyed much of human civilization, opening the way for apes to rule the planet. Meanwhile, an ape army mounts a full-scale assault on the underground civilization, which is defended primarily by telepathically transmitted illusions that are not fully effective on apes. In the cataclysmic final scene, Brent and Taylor battle the humans who are trying to set off the doomsday bomb and are both killed. However, as he dies, Taylor himself sets off the device, which will ignite Earth's atmosphere and burn the entire planet to cinders, destroying all life.

Escape from the Planet of the Apes (Don Taylor, 1971) reverses the scenario of the first two films by featuring a crew of apes from the future who fly a spacecraft (having escaped the conflagration of the second film) to the human-ruled Earth of the 1970s. Now it is the apes who are the sympathetic protagonists and the humans who greet them in a mode of savage xenophobia. Indeed, all three ape astronauts are killed in the course of the film, including Cornelius and Zira (again played by Roddy McDowall and Kim Hunter). In the meantime, however, Zira gives birth to a male infant, which she swaps with a baby chimp in a circus run by one Armando (Ricardo Montalban). The intelligent infant is thus saved from destruction, setting the stage for future developments.

In *Conquest of the Planet of the Apes* (J. Lee Thompson, 1972), the baby chimp from the previous film grows up in Armando's care, ultimately taking the name Caesar as an adult (when he, like his father Cornelius before him, is played by McDowall). The action is set in 1991, eight years after a worldwide plague (caused by a virus brought back from outer space) has killed every dog and cat on Earth. In response, humans have adopted apes (immune to the virus) as pets, but over the years, the apes have gradually become slaves, doing much of the menial work formerly done by humans. Indeed, slavery is a major motif in this film, and the brutal treatment of the enslaved apes clearly parallels the earlier treatment of human slaves in America. If this point were not clear enough, it is openly stated by MacDonald (Hari Rhodes), an African American character who is one of the few humans in the film who are sympathetic to the plight of the apes. When the humans discover that Caesar is intelligent and can talk, they quickly move to kill him, but he escapes and leads a general rebellion that leaves the apes, at least momentarily, in charge of Los Angeles. As the film ends, Caesar is confident that their local success will trigger a successful worldwide ape rebellion.

Battle for the Planet of the Apes (J. Lee Thompson, 1973) is set several years later, after a nuclear holocaust has largely destroyed human civilization.

Caesar has led a mixed band of apes and humans out of a ruined and radioactive Los Angeles into the countryside, where they establish a community, apes and humans living in relative harmony under his leadership. However, the gorillas in the community are growing increasingly warlike and antihuman under the influence of their leader, General Aldo (Claude Akins). When Caesar leads an expedition into Los Angeles to try to discover the information about Earth's future that had been brought back by his parents, they are discovered by a group of humans (the ancestors of the subterranean humans of *Beneath the Planet of the Apes*) living beneath the surface. Feeling threatened, the humans follow Caesar's group back to their community and decide to mount an all-out assault in an attempt to destroy it. The apes emerge victorious in the ensuing battle, while Caesar wins the battle with Aldo for control of the community. These two victories pave the way for peaceful cooperation between apes and humans, as we learn in a final cut to the year 2670, where the Lawgiver (a sort of ape Moses, played by John Huston) reveals that this peace has held for more than 600 years. The implication (though there is some ambiguity) is that Caesar's appearance and actions in the past may have altered the course of history, preventing the baleful consequences outlined in the first two *Apes* films.

6

Star Wars

Released 1977; Director George Lucas

Star Wars, with its groundbreaking special effects and staggering commercial success, may be the most influential science fiction film in history. Its characters became icons of American popular culture, its language became part of the American vernacular, and its simple, but powerful, story became one of the best known in American history. It inspired a string of sequels that together now constitute the most commercially successful franchise in film history. Meanwhile, science fiction film, once a low-budget genre seeking a niche audience, was transformed into a genre of big-budget blockbusters, often relying more on spectacular special effects than on thoughtful scenarios, compelling plots, or believable characters. To this extent, the massive influence of *Star Wars* has not been entirely positive, even though the film certainly breathed new life into a genre that seemed at the time relegated to relatively minor status in American culture.

THE STORY: GOOD VS. EVIL

This very familiar film begins with the famous on-screen announcement that the events of the film take place "A long time ago in a galaxy far, far away...." The world of the film is thus divorced from the here and now, in line with Lucas's clear intention to produce a film with mythic, rather than historical, resonance. This opening is also reminiscent of the standard opening of fairy tales, and the film clearly has a number of fairy-tale dimensions. Meanwhile, the "long-ago" setting is also consistent with the fact that *Star Wars*, despite its futuristic look, is very much a nostalgia film that looks lovingly back to its predecessors in the science fiction serials of the 1930s. Then the well-known rolling text of the opening sets up the basic scenario: rebel forces are currently engaged in a civil war against "the evil Galactic Empire." Meanwhile, we learn that, during a recent victory, rebel forces have stolen the secret plans to the "Death Star," the Empire's ultimate weapon, an armored space battle station with enough power to destroy an entire planet. Princess Leia Organa (Carrie Fisher) is rushing through space to deliver the plans to her father and the other rebel leaders, but is being pursued by forces of the Empire.

As the action begins, Princess Leia's small ship is pursued and caught by a much larger imperial cruiser, announcing the David vs. Goliath character of the Empire–rebel opposition of the film. On her ship, we first meet the charming (and bickering) robots (or "droids") C–3PO (Anthony Daniels) and R2–D2 (a mechanical costume with dwarf Kenny Baker inside), two of the iconic figures of the *Star Wars* universe. On the imperial cruiser, we meet another central figure, the evil Darth Vader (voiced by James Earl Jones, but physically played by champion bodybuilder David Prowse), who will eventually be revealed (in *The Empire Strikes Back*) to be a Jedi Knight gone over to the dark side. The smaller ship is caught, then boarded by imperial stormtroopers, themselves looking almost robotic in their white helmets and body armor, suggesting that they are in the service of inhuman forces. A search of the ship does not unearth the stolen plans, though Princess Leia is taken captive. The droids manage to get away in an escape pod. Leia angrily claims diplomatic immunity as a member of the Imperial Senate on a diplomatic mission, but Lord Vader is unimpressed. He concludes that the plans must be in the escape pod and orders his forces to pursue it to the nearby desert planet of Tatooine to retrieve them.

Down on the desolate planet, C–3PO and R2–D2 are soon captured by Jawas, diminutive, hooded traders in salvaged robots and other scavenged machinery. Then, still unaware that imperial forces have followed them to the planet, they are sold to Uncle Owen (Phil Brown) and his young ward and nephew, Luke Skywalker (Mark Hamill). Luke badly wants to leave the planet to go to the "Academy" as a first step in his quest for adventure and opportunity, but he is needed by his uncle to help with the harvest. He is thus highly excited to learn that the droids have been involved in the rebellion against the Empire, and especially intrigued when, as he works on R2–D2, he accidentally activates a projected hologram of Princess Leia, repeating "Help me, Obi-Wan Kenobi. You're my only hope." This message eventually leads Luke and the droids into the deep desert, where it is rumored that a strange old hermit named Ben Kenobi is living.

In the desert, Luke is attacked and knocked unconscious by Sand People, vicious denizens of the desert. However, he is rescued when an old, hooded man approaches, causing the Sand People to flee. The old man is soon identified as Obi-Wan Kenobi (Alec Guinness). He reveals that he and Luke's father ("the best star pilot in the galaxy") were both Jedi Knights who fought in the Clone Wars. They were good friends. He gives Luke his father's light saber, the weapon of choice of the Jedi Knight, though Uncle Owen had forbidden it, fearing that it would inspire Luke to follow in his father's footsteps. He tells Luke that the Jedi Knights were hunted down and destroyed with the help of Darth Vader, who betrayed and killed Luke's father using the dark side of the "Force," an "energy field created by all living things. It surrounds us and penetrates us. It binds the galaxy together."

Obi-Wan realizes that R2–D2 must be delivered safely to the planet of Alderaan so that the plans for the Death Star can be retrieved by the rebels. Uncle Owen and Aunt Beru having been killed by stormtroopers searching for the droids, Luke is free to go along. First, however, they must find a starship to take them there, so they travel to Mos Eisley spaceport, described by Obi-Wan as a "wretched hive of scum and villainy." They are stopped by stormtroopers, but Obi-Wan uses the Force to influence the troopers to let them pass.

In one of the film's best known scenes, the heroes enter a cantina frequented by a wide variety of space-faring alien rogues, though the droids are sent away. "Their kind" are not welcome in the lounge, though it seems to cater to the dregs of space. One of patrons of the cantina brags of his status as a notorious criminal, then threatens Luke. Obi-Wan intercedes, lopping off the alien's arm with his light saber, though it is not clear why the Jedi couldn't simply have used the Force, as he had earlier done with the stormtrooper, to mollify the attacker. In the meantime, Obi-Wan has met the large, hirsute Chewbacca (7' 3" Peter Mayhew), a Wookiee, who is first mate on a fast starship captained by Han Solo (Harrison Ford). Obi-Wan and Luke negotiate with Solo, hoping to use his ship, the *Millennium Falcon* (a sort of outer-space hot rod), to travel to Alderaan. All of the major characters who participate in *Star Wars* are now in place.

Solo and Chewbacca transport the others to Alderaan, only to find that the planet has been destroyed by the Death Star as a warning to those who would oppose the power of the Empire. Then the *Millennium Falcon* is caught in a tractor beam and brought aboard the huge battle station, where the heroes manage to rescue Princess Leia, though they nearly perish in a famous scene in which they are almost crushed in a garbage compactor. Obi-Wan is struck down in a light saber duel with Darth Vader, though there are signs that he simply ascends to a higher plane of existence, whence he is still available to provide spiritual and moral support to Luke in times of crisis.

The heroes travel to the key rebel base, on the planet of Yavin. On the trip there, Han (devoted to his own personal interests) and Leia (devoted to the good of her people and the galaxy) constantly bicker, but there is obviously an attraction between them, introducing a new element to the plot. At the base, the rebel leaders download the plans for the Death Star from R2–D2. Experts examine the information and conceive a plan for an attack on the station. Meanwhile, the Death Star has followed them to the planet, where it goes into orbit. The experts conclude that the battle station has a potentially fatal weakness: if a small one-man ship can get through the defenses and fire a proton torpedo down a mall thermal exhaust port, the torpedo will travel through a shaft directly to the reactor system, starting a chain reaction that will destroy the station. Rebel pilots mobilize to mount the attack, though Solo prepares to take his reward and leave. Luke is unable to convince him to join the attack. R2–D2 goes with Luke to help provide computer control for his ship. Luke hears the voice of Obi-Wan, telling him that the Force will be with him on the mission.

The rebel fighters battle imperial fighters and the anti-aircraft defenses of the Death Star. Eventually, one fighter gets a shot at the exhaust port, but misses. Luke next approaches the port, with Vader in pursuit, sensing that "the Force is strong" in Luke. Obi-Wan's voice implores Luke to relax and use the Force, so Luke switches off his targeting computer and decides to trust the Force. Vader closes in on Luke, but is distracted when Solo, in the *Millennium Falcon*, suddenly (and predictably) joins the fray. The Death Star is about to blast Yavin, when Luke fires a shot down the exhaust shaft. The Death Star is destroyed. Obi-Wan reminds Luke: "Remember: the Force will be with you, always."

Back at the rebel base, a damaged R2–D2 is repaired. Luke, Han, and Chewie are given medals by the princess before a triumphant gathering of the rebel troops—a scene that more than one critic has argued seems to derive from Leni Reifenstahl's masterpiece of Nazi propaganda, *Triumph of the Will* (1934). The film ends just as the rebellion is gaining momentum, clearly paving the way for a coming sequel, though the filmmakers could not have known at the time just how successful the *Star Wars* franchise was going to be.

THE SOURCES OF THE MOVIE

Star Wars is based on an original story and script by director Lucas. However, the film and its sequels draw upon numerous predecessors, and the link between *Star Wars* and its various indirect sources is among the most widely discussed aspects of the film. For example, Joseph Campbell's writings on myth have frequently been cited as a source for the film, and Campbell himself was once quoted to the effect that Lucas was the best student he ever had. The most obvious source for *Star Wars* lies in the *Flash Gordon* and *Buck Rogers* science fiction serials of the 1930s, though other pulp science fiction sources from that era (such as the space operas of E. E. "Doc" Smith) have also been identified. Other sources in film include the works of Akira Kurosawa, especially *The Hidden Fortress* (1958), which contains many of the plot elements later used by Lucas in *Star Wars*. Other sources can be identified as well, including J.R.R. Tolkien's *Lord of the Rings* trilogy and such classic films as *The Wizard of Oz* (1939). All in all, while few specific elements of *Star Wars* may be particularly original, the film is unique in its effective combination of ingredients from so many sources.

ANTICIPATING REAGAN: NOSTALGIA FOR THE FUTURE IN *STAR WARS*

The commercial success of *Star Wars* is virtually legendary. It quickly became the highest-grossing film of all time (though it now ranks second to James Cameron's *Titanic*), while the merchandising campaign that accompanied the film became an unprecedented success and changed the phenomenon of film merchandising forever. Meanwhile, other spinoffs, such as novels and comic books, created an "Expanded Universe" that goes well beyond the films. *Star Wars* achieved considerable critical success as well. It garnered ten regular Academy Award nominations, winning six, plus an additional Special Achievement award for Ben Burtt's sound effects in the creation of the alien, creature, and robot voices. In addition, while the film lost the Oscar in the prestigious categories of Best Picture, Best Director, and Best Screenplay, the nominations in these categories were unprecedented for a science fiction film, especially one perceived, at least initially, as a film for children. *Star Wars* ranked fifteenth on the 1998 American Film Institute list of the greatest American films, making it the highest rated SF film on the list.

The special effects for *Star Wars*, created by a team headed by John Dykstra (who had worked under special effects legend Douglas Trumbull on the 1972 SF film *Silent Running*) were particularly impressive. The new techniques they developed in conjunction with Lucas were applied in any number of subsequent films, while they continued to develop more new techniques as the sequence of sequels was made. Thus, while the initial *Star Wars* effects relied primarily on sophisticated new uses of models and matte paintings, the company came to use more and more computer-generated images as time went by. Industrial Light and Magic, the company founded by Lucas to produce the special effects for *Star Wars*, would go on to become the dominant special effects company in American film, producing the effects for any number of subsequent films, including such major SF films as *E.T. the Extra-Terrestrial* (1982), *Terminator 2: Judgment Day* (1991), most of the *Star Trek* films, *The Abyss* (1989), *Total Recall* (1990), *Jurassic Park* (1993), *Artificial Intelligence: A.I.* (2001), and *Sky Captain and the World of Tomorrow* (2004). They also did the special effects for such effects-driven non-SF films as the *Indiana Jones* series, the *Harry Potter* series, and *Titanic* (1997).

There is no doubt that the much-discussed special effects of *Star Wars* were a large part of the film's success with moviegoers. However, while these effects were unprecedented, they also represented a sort of throwback, allowing audiences to experience the kind of amazement at movie magic that had enthralled audiences in the early decades of film. Indeed, *Star Wars* points backward in a number of ways, and it is clear that, despite its futuristic look, *Star Wars* is very much a nostalgia film, somewhat in the mold of Lucas's own *American Graffiti* (1973). *Star Wars* is, one might say, the sort of science fiction film that filmmakers of the 1930s might have made had they had available to them the special-effects resources (technological and financial) that were available in the late 1970s.

Indeed, while much has been made of the mythic dimensions of *Star Wars*, its simple, black-and-white, good vs. evil plot, enacted by quasi-allegorical characters, derives as much from classic Hollywood film as it does from any source in myth. This is not to say, of course, that classic Hollywood film does not itself derive much of its energy from its ability to tap into the same sort of basic, archetypal images and motifs as myth. It does, however, emphasize the fact that *Star Wars* is an unabashed work of popular culture and that much of the film's success can be attributed to its unpretentious celebration of the kind of simple, straightforward oppositions that had given the pulp fictions of the 1930s their innocent appeal. This simplicity and innocence helped the film appeal to children, but *Star Wars* also had a great appeal for adult audiences in the United States in the late 1970s. After the trying times of Vietnam and Watergate, American audiences were eager for the kind of reassurance provided by simple verities and uncomplicated expressions of the ultimate power of good to defeat evil.

This same hunger on the part of American audiences led fairly soon after the release of *Star Wars* to the election of Ronald Reagan to the U.S. presidency, and the Reagan message—with its call for a return to traditional values, its presentation of international politics as a simple opposition between good and evil, and its belief in the fundamental value of free enterprise—appealed to very much the same sort of desires as did *Star Wars*. Indeed, *Star Wars*, perhaps more than any other single science fiction film served as a harbinger of social change in America. The early 1970s had been marked by dark, dystopian SF films, such as *A Clockwork Orange* (1971), *The Andromeda Strain* (1971), *The Omega Man* (1971), *Silent Running* (1972), and *Soylent Green* (1973), reflecting the pessimistic tenor of late-Vietnam and Watergate era America. The success of *Star Wars* announced a new desire for an optimistic, reassuring message that announced the possibility of a better future, a message also delivered by the Reagan campaign and, later, the Reagan presidency.

The very language of the Reagan administration often closely echoed that of the film, as in the famous characterization of the Soviet Union as an "evil empire." Little wonder, then, that the most important attempt on the part of the Reagan administration to expand the technological capabilities of the United States to fight "evil" involved a proposal to develop a science fiction-like network of laser-based orbiting space weapons that came to be known as the "Star Wars" program. This label (first derisively attached to the program by Senator Edward Kennedy, but later embraced by the Reagan administration) is no mere coincidence in terminology: there is evidence that Reagan's vision of the system (and most other things) was strongly influenced by Hollywood films, including *Star Wars* itself, but also going all the way back to the 1940 film *Murder in the Air*, in which Reagan himself played a Secret Service agent who prevents a foreign spy from stealing the plans for a powerful new defensive weapon that could stop and destroy any attacking vehicle or missile.

On the other hand, the politics of *Star Wars* are somewhat more complex than they might first appear. To some extent, it is true that the galactic political situation portrayed in the film draws upon the rhetoric of the Cold War, with the Soviet Union replaced by the Galactic Empire. However, *Star Wars* is hardly a simplistic allegory of individualist Western rebels opposed to totalitarian Eastern despots. Indeed, in many ways the rebels appear more Eastern, while the Empire appears more Western. For one thing, the real empire builders of world history have been Great Britain, France, and the United States, all members of the anti-Soviet Western bloc during the Cold War. Moreover, much of the representation of the heroic rebel alliance seems to draw upon the rhetoric of anticolonial resistance, an historical phenomenon that drew much of its theoretical inspiration from the Marxist critique of global capitalist expansion. It is certainly the case that the forces of the Empire, with its advanced technology and superior resources, clearly have much in common with the capitalist West, while the rebel forces often resemble less well equipped anticolonial forces, such as the Viet Cong in Vietnam or the National Liberation Front of Algeria.

The Jedi Knights, who are so crucial to the texture of the *Star Wars* universe (though they have been virtually eliminated before the film begins), are clearly more reminiscent of Japanese samurai than of Western medieval knights, while the religious and philosophical resonances of the Force that lies behind the Jedi are much more Buddhist and Taoist than Christian. It would, however, be a serious mistake to see *Star Wars* as a simple celebration of Eastern mysticism as opposed to Western materialism. Luke Skywalker, as the young prince coming of age and assuming his full capabilities and responsibilities, is a stock figure from Western fairy tales, just as Leia (eventually revealed in *The Return of the Jedi* to be his sister) is essentially the stereotypical damsel in distress, though one with considerable resources of her own. Han Solo is a stock figure from American film, especially Westerns, in which individualist loners (usually played by actors such as John Wayne or Clint Eastwood) frequently become reluctant heroes when confronted by evil.

To a large extent, the opposition in *Star Wars* is couched not in terms of East vs. West, but of human (the rebels) vs. inhuman (the Empire). Emperor Palpatine, looking somewhat like the grim reaper with his dark-hoodly cadaverous visage, seems anything but human. Darth Vader, the most prominent villain in the original three *Star Wars* films, has literally lost his humanity: as announced by the signature whooshing of his mechanical respirator, he is in fact mostly machine, the majority of his body replaced by mechanical parts. Even all those legions of imperial storm troopers, who are presumably human, seem inhuman because of the armor they wear, making it more acceptable to have them serve in the film largely as cannon fodder.

This human vs. inhuman structure represents an us vs. them mentality that reinforces the good vs. evil polarity of the film. However, it also makes the seemingly clear moral message of the film somewhat problematic in that it tends to send an almost subliminal suggestion that those who are like us are good, while those who are unlike us are evil. For example, the imperial storm troopers (who are slaughtered en masse in the film) seem to be human, but the film intentionally dehumanizes them in ways that seem to invite us to ignore the humanity of those whom we have identified as enemies. This same kind of thinking can also be seen in the representation of aliens in the film. As the famous cantina scene makes clear, the faraway galaxy in which *Star Wars* is set is populated by a number of intelligent alien species. However, these aliens appear to play a very marginal role in galactic politics, where humans (or former humans) remain the only major players. The very fact that the film's most memorable portrayal of aliens occurs in the cantina scene (where most of the alien patrons seem to be criminals or outcasts of one kind or another) may be very telling. Other aliens depicted in the film and its sequels (Jabba the Hut, the Sand People, the Jawas) tend to be criminals or outlaws as well. Whenever aliens are portrayed sympathetically (Chewbacca or the Ewoks of *Return of the Jedi*) it is with a substantial amount of condescension (they tend to resemble cuddly pets or perhaps stuffed animals) that clearly marks them as subsidiary to humans.

The ancient Jedi master Yoda (who appears only in the sequels and prequels, not in the original film) is the only major exception to this formula. Impossibly wise and surprisingly formidable (but also small, ugly, and green), the diminutive Yoda seems to embody the very positive message that we should not judge others by their appearance, especially if it is different from our own. On the other hand, though Yoda is clearly gifted with a variety of superhuman abilities, he nevertheless comes across as something of a pet, adorable to children, somewhat in the mode of his puppet predecessor, the Muppet Kermit the Frog (also small and green, and a legitimate forerunner of Yoda in that Frank Oz was a central player in Jim Henson's troupe of Muppeteers—though Oz operated Miss Piggy opposite Henson's Kermit).

If *Star Wars* is, from this point of view, anything but an endorsement of otherness, it is also the case that the film's glorification of the rebels and their tactics carries a potentially subversive charge within the context of recent American history. After all, while the United States has consistently celebrated its own revolutionary origins, by 1977 the very concept of revolution had come primarily to be associated with socialist revolutions, a series of which (beginning with the Russian Revolution itself) had been one of the defining political phenomena of the twentieth century. From the retrospective view of the early twenty-first century, the Empire, with its vastly superior resources and technology, would seem to play the role in galactic politics that the United States now plays in world politics. Similarly, the underequipped but staunchly determined rebels seem less like the revolutionaries who founded the United States than the anticolonial fighters of the second half of the twentieth century and various Third World resistance movements of today, such as the Zapatistas of Mexico or even the dreaded Al-Qaeda, who, like Luke and Obi-Wan, emerged from their desert homes, buoyed by their spiritual beliefs to think they can fight an opponent with vastly superior technological resources.

If the latter comparison seems particularly far-fetched, or even odious, one need only consider the crucial final battle of *Star Wars*, in which the desperate rebels attack the imposing Death Star with a few small craft piloted by determined individuals who know they will probably not survive the attack. They are essentially suicide bombers, and the stunning blow they strike when Luke Skywalker, with a single shot, triggers a chain reaction that destroys the gigantic Death Star, resembles nothing in world history more than the shocking events of September 11, 2001, when a few Al-Qaeda operatives managed to take down the mighty World Trade towers in New York City. Granted, the Death Star is a military target, a deadly offensive weapon. We should not forget, however, that the giant battle station no doubt contains thousands upon thousands of human beings who are killed when the station explodes, even if most of them are the faceless stormtroopers for whom we have been conditioned to feel little sympathy throughout the film. (The Al-Qaeda rebels also attacked the Pentagon, surely a military target, while the World Trade Center was a central nodal point of American business, as key to the power of global capitalism as the Death Star had been to the power of the Empire.) The subsequent attempts of the Empire to hunt down and exterminate the rebels in the first two sequels then resemble nothing more than the American global hunt for terrorists in the wake of the September 11th bombings.

This is not, of course, to suggest that *Star Wars* counsels us to sympathize with the bombers of the World Trade Center, not the least because the film was made more than a decade before the founding of Al-Qaeda—as an anti-*Soviet* guerrilla group in Afghanistan in 1988. Indeed, in the much later prequels to the original film, Lucas seems to go out of his way to portray the "rebels" as defenders of conventional political authority in the galaxy, while the Empire is actually an upstart regime that has illegally seized power from the preceding Republican government, somewhat in the mold of the fascist regime in Spain that seized power in Spain in the 1930s. These later films celebrate legitimacy in other ways as well, including the fact that the Force apparently turns out to be available only to those with the proper inherited bloodlines. Nevertheless, the very fact that the rebels *do* employ terrorist tactics in the interest of a presumably virtuous cause asks us to reconsider some of our own recent demonization of terrorists and to remember that they may have a point of view that is more complex than the mere pursuit of evil for its own sake.

This ability to encourage us to rethink even our most entrenched notions about the world (a phenemonon literary critics refer to as "cognitive estrangement") is perhaps the central most important resource of science fiction as a cultural form. Because of the nature of science fiction as a genre, even a seemingly regressive work such as *Star Wars* asks us to imagine a world different from our own, an exercise that in itself forces us to adopt perspectives that are different from those we habitually inhabit. If nothing else, this experience reminds us that perspectives different from ours do exist and might perhaps be perfectly legitimate. Similarly, by asking us momentarily to imagine a different reality from our own, science fiction reminds us that reality *might* in fact be different than it is and that our contemporary world developed as the result of historical events that might have been otherwise. By extension, this same lesson teaches us that it might very well be possible for our own reality (social, political, cultural) to change further as a result of future historical events.

In *Star Wars*, the apparent reliance on simple moral verities works well with the mythic and fairy-tale elements of the film. However, the generic tendency of science fiction to challenge easy assumptions works directly against the straightforward good vs. evil oppositions for which the film is famous. Then again, a close examination of certain aspects of the film—such as the mass killings involved in the destruction of the Death Star—already undermines those easy oppositions, reminding us of the kinds of atrocities that can be committed by those who are unequivocally convinced of the rightness of their actions.

TRANSFORMING A GENRE: THE LEGACY OF *STAR WARS*

Any number of subsequent films (not to mention television series such as *Battlestar Galactica*) show an obvious *Star Wars* influence, especially in their use of special visual effects. For example, the first films in the *Star Trek* film sequence (beginning with the original *Star Trek: The Motion Picture* in 1979) probably owe more of their look to *Star Wars* than to the original *Star Trek* television series. The military scenario of *Star Wars* influenced numerous films, perhaps most obviously Roland Emmerich's *Independence Day* (1996). And the lovable robots of *Star Wars* spawned a barrage of imitations, such as chattering Twiki of the television series *Buck Rogers in the 25th Century* (1979–1981) and the cute-but-courageous Vincent (voiced by SF veteran Roddy McDowall, who sounds a lot like Daniels's C–3PO) in Disney's *The Black Hole* (1979). It should be pointed out, however, that the droids of *Star Wars* were themselves preceded and probably influenced by the charming robots of Douglas Trumbull's *Silent Running* (1972).

Numerous films, such as Steven Spielberg's *E.T.* (1982) and Tobe Hooper's *Poltergeist* (1982), have incorporated direct allusions to *Star Wars* as a sort of nod to their illustrious predecessor (which in these films seems to stand in for American popular culture as a whole), while films such as Mel Brooks's *Spaceballs* (1987) have spoofed *Star Wars* and its sequels. *Star Wars* also renewed interest in the science fiction serials of the 1930s, leading to the production of such works as television's *Buck Rogers in the 25th Century* and culminating in Kerry Conran's *Sky Captain and the World of Tomorrow* (2004), the ultimate nostalgia tribute to the pulp science fiction of the 1930s.

Of course, *Star Wars* itself is part of an elaborate sequence of works that includes two immediate sequels, then a second trilogy of "prequels." This second trilogy, labeled Episodes I–III, retroactively makes *Star Wars* the fourth installment in a narrative sequence, and the original film is now officially titled *Star Wars Episode IV: A New Hope*. The first sequel, *The Empire Strikes Back*, is thus Episode V in the sequence, while *The Return of the Jedi* is Episode VI.

The Empire Strikes Back (1980) is set soon after the first film, featuring essentially the same cast of characters (and actors), though this film was directed by Lucas's old film-school teacher Irvin Kershner, with Lucas now serving as executive producer. Luke Skywalker has now become an important leader in the resurgent rebel alliance, while Darth Vader plays the leading role in the attempts of the Empire to crush the rebellion. These attempts increasingly focus on Luke himself, as Vader convinces the Emperor of the advantages of winning the young man, with his strong connection to the Force, over to their side. Meanwhile, Luke advances in his Jedi training under the tutelage of the irascible Yoda, the most important new character added in this film. Han Solo plays an increased role in this film, becoming one of the classic swashbuckling heroes of American film. Meanwhile, love blooms between Solo and Princess Leia, making him a romantic hero as well—and leading to Harrison Ford's breakaway success as a leading man in *Raiders of the Lost Ark* (written and executive produced by Lucas and directed by science fiction superstar Spielberg) the following year. Little is resolved in this film, which ends with the war between rebel and imperial forces still underway, though the Empire does seem to have gained ground. The film does, however, include one major revelation: that Darth Vader is the former Anakin Skywalker, Luke's father, gone over to the dark side of the Force. We also learn that the nefarious Vader harbors a secret plan to overthrow the emperor and seize control of the galaxy for himself, perhaps with the aid of his son, though Luke staunchly resists recruitment by his newly-identified father.

The Return of the Jedi (1983), directed by Richard Marquand, continues the original *Star Wars* sequence to its conclusion. Here, Luke and Leia manage to rescue Han after he had been (at the end of the previous movie) frozen in carbonite and handed over to Jabba the Hut as a sort of trophy. Meanwhile, aided by the lovable (but feisty) Ewoks, the rebel forces emerge triumphant after Vader (saving his son with a last-second change of heart) manages to kill the evil Emperor Palpatine before dying himself, while the rebel spacefleet destroys a second Death Star. We also learn that Leia and Luke (though they had not themselves previously known it) are twin siblings.

In the first prequel, *Star Wars: Episode I—The Phantom Menace* (1999), Jedi Kight Qui-Gon Jinn (Liam Neeson) and his Protégé, a young Obi-Wan Kenobi (Ewan McGregor) come to the aid of Queen Padmé Naberrie Amidala (Natalie Portman) of the planet Naboo to free her planet from domination by the nefarious Trade Federation. However, *The Phantom Menace* is mainly interesting not for that plot but for the background it provides to the earlier *Star Wars* films. It introduces a young (and mysteriously gifted) Anakin Skywalker, who also helps out and who, in the end, becomes the Protégé of Obi-Wan, though we know he will ultimately go over to the dark side and become Sith Lord Darth Vader. The film also shows us the first meeting between C–3PO (built by young Anakin) and R2–D2. It also gives us early looks at Jabba the Hutt and Yoda and some hints at the workings of interplanetary politics.

Star Wars: Episode II—Attack of the Clones (2002) is set ten years after the events of Episode I, when the political situation in the galaxy has grown even more tense. The Trade Federation and their allies in the Commerce Guild, now led by former Jedi knight Count Dooku (Christopher Lee), gather an army of droids and prepare to move against the Republic. Obi-Wan Kenobi (Ewan McGregor) is now a seasoned Jedi knight and Anakin Skywalker (Hayden Christensen) is now a young man nearing the end of his Jedi training. Padmé Amidala (Natalie Portman) has served her term as Queen of Naboo and is now a Senator in the Galactic Senate. As the film begins, an attempted assassination of Senator Amidala leads Anakin and Obi-Wan to be called in as her bodyguards. Their investigation of the situation leads Obi-Wan to discover that a giant army of clones is secretly being prepared for the use of the Republic. Meanwhile, Anakin and Padmé fall in love, while the murder of Anakin's mother begins to turn him toward the dark side. That side, as it turns out, has already taken control of Dooku, who is now secretly Sith lord Darth Tyranus. Meanwhile, there are continuing hints that Supreme Chancellor Cos Palpatine (Ian McDiarmid), who will go on to become emperor, also has connections with the dark side. A sword-toting Yoda (still voiced by puppet master Oz, though now imaged by computer animation instead of puppetry as in the earlier films) leads the clone army in a victorious assault that saves Anakin, Padmé, and Obi-Wan, all of whom had been taken captive by Dooku and his minions. However, the galactic situation is far from rosy; indeed, the film ends just as the galactic war is beginning. The film includes lots of explosive action and is darker than Episode I, but it is still largely a film for kids.

Star Wars: Episode III—Revenge of the Sith (2005) is the darkest (both thematically and visually) of all the *Star Wars* films. It is also presumably the last of those films, completing the second trilogy and setting the stage for the first. Here, the Republic completes its descent from democracy into repression, becoming the evil Galactic Empire under the leadership of Palpatine, who now clearly emerges as Sith Lord Darth Sidious. Some have seen Palpatine's use of patriotism to stir support for his imperialistic schemes as a commentary on the politics of the Bush administration, but this film is primarily devoted to spectacular action (with the best special effects of any *Star Wars* film) and to providing backstories for the major characters and situations of the original *Star Wars*. The fate of Anakin Skywalker (Christensen) mirrors that of the Republic, as he completes his turn to the Dark Side and transformation into the Darth Vader so familiar from the first trilogy. As the film ends, Anakin's body is destroyed in a climactic duel with his old master Obi-Wan Kenobi (McGregor), though he is rescued by his new master Palpatine (McDiarmid) and rebuilt into the black-helmeted cyborg Vader. The end of the film also includes the births of Luke and Leia, the children of Anakin and Padmé (Portman). Their mother having died in childbirth, the two infants are spirited away to safety by Obi-Wan and Yoda, the only remaining Jedi who have not been destroyed by the treacherous Palpatine and his minions. Leia goes to live with her adoptive parents, while Luke is taken to live with his aunt and uncle on Tatooine. Obi-Wan goes to live in seclusion on Tatooine (to help look after Luke), while Yoda goes into hiding, leading to the situation that prevails at the beginning of the first trilogy.

7

Close Encounters of the Third Kind

Released 1977; Director Steven Spielberg

Close Encounters of the Third Kind was a groundbreaking film that solidified the reputation of Steven Spielberg (who had just come off of the making of *Jaws*, his first big hit) as a master storyteller and an accomplished director of well-crafted blockbusters. Further, coming hard on the heels of the summer megahit *Star Wars*, *Close Encounters* ended the 1977 movie year with a rousing verification that science fiction film offered abundant opportunities for box-office success. These two films would be quickly followed by a string of high quality, high profit SF films—including *Star Trek: The Motion Picture* (1979), *Alien* (1979), *Blade Runner* (1982), and *E.T. the Extra-Terrestrial* (1982)—that together made the period from 1977 to 1982 the richest five-year span in the history of the genre.

THE STORY: SEEKING A HIGHER POWER

Close Encounters of the Third Kind begins as United Nations investigators scramble to a site in the Sonora Desert of Mexico, where a group of World War II-vintage American airplanes have suddenly materialized as if out of nowhere. The investigators are led by Frenchman Claude Lacombe (François Truffaut), who has enlisted American cartographer David Laughlin (Bob Balaban) to translate for him because of his poor facility with English. They quickly determine that the planes were the ones that had been lost during a training mission (Flight 19) out of a naval air station in

Ft. Lauderdale in 1945. The planes and their contents look brand new, and the engines are still in perfect working condition. There are no pilots or crew.

This scene sets the tone of mystery that will continue throughout the film. Our contemporary inability to cope with mystery is then quickly emphasized in the next scene, in which an apparent UFO is spotted by pilots and air traffic controllers near Indianapolis. All involved decline to report the sighting and decide to ignore it, fearing that they will be regarded as crackpots. Their attitude is clearly meant to recall the official U.S. government policy of regarding the numerous reports of such sightings as lacking verification.

The film then cuts to a farmhouse in Muncie, Indiana, where a sleeping boy, Barry Guiler (Cary Guffey), is awakened by lights dancing on his face. The young boy, despite his name, is entirely without guile, and his innocence makes him open to phenomena that the more sophisticated adults in the previous scene chose to ignore. He looks toward an open window, while his mechanical toys all suddenly begin to turn on and operate. He goes downstairs and finds the front door open and the kitchen trashed, a doggie door swinging as if something just passed through it. The commotion awakes the boy's mother, Jillian Guiler (Melinda Dillon), who comes to look for him and sees him running away from the house, laughing happily.

This almost magical scene is then immediately contrasted with a scene of domestic routine, helping to establish the confrontation between the marvelous and the ordinary that will provide much of the film's special energy. In this scene, 8-year-old Brad Neary (Shawn Bishop) asks his father Roy Neary (Richard Dreyfuss) for help with his math (he has trouble with fractions), but Roy would rather play with his toy trains. Neary's wife, Ronnie (Teri Garr) reminds him of a promise to take everyone to a movie that weekend. He excitedly suggests that they see *Pinocchio* (1940), announcing the theme of Disney-like magic and wonder that will be crucial to the film. Brad, however, is uninterested in magic: he objects to having to see a boring G-rated film. The younger son, Toby (Justin Dreyfuss, nephew of Richard) joins Brad in voting to play Goofy Golf rather than see the movie. All the while, Cecil B. DeMille's *The Ten Commandments* (1956) plays on the TV in the background, but is largely ignored. Religion will be a crucial theme in *Close Encounters*, but the DeMille film, especially when reduced to television form, also announces a culture for which religion has become just another commodity, a form of popular entertainment rather than true spirituality. Then a call comes in for Neary, a lineman for the electric company, to come in to work to help fight a power outage that is sweeping across the area.

Back to Jillian Guiler, now looking for Barry in the woods with a flashlight. Neary, meanwhile, drives through the dark countryside, then suddenly stops. "Help, I'm lost!" he cries (though with good humor) to no one in particular, and he is clearly lost in more ways than one. Not only is he unable to find his destination of the moment, but he has also lost sight of any real destination or meaning in his life. He stops and looks at his maps. After what seems to be a UFO passes overhead, a row of mailboxes beside the road starts to shake violently back and forth, the doors flapping open. A bright light from the sky envelopes Neary's truck, flashing as he looks upward. A railroad crossing alarm goes off and the items inside his truck start to fly around, the radio going haywire. Then it all stops. Looking upward through his windshield, Neary sees a strange craft gliding overhead. It beams another light down on the road ahead. Then Neary's truck starts by itself and his radio comes on, filled with frantic reports of strange happenings. As he drives forward the shadow of the craft moves across the landscape. The Guiler and Neary plot strands then converge as Neary almost runs over Barry, whose mother manages to knock him out of the way in the knick of time.

The Guilers and Neary then join a small gathering of people who observe as a series of small UFOs flies by. Neary excitedly rushes home to tell Ronnie what happened. A "sensible" woman (unreceptive to magic), she is skeptical of Neary's report—and will remain so throughout the film. He drags her out of bed to take her back to see what is going on. He rouses the kids as well, and they all go out and get in the truck. Ronnie notices that Roy is oddly sunburned on one side of his face. At Roy's insistence, they drive back to the spot where Roy and the others saw the series of small craft flying by, but they see nothing out of the ordinary. Ronnie, trying to be patient, suggests a "snuggle," then starts to kiss Roy as if to offer consolation. There is a certain condescension in her affection, as well as a hint that she is trying to use sex to lure Roy back into the fold, encouraging him to drop his quest for the marvelous and return to the world of the mundane.

After this scene of wedded domesticity, we cut (in a scene added especially for the 1980 Special Edition of the film) to the Gobi Desert of Mongolia, where a man leads a camel up a sand dune. Suddenly three station wagons with UN markings come bursting over the dune followed by two helicopters. Excited desert-dwellers lead them to a site where an ocean-going ship has materialized in the desert. Echoing the lost planes found in Mexico, the ship is the Cotopaxi, a long-lost seagoing cargo vessel, obviously out of place in the middle of the desert. Back in the Neary home, Roy is becoming increasingly obsessed with the UFO sightings, and in particular with a certain shape that he keeps seeing in objects around him, such as shaving cream and mashed potatoes. Apparently due to this obsession, he loses his job.

The next scene continues the pattern of cuts between an almost stifling domesticity and a potentially inspiring aura of mystery. The UN team now arrives in Dharmsala, Northern India, where a gathering of locals sits and chants a now-famous series of five tones they recently heard coming from the sky. Their seeming spiritual tranquility contrasts sharply with the sight of UN investigators walking among them carrying high-tech microphones to record the chanting. Asked where the tones came from, the Indians, as one, point toward the sky. Lacombe and his team then bring the recording back to play for a gathering in the United States. Lacombe demonstrates how the sign language developed by Zoltan Kodaly can be used to represent the tone sequence visually, thus indicating that ingenuity can overcome obstacles to communication. However, the auditorium in which Lacombe makes his presentation is nearly empty, signifying the lack of interest in such phenomena in the West.

By this time, Lacombe has clearly been established as a crucial symbolic figure, standing in for the scientific quest to understand the film's strange phenomena in a rational way, while Neary and Jillian Guiler represent a more emotional, even spiritual quest. At this point, the domestic and the mysterious start to converge as we cut from Lacombe's scientific briefing to Neary as he joins a crowd that night, on the lookout for UFOs. Jillian sees and greets him: she has the same sunburn, though hers is on both sides. Neary notices that Barry, playing in the dirt, is sculpting the same shape he saw in his shaving cream.

An astronomical station has been sending out signals made of the tone sequence from India. In return, they receive a series of signals containing numbers, which they eventually understand as a latitude and longitude. They fetch a giant globe and locate the coordinates as a point in Wyoming, at the base of the Devils Tower National Monument, a mysterious-looking formation that will play a crucial role in the rest of the film. The government quickly mobilizes to respond to this information, concluding that the coordinates indicate the site where the aliens hope to meet officially with humans for the first time.

Back in the Guiler home, Jillian, something of an artist, sketches in charcoal the same shape that has been fascinating Neary, while her son plays the five-tone sequence on his xylophone. Clouds begin to boil overhead and light appears through them. "Toys!" shouts Barry, gleefully, looking to the skies. Jillian is less certain. She locks the windows and barricades the doors. A orangish light comes through the keyhole. Barry opens the door to find that the outside is infused with orange light. Jillian pulls him in and relocks the door. Bedlam breaks loose in the house, and bright light pours through every opening. Barry is thrilled as household appliances begin to operate on their own, but his mother is frantic. She picks up the phone, but can hear nothing on it but the five-tone sequence. The refrigerator and stove shake and rattle. Barry heads out through the doggie door in the kitchen, into the orange light, his mother unable to stop him. The commotion suddenly halts. Jillian rushes outside, but Barry is nowhere to be found.

Neary keeps thinking of the mysterious shape, a sort of stubby mountain, drawing it on his newspaper. At dinner, he sculpts the shape from his mashed potatoes, then begins to cry, seeming more and more unbalanced—especially to his relatively unimaginative wife and children. Ronnie, unable to believe in the genuinely marvelous, is increasingly convinced that her husband is going insane. Roy makes a clay model of the shape, becoming agitated by his inability to understand what it means, rushing out into the night to sit in a swing (again signifying his childlike side). Ronnie awakes in the middle of the night and finds him sitting in the tub, fully clad, with the shower on. She urges him to go to family therapy. The children come in and become violently upset at the sight of their father in such a state. Ronnie screams at them to go away. Roy begs Ronnie for help, but she becomes angry and screams at him: "You're ruining us! You're ruining us!"

In the next scene, Roy watches a cartoon in which Daffy Duck battles an alien (1953's *Duck Dodgers in the 24 ½th Century*), then suddenly concludes that his recent fascination is mere childish silliness, like the cartoon. He starts to rip up his clippings of UFO reports and his other UFO materials (we see that he has a model of the *U.S.S. Enterprise* from *Star Trek* hanging from the ceiling). After we see a Pinocchio music box that, tellingly, plays "When You Wish Upon a Star" (the theme song from the Disney movie), he even begins to tear apart the clay sculpture, but suddenly realizes that, with the top taken off, leaving it flat, it has the right shape at last. He awakens the family that morning as they hear him ripping up the shrubbery around the house. Seeming completely insane, he begins tossing the plants through the kitchen window. He throws dirt and bricks through the window as well. Neighbors look on at his bizarre antics as he wrestles a garbage can away from the garbage man, dumps half the garbage out in the street, then dumps the rest, and the can, through the kitchen window. He rips up the wire fence from around his neighbor's duck pond and tosses that into his kitchen as well. Ronnie, having had enough, rushes the three kids into the car, orders them to lock the doors, then drives away, leaving Roy behind, even after he leaps on the hood of the vehicle to try to stop her.

Neary himself climbs through the kitchen window, then uses the materials to build a large sculpture of the mysterious shape in his living room. As he works, the television is on, as it usually is in the domestic scenes of the film. Then a TV news report about a government-planted story about a nerve gas spill near Devils Tower comes on as Roy talks to Ronnie on the phone, hoping to get his family to come home. Devils Tower itself appears on the TV behind him. Ronnie hangs up, and Roy finally notices the image on the screen, immediately realizing that this is the shape that has so occupied his mind. He rushes to his station wagon (emblem of domesticity) and heads for Wyoming, now identified as the locus of the mysterious.

When Neary arrives in the vicinity of Devils Tower, he meets up with Jillian, and the two of them proceed toward the Devils Tower, evading government attempts to clear the area. Eventually, however, they are detained by the authorities. Neary and Lacombe finally come together as the scientist questions Neary via his interpreter, Laughlin. Lacombe asks Neary whether he has various medical conditions and if he has recently had a "close encounter." Neary's only response is to ask, "Who are you people?" They show him pictures of a number of people, including Jillian. All but she are strangers to him. He admits that he and Jillian felt compelled to come to the area to seek "an answer," though he can explain no further.

Neary is taken out and put in a helicopter with a number of others (including Jillian) wearing gas masks. There are twelve of these "pilgrims," who seem to have been called to the scene from all over the country, feeling compelled to do so by the same vision of Devils Tower. This is an auspiciously religious number, though Lacombe expresses confidence that there must have been hundreds of others who simply didn't make it this far. Neary takes off his mask and discovers that the air is fine. Jillian and another man, Larry Butler (Josef Sommer), follow suit, bolting from the helicopter as it waits to take off. They run off toward Devils Tower, with Lacombe watching, thoughtful, out a window.

The three escapees climb toward Devils Tower as helicopters sweep overhead, dropping a sleeping gas that knocks out Larry, though Roy and Jillian evade it and continue their climb. Roy barely makes it up a slippery incline. They reach a point where they see a huge lighted arena at the foot of Devils Tower and hear a voice over a loud speaker directing everyone to take their positions and ordering the lights in the arena to be dimmed. The speaker directs everyone to watch the skies. Swirling lights approach the "arena"; three ships hover over it. The humans repeatedly play the five-tone sequence over a speaker, but get no response from the ships. Suddenly, the ships play the tone sequence in response, then fly away.

Roiling clouds approach with dancing lights inside. Several small ships swoop over the arena, apparently scouting it out in advance. One passes slowly just over the heads of the personnel on the ground, then moves away. Neary decides to go down to the arena, though Jillian elects to stay behind. They kiss, but as spiritual comrades rather than lovers. As Neary climbs down to the arena, the huge alien mother ship appears over Devils Tower, bearing numerous blue and orange lights. It slowly moves down to the arena and comes to a stop just above the ground. The humans waiting on the ground play the tones; the craft answers with a different sequence of tuba-like blasts, one of which is so powerful it blows out the glass in a tower. The two sides exchange several sequences of musical tones, as if the aliens are trying to teach the humans "a basic tonal vocabulary."

Jillian finally climbs down to the arena and joins Roy. Bright lights come on beneath the craft; suddenly human figures begin to come down a landing ramp that is lowered from the craft and emerge from bright light. They are the crewmen from the 1945 naval flight exercise (Flight 19) from the film's opening. Other humans, civilians, emerge, including Barry, who happily rushes to his waiting mother. Lacombe sees Neary and asks him what he wants. "I just want to know that it's really happening," replies Neary. Lacombe tells Neary that he envies him, apparently concluding that Neary has received a special call to come to the scene that the rational Lacombe has not. Suddenly, an alien emerges from the light, with long spindly arms and legs and making gestures of peace. Then a group of small, childlike aliens emerges, very different from the first alien, indicating that the alien society includes different species. The humans watch expectantly as the aliens mill about. Jillian, her eyes tearing with joy, snaps photographs of the amazing event.

Cut to a chapel service among a group of individuals who seem to have either volunteered or been chosen to be sent off aboard the alien craft, including Neary, presumably the only one of the group to have been called by the aliens themselves (as the authorities apparently did not allow the other pilgrims onto the site). These "ambassadors" (many of them appear to be almost identical-looking military men) are then led out to the arena wearing red jump suits. In what appears to be a continuity error, there at first seem to be thirteen of the red-suited figures, though later there appear to be only twelve, two of whom are women and one of whom is an African American man. Several of the small aliens take Neary by the hand and lead him (his arms outstretched, Christlike) into the light beneath the mother ship as a strain from "When You Wish Upon a Star," oddly conflating Christian imagery with Disney, drifts whimsically into the background music. Neary looks back toward Jillian with a look of peace and contentment, then steps up the ramp into the craft. The other ambassadors are never shown boarding the craft, and it is not in fact clear that they do so. An alien of still another species (looking a bit like the "greys" associated with the supposed crash of an alien craft near Roswell, New Mexico, in 1947, but also a little like a relative of the later E.T.) emerges from the light. This alien, whom Spielberg dubbed "Puck," was in fact designed by Carlo Rambaldi, who would ultimately design the title character of *E.T.* Puck exchanges the five-tone sequence with Lacombe, using the Kodaly sign language; the alien then goes back into the ship. Barry calls "Bye" as the craft lifts off into the skies.

THE SOURCES OF THE MOVIE

Close Encounters is based on an original screenplay by Spielberg and has no other direct sources. However, in the making of the film Spielberg drew significantly upon UFO lore and in particular on the work of scientist J. Allen Hynek, who served as technical advisor on the film. Hynek's 1972 book *The UFO Experience: A Scientific Inquiry* (based on his twenty years of work as a consultant to the U.S. Air Force investigating UFO sightings for Project Blue Book) is still regarded as a classic of the field and is, among other things, responsible for the terminology that gave the film its title. (Close Encounters of the First Kind involve close-range UFO sightings with no physical manifestations; Close Encounters of the Second Kind involve sightings and physical phenomena such burn marks or interference with electrical equipment; Close Encounters of the Third Kind involve sightings of actual aliens.)

GOOD ALIENS, BAD TELEVISION: ALIEN INVASION AND THE BANALITY OF EVERYDAY LIFE IN *CLOSE ENCOUNTERS OF THE THIRD KIND*

Close Encounters of the Third Kind became, on its initial release, the largest grossing film in the history of Columbia Pictures, a success that bailed the company out of considerable financial difficulty and propelled director Spielberg to superstar status. The film also garnered eight Academy Award nominations, including a Best Director nomination for Spielberg and a Best Special Visual Effects nomination for Douglas Trumbull and his effects crew. However, of these awards the film won only for the cinematography of Vilmos Zsigmond, though it also won a special Oscar given to Frank Warner for sound effects editing. In addition to this initial success, the film has also shown considerable staying power and remains one of the most beloved and respected American science fiction films more than a quarter century after its first release.

While *Close Encounters of the Third Kind* leaves many questions unanswered, its message is in most ways relatively straightforward and simple. Indeed, any uncertainties that remain are simply part of the central message, which is not merely that we need not fear invasions by aliens, but that we should in general be open to new things, even if they go beyond what can be encompassed or understood by our previous experience. To an extent, one can interpret this message as a religious one. Thus, film critic J. P. Telotte, in his book *Science Fiction Film* (Cambridge University Press, 2001), describes the film as a "story of belief, acceptance, and quasi-religious affirmation" (144).

Telotte goes on to outline the ways in which the film, with its vision of benevolent, childlike aliens who nevertheless possess powers far beyond our own, seeks to provide a reassuring vision of order in the universe amid the seeming chaos of our own postmodern lives. Any number of critics have been even more forceful about seeing a strong religious message in the film, which, while it conveys the point of view of no particular religion, does seem to urge the value of belief in something larger than ourselves. Other critics have been less generous, however. Andrew Gordon, in a 1980 article in the journal *Literature/Film Quarterly* (Vol. 8, No. 3, pp. 156–64), provides one of the more negative readings of the film when he charges that Spielberg presents a "purified, Disneyized version of religion" that cashes in on a number of popular (and highly commercial) quasi-mystical fads of the late 1970s (156–57). Tony Williams, in a 1983 article in the film journal *Wide Angle* (Vol. 4, No. 5, pp. 23–29) finds an ominous political message in the film's endorsement of belief, which he sees as an expression of an immature yearning for the security of control by authoritarian power.

Of course, some of the "religious" content of the film may be supplied as much by the film's audience as by the film itself, so whatever yearnings are expressed by this content could be those of the viewers rather than the filmmakers. In the wake of Vietnam and Watergate (and the seeming collapse of the idealistic political movements of the 1960s and early 1970s), American audiences, in particular, were ready for the marvelous and for a message of hope, open to suggestions that all could be made well by the intervention of higher powers. It is certainly the case that *Close Encounters* includes absolutely no overt expressions of religious belief, and the only "higher" power actually shown in the film is that represented by the aliens themselves. However, these aliens are not presented as supernatural; they are simply extremely advanced in a technological sense. Indeed, Spielberg seems to have gone out of his way to make this point, especially in his representation of the mother ship, the design of which (by various accounts based either on an oil refinery or a power-generating station) includes a vast amount of what appears to be complex machinery. Granted, the aliens themselves, with their air of playful childlike innocence, hardly seem capable of developing and building the kind of high-tech machinery embodied in the mother ship—though the interior shot in the 1980 Special Edition does seem to show many of them busily working, rather than playing. Then again, perhaps the humans of the film see only what the aliens want them to see. Perhaps the childlike innocence is either a calculated gesture of friendship or (more ominously) an intentional ruse designed to secure the trust of the humans.

The film does seem determined to make the behavior of the aliens appear inscrutable, and many of their strategies do not seem to make sense from a human perspective. Among other things, the aliens seem remarkably oblivious to the pain and suffering they might have caused to human beings in their decades-long program of abductions of humans. Nor do they seem concerned about the lives and families (like the Nearys) that might be wrecked by the oddly mysterious nature of their arrival. One would think, after all, that a culture advanced enough to have built a starship (and that has had decades to study abducted human beings) would have developed a more unambiguous means of communication—unless, of course (echoing the linguistic imperialism that typically informed the attitudes of Western colonial powers on Earth), they regard human beings as so inferior that it is not worth stooping to their level or using their languages.

In any case, if there is a supernatural power at work in the events of the film, that power would appear to be not the aliens themselves but a god-like agency that oversees the alien arrival on earth and attempts to mediate the encounter between the two sides. That interpretation might explain the fact that the humans on earth seem to be receiving two entirely different sorts of messages from extrahuman forces. On the one hand, there are innocents and artists (like Roy Neary and Jillian Guiler) who seem to receive intuitive, spiritual calls announcing the alien arrival. On the other hand, the aliens also send mathematical codes to scientists on earth explaining exactly where they would like to meet. At times, however, these two modes of communication collapse into one. For example, the five-tone sequence that is so central to the film is both mathematical and musical. While we are clearly meant to understand that the crowd of Indian mystics shown early in the film is especially receptive to the sequence because of their greater spirituality (relative to Americans, with their highly materialistic culture), it is also the case that actual communication with the aliens seems to be established not by spiritual communion but by the use of a high-tech computer system that is programmed to interpret the alien tonal codes and respond in kind.

The film's use of Indian mysticism as an emblem of spirituality is itself a cliché of Western popular culture, echoing an image popularized in such events as the famous visit of the Beatles to India in 1968 to confer with the Maharishi Mahesh Yogi. If this image suggests the kind of commodified pop spirituality criticized by Gordon, it is also problematic in that the film, especially in its portrayal of Roy Neary and Barry Guiler, clearly seeks to associate spiritual openness with childlike innocence. As a result, the suggestion of greater Indian spirituality is also a suggestion of Indian childishness, which quite directly echoes any number of Western racist and colonialist stereotypes about the simplicity of the nonWestern mind.

Close Encounters is a film that repeats a number of such offensive stereotypes, presumably inadvertently. In addition to its problematic treatment of cultures, the film's depiction of women is troubling as well. Ronnie Neary, depicted as the prototypical ball-and-chain who seeks to domesticate her man and curb his desire to dream (then abandons him when he dreams nevertheless), is the obvious case here. The film clearly sides with

Roy against Ronnie, and nothing is made of the fact that the former abandons his familial responsibilities to go off in search of a pipe dream. The film is also careful to avoid any questions about responsibility with Jillian Guiler, the stereotypical "good" woman who, in clichéd contrast with Ronnie, understands Neary's need to follow the call he has heard. But Jillian has no husband to abandon, and she goes to Devils Tower to retrieve her son, rather than to leave him behind. Finally, that the male pilgrim Roy is given the crucial role of ambassador to an alien civilization, while the female Jillian simply comes to pick up her child (then happily, like a good soccer mom, snaps photographs) privileges the male role in a rather traditional way.

Granted, one might take the seeming benevolence of the highly advanced aliens as a rebuke to the Western legacy of self-serving colonial exploitation of the rest of the world. But any attempt to read *Close Encounters* as a critique, rather than a repetition, of Western colonialist ideology runs afoul of the film's complete failure to challenge the stereotypes it repeats. In addition, the film never mentions the fact that Devils Tower is a powerful spiritual symbol for several Native American cultures, the site having apparently been selected by the filmmakers purely for its visual effect rather than its spiritual resonances. Then again, the very fact that the site is a national monument is itself problematic and suggests the appropriation of a sacred Native American site for use essentially as a tourist attraction. From this point of view it is significant that the television feature report that Near sees on Devils Tower describes it as "the first national monument erected in this country by Theodore Roosevelt in 1915" as if the impressive natural geological phenomenon, which plays an important role in Plains Indian myth and folklore, was somehow constructed by the federal government. To make matters worse, the report even includes the wrong date: Roosevelt designated the site as a national monument in 1906, not 1915.

This inaccurate media report can be taken as part of the film's overall critique of television. As Neary works on the large (and impressive) sculpture of Devils Tower in this living room, it is not clear whether he has discovered his latent gifts as a sculptor or whether those gifts have been bestowed upon him by forces from beyond our world. Meanwhile, the soap opera *Days of Our Lives* plays on the television, its emblem of sand passing through an hourglass symbolizing the way in which Neary and his fellow suburbanites have merely been marking time, drifting through their empty lives. As if to emphasize this point, Neary looks out the window at his neighbors as they go about their various humdrum tasks, realizing as he does how distant he feels from them now that he has a calling from beyond the ordinary. The television then switches to a Budweiser beer commercial, again emphasizing the banality of suburban life, while at the same time suggesting the vapid commercialism of most television programming. One could, of course, find religious (especially Christian) significance in the Budweiser commercial that Neary hears, especially in the words of its jingle: "The king is coming: let's hear the call." But if those words could be taken to associate the alien arrival with the second coming of Christ, they surely do so in the most debased of ways. What they really suggest is the appropriation of even the most sacred of symbols by American corporate capitalism for use in even the most profane of missions, such as selling beer.

The news bulletin that follows the commercial is in many ways even more powerful than the soap opera or the beer commercial as a critique of the workings of American television. Not only does the feature report on Devils Tower show an obliviousness to Native American spiritual concerns (or, for that matter, simple facts), but the news report of a train derailment is entirely fabricated; it does nothing more than convey a lie concocted by the government, indicating the complicity of the media in official attempts to mislead the public. Meanwhile, the news reporter who announces the apparent calamity of a massive nerve gas spill in the cattle lands of Wyoming (possibly contaminating the beef supply) ends his account by making the event into a joke: "This means order your steak well done, Walter." It is not clear whom he is addressing, by the way, since the anchor man who introduces him is ABC's Howard K. Smith, not CBS's Walter Cronkite; the situation is even further confused later when Neary, during his interrogation by Lacombe, admits that he has come to the area to investigate a "Walter Cronkite story."

Given this portrayal of the media, perhaps it comes as no surprise that the television report does not mention the importance of Devils Tower in Native American culture. But the film itself does not mention this importance, either, perhaps because to mention the importance of Devils Tower to Native Americans would call attention to the virtual destruction of Native American cultures by the intrusion of technologically superior Western powers. In so doing, the film might have undermined its own message that we should welcome the benevolent alien invaders. After all, the U.S. Army forces that originally decimated the Native American tribes living in the region of Devils Tower carried with them a narrative of national benevolence that did not prevent near genocide. If the United States, standard bearer of liberty and justice, could essentially eradicate the less technologically advanced plains Indians, then what is to prevent the advanced aliens from doing the same to the United States, especially given that American culture is depicted throughout the film as spiritually impoverished and almost irredeemably corrupt?

If the inclusion of Native Americans in the film might have confused its message, it is also the case that *Close Encounters* is, in fact, a confused film in a number of ways. It is especially clear and quite powerful in its condemnation of American capitalist society as driven by materialist demands that leave the general population spiritually bereft. It is less convincing, however, when it attempts to offer alternatives to everyday American life, the option of simply waiting for alien (or divine) forces to save us seeming less than practical. Ultimately, of course, the real magic promoted by the film as an antidote to American capitalism comes not from gods or aliens, but from Hollywood. In *Close Encounters*, film itself is marvelous, especially as opposed to television, its main cultural competitor. Indeed, television in the film is depicted as so insipid that even a religious epic like *The Ten Commandments* loses much of its magic when it is reduced to the small screen, as we can see from the scene in which Roy, desperate for magic, pleads with Ronnie to let the kids watch a few-minute snippet of the nearly four-hour film, thus depriving the film of its overall context and impact, reducing it instead to a bite-sized television portion.

Close Encounters can be read as offering film as a potentially magical alternative to the commercial banalities of television, whether in classic Disney films like *Pinocchio*, with their evocation of childhood magic, or in magical films like *2001: A Space Odyssey*, which *Close Encounters* visually and lovingly echoes at several points. It was precisely with an eye toward such echoes that Spielberg, a fascinated admirer of the Kubrick film, sought out Trumbull (who played a key role in designing the special effects for *2001*) to be his special photographic effects supervisor. Indeed, Spielberg reportedly watched and rewatched *2001* obsessively during the filming of *Close Encounters*, which can be seen as a sort of homage to Kubrick—one that would be repeated in different form when Spielberg assumed the directorship of the 2001 film *Artificial Intelligence: A.I.*, which Kubrick had planned to direct before his death in 1999 (and which also, for that matter, draws on *Pinocchio* in significant ways).

Of course, the central emblem of movie magic in *Close Encounters* is *Close Encounters* itself, which asks viewers to regard the film they are watching as precisely the kind of extraordinary phenomenon that the film so thoroughly endorses. For example, audiences are perfectly well aware that the magnificent alien mother ship was actually constructed not by childlike aliens but by Spielberg and Trumbull. (If this were not clear enough, the filmmakers left several "signatures" on the mother ship, which, among its busy high-tech accoutrements, includes glued-on models of the robot R2–D2 and Darth Vader's spaceship from *Star Wars*, as well as a model of a Volkswagen Beetle.) But the magic of *Close Encounters* resides as much in its dare-to-dream theme as in its special effects. Then again, even this aspect of the film is a bit contradictory. By presenting film as a sort of escape from the suffocating routine of daily life under capitalism, *Close Encounters* delivers a ringing endorsement of the notion of Hollywood as America's Dream Factory, even as the overt critique of capitalism in the film makes the "factory" portion of this image problematic. Further, the film's preference for the imagination over commerce ignores the fact that it was a big-budget production that would reap huge profits for its corporate sponsors. Nevertheless, *Close Encounters* remains a powerful and special film, one that reminds us that, however routine life may have become in the modern workaday world, glimmers of hope for a magical future still remain.

NOTE ON ALTERNATIVE VERSIONS

It should be noted that three different versions of *Close Encounters of the Third Kind* have been released. The original theatrical version, much to Spielberg's dissatisfaction, was rushed into distribution in November so that the financially troubled Columbia could cash in on the lucrative Christmas season market. In 1980, a "Special Edition" of the film was released to theaters, involving the deletion of some scenes from the original, the addition of some scenes wanted by Spielberg, and the addition of an interior shot of the alien mothership at the insistence of the studio. The "Collector's Edition" was originally released to theaters in 1997 for the film's twentieth anniversary, then released on VHS and laserdisc the following year. That edition was released on DVD in 2001 and is the edition included in the currently available two–DVD set as well as its original one–disc version. This version omits the interior shot of the alien ship and includes a few other editorial changes that added a net total of about five minutes to the running time of the film. The above discussion applies specifically to this Collector's Edition.

CRAFTSMANSHIP AND THOUGHTFULNESS: THE LEGACY OF *CLOSE ENCOUNTERS OF THE THIRD KIND*

In addition to its numerous echoes of *2001: A Space Odyssey* and the central thematic role played by *Pinocchio, Close Encounters* contains direct or indirect references to a number of other films, such as *Metropolis* (1927) and Alfred Hitchcock's *North by Northwest* (1959). *Close Encounters* has also exerted a strong influence on subsequent films. Visually, it was a landmark film that changed forever the way the movies would represent aliens and UFOs, influencing the look of any number of subsequent SF films, in addition to television's *The X-Files*. The benevolent alien motif of *Close Encounters* recalls such films as *The Day the Earth Stood Still*, but poses a direct challenge to such films as *Invasion of the Body Snatchers*. The film that is most directly and obviously related to *Close Encounters* is Spielberg's later *E.T. the Extra-Terrestrial* (1982), which also conveys the notion of be- nevolent alien visitors, as does John Carpenter's *Starman* (1984). James Cameron's *The Abyss* (1989) also features benevolent (though apparently more interventionist) aliens, while its visual effects sometimes recall *Close Encounters* as well. On the other hand, the hugely successful *Independence Day* (1996) is a sort of anti–*Close Encounters* that avowedly returns to the 1950s days of hostile alien invaders. Similarly, Spielberg's own *War of the Worlds* (2005) features hostile aliens bent on the extermination of the human race, which they apparently plan to use as fertilizer.

8

Alien

Released 1979; Director Ridley Scott

Alien had already been in development for some time before the huge success of *Star Wars* in 1977, but that success encouraged Twentieth Century Fox to push for the production of *Alien* with a stepped-up budget and timetable. The result was another of the signature science fiction films of the American cinema, though it was a film that could not have been more different from *Star Wars*. Ridley Scott combined horror with science fiction to produce a film with a dark theme and a dark look, while also introducing one of the most compelling characters in SF film, Sigourney Weaver's vulnerable but tough-as-nails Ellen Ripley. Though not as popular as *Star Wars, Alien* was still a big commercial success, demonstrating that science fiction films could make money, even when aimed at adult audiences. Meanwhile, the distinctive dark, industrial look of *Alien* influenced any number of subsequent films, including one of the most successful sequences of sequels in SF film history.

THE STORY: IT CAME FROM OUTER SPACE

Alien begins with a quick tour of a spacecraft, which on-screen text identifies as the *Nostromo*, a "commercial towing vehicle" with a crew of seven and a cargo of 20,000,000 tons of mineral ore that is being returned to Earth. The ship has a highly industrial, used, and run-down look, very much in contrast to the shiny, immaculate spacecraft of predecessors such as

2001: A Space Odyssey (1968) and *Star Wars* (1977). Eerie views of the seemingly empty ship are followed by a shot of the crew awakening from hibernation, their pods springing open on the order of "Mother," the ship's main computer. After they awake, the crew gathers for breakfast, giving us a chance to meet them. Appropriate to their ship, they are a far cry from the dashing heroes of much science fiction. Envisioned by the filmmakers as a group of "truckdrivers in space," they are not in space to seek adventure or knowledge; they're simply there to collect a paycheck. Introducing the theme of economic motivation that will be crucial to the entire film, we learn early on that some of the crew are being paid more than others, much to their displeasure. Thus, Brett (Harry Dean Stanton) and Parker (Yaphet Koto), bring up their contention that the "bonus situation" is not equitable because they are only receiving half shares. Captain Dallas (Tom Skerritt) simply replies that they are getting what they contracted for, without commenting on the fairness of the contracts. This scene also introduces the second officer Kane (John Hurt), the third officer Ripley (Sigourney Weaver), the science officer Ash (Ian Holm), and the navigator Lambert (Veronica Cartwright).

Soon the crew members discover that they have not been awakened because they are approaching Earth, as they had expected. Instead, they are in a strange solar system, where Mother has picked up what may be a distress beacon. When the crew complains about the diversion (and Parker suggests that he should be paid extra for it), Ash explains that they are contractually obligated to investigate any signs of intelligent life, on penalty of total forfeiture of shares. They home in on the signal and find that it is coming from a small planetoid, so they undock from the refinery they are towing and land the *Nostromo* on the planetoid, near the source of the signal.

The ship is damaged in the rough landing, necessitating repairs by Parker and Brett, the working-class members of the crew—who greatly resent the fact that Ripley joins them on the lower decks as they work, though the resentment seems to be more because she is an officer than because she is a woman. They seem to feel that she is invading their territory, thus implicitly challenging their professional competence. Meanwhile, Lambert, Kane, and Dallas suit up and go outside to seek the source of the signal. They struggle through a weird, stormy, low-visibility landscape and trace the signal to the wreck of a strange, almost surreal, alien spacecraft. Inside, they find what seem to be the fossilized remains of an alien pilot, looking as if it had exploded from the inside. Kane then discovers a hot, damp chamber that seems to be full of some sort of eggs. When he examines one of them, it stirs with life, then opens up, revealing a pulsating mass, which suddenly leaps from the egg onto the faceplate of Kane's helmet. Dallas and Lambert rush him back to the landing craft. Ripley is reluctant to allow them inside with the alien life form attached to Kane, due to quarantine regulations. Ash, however, opens the hatch (presumably out of humanitarian motives, though we later realize that he simply wants to retrieve the alien), even though Ripley outranks him.

Inside, Ash and Dallas crack open the faceplate of Kane's helmet and find a weird, tentacled creature attached to his face. They work inside the ship's medical facility to get the thing off, while the others look on from outside. Unable to remove the creature, they scan Kane's body, finding that the creature has an appendage down Kane's throat, apparently feeding him oxygen. Dallas orders the creature removed from Kane; when Ash tries to cut through a tentacle, a yellowish fluid, apparently the creature's blood, spills out of it and eats through the floor, drops to the next deck, and begins to eat through there as well. Dallas concludes that the fluid must be some sort of "molecular acid."

Parker and Brett continue to work to repair the *Nostromo*, while Ash continues to examine the strange creature, which he finds has the ability to shed its cells and replace them with polarized silicon, which gives it a "prolonged resistance to adverse environmental conditions." Soon afterward, though, it spontaneously drops off of Kane's face and dies. Ash begins to dissect it as Dallas and Ripley look on. Ripley wants it off the ship, but Ash regards it as a valuable scientific specimen. Dallas sides with Ash, telling Ripley that Ash has authority in scientific matters.

Dallas insists that they take off immediately, though the repairs are not fully complete. They make it back to the orbiting refinery, where Lambert calculates that they are still ten months from Earth. Kane, meanwhile, regains consciousness and seems to be recovering well. The crew decides to have a meal before going back into hibernation and heading for Earth. As they eat, Kane seems to be choking. They lay him on the table and restrain him. Suddenly, blood spatters from his chest as he thrashes wildly about. A weird, bloody alien creature emerges from his chest as the others look on in horror, then takes off, skittering across the room.

The remaining members of the crew place Kane's body in a coffin and eject it from the ship, while the creature remains loose on board. They mobilize to search for it; in the process, Brett is snatched by the alien, now grown much larger, and taken into an air duct. The others, realizing that the alien is using the air ducts to move about the ship, decide to hunt it there. Dallas goes into the duct system with a flamethrower, making his way forward as the others close hatches behind him, presumably cornering the alien. The others monitor his progress, but lose his signal as he comes upon the creature. When they investigate, they find only his flamethrower. Ripley, now the senior officer on the ship, wants to continue Dallas's plan of driving the alien through the airshafts to an airlock. However, she first goes into the console room—a chamber of flashing lights that might have looked at home in *2001: A Space Odyssey*—to consult Mother. The appearance of this room is entirely appropriate, because Mother herself is a sort of descendant of the earlier film's infamous HAL. Ripley discovers that Mother, in league with Ash, has ordered the return of the alien for study at all costs, the crew having been declared expendable. Furious, Ripley confronts Ash with this information. They struggle. He weirdly attempts to kill her by shoving a rolled-up girlie magazine down her throat in a symbolic rape that also recalls the attack of the original alien on Kane. The others arrive to join the fray. Parker slugs Ash, who begins to go wild and to spew white fluid from his mouth. Parker knocks his head off, finally stopping him. Ash is a robot. The robot, head dangling, attacks Parker, but they finally deactivate it.

Ripley theorizes that the company wants the alien for its weapons division and that Ash has been protecting it all along for that reason. They manage to reactivate Ash in order to interrogate him about his orders from the company. He explains that he was ordered to bring back the creature, "all other priorities rescinded." Parker angrily sums up the film's verdict on the company: "The damn Company. What about our lives?"

Ash further warns them that the creature cannot be killed: "It's a perfect organism. Its structural perfection is matched only by its hostility." He admits that he admires its "purity," because it is "a survivor, unclouded by conscience, remorse, or delusions of morality"—much like the Company itself. In response, Ripley decides that they should blow up the ship and try to get back to Earth in the shuttle. She sends Lambert and Parker off to gather coolant for the shuttle's air support system, then prepares to set the *Nostromo* to self-destruct, which will leave them ten minutes to escape. First, though, she goes off in search of Jones, the ship's cat—which has appeared in the film mostly as a sort of snarling beast, sometimes mistaken for the alien, accompanied by hints that it might have been impregnated like Kane or otherwise somehow possessed by the alien. In the meantime, the alien attacks (and apparently kills) both Lambert and Parker. Ripley keys in the emergency self-destruct sequence, then prepares to leave the *Nostromo*. On the way out (in a gruesome scene added for the 2004 Director's Cut), she discovers Dallas and Brett, formerly presumed dead, encased in some sort of cocoon-like mass, where they will apparently be used as hosts for the gestation of more creatures. This fate is clearly more horrifying than simple death, and Dallas begs Ripley to kill him. His pleading "Kill me," clearly echoes the pitiful "Help me" cry of the human-fly hybrid caught in a spider web at the end of the 1958 horror classic, *The Fly*. Ripley blasts him and Brett with a flamethrower.

Ripley finds her path to the shuttle blocked by the alien. She runs through the dark ship, as the option to override the detonation procedure expires. Mother announces that the ship will detonate in five minutes. "You bitch!" screams Ripley, smashing a panel. Then she again heads for the shuttle. On the way, she manages to retrieve Jones, thus planting the suggestion that she might thereby be taking the alien aboard the shuttle. The shuttle takes off as the countdown on the *Nostromo* reaches twenty seconds. They get clear in time to watch the explosion of the ship. "I got you, you son of a bitch," Ripley mumbles (apparently regarding the alien as male).

She and Jones appear to be heading safely for home. She puts the cat in a hibernation chamber, then undresses and sets various shuttle controls as she prepares to hibernate as well. Suddenly, an alien claw pops out of a console. The creature is on board, after all, though not via Jones. Terrified, Ripley slowly slips into a spacesuit. Trying to hold it together, she haltingly sings "You are my lucky star" as she straps herself in and evacuates the ship, propelling the alien out into space. It grabs the hatchway as it leaves, so she shoots it with a grappling hook, knocking it into space, but leaving it tethered to the ship by the line attached to the grapple. It tries to climb back in through a rocket exhaust. Ripley lights the rocket and blasts the creature away into space once and for all. Peaceful music announces her victory.

Ripley records her final report before going into hibernation, noting the destruction of the *Nostromo* and the rest of the crew. She also indicates that she plans to reach the "frontier" in about six weeks, hoping the "network" will pick her up. She goes into hibernation, as the end credits roll over a starry spacescape.

THE SOURCES OF THE MOVIE

The exact source of *Alien* is the subject of some controversy. The film was ostensibly based on an original story idea by Dan O'Bannon and Ronald Shusett, scripted for the screen by O'Bannon. O'Bannon and Shusett freely admit that they were greatly influenced by previous science fiction films, among which *It! The Terror from Beyond Space* (1958) probably deserves the most prominent mention, though the SF comedy *Dark Star* (1074, scripted by O'Bannon and directed by then-newcomer John Carpenter) is also an especially important predecessor. In addition, science fiction pioneer A. E. Van Vogt filed suit after the release of the film, claiming that it was inspired by his short stories "Black Destroyer" and "Discord in Scarlet" (both 1939), which were folded into the 1950 novel *Voyage of the Space Beagle*. He may have had a point. "Black Destroyer" features a deadly alien creature that stows away aboard a human ship, while another stowaway killer alien in "Discord in Scarlet" lays eggs inside human hosts. In any case, Van Vogt settled out of court (for a considerable monetary settlement), and his stories are now widely considered to be one source for *Alien* and its sequels. On the other hand, the elements that make *Alien* truly special as a film (the design of the alien itself, the female protagonist, the evil Company, the industrial-looking spaceship) are entirely missing from the Van Vogt stories.

MONSTERS, MACHINERY, AND MIXED GENRES IN *ALIEN*: SCIENCE FICTION GOES POSTMODERN

Alien was a highly successful film that won an Oscar for best special effects and was nominated for another for best art direction and set decoration. In general, however, it made far less of a splash than had *Star Wars*, its direct predecessor at Fox. Over the years, however, *Alien* has joined Scott's later *Blade Runner* (1982) as the two SF films to have received the most serious attention from academic critics. In addition to its innovative visual style, *Alien* has attracted significant critical attention for a number of reasons, including its mixture of genres and other postmodern elements, its thematic treatment of gender and sexuality, and the implications of its representation of the predatory Company.

Certainly, one of the most important elements in the success of *Alien* involves the decision to make the *Nostromo* look like a working piece of industrial hardware. Ron Cobb's design of the ship's interior adds a great deal to the believability of the film, while also helping to reinforce the film's dark vision of the future and to enhance the film's sense of terror. Thus, the gloomy, dank, claustrophobic passages and chambers through which the crew of the *Nostromo* pursue (or are pursued by) the alien surely work better for the purposes of this film than would the gleaming, spacious corridors of the large ships in *Star Wars* or *Star Trek*. In addition, all the visible (and slightly worn and dirty) machinery that we see aboard the *Nostromo* helps to remind us that this is a working vessel and that the humans in the crew are simply trying to get home to collect a paycheck.

The design of the alien itself (in its various transformations), as well as the design of the alien ship on which it is first found, are among the most memorable designs in all of SF film. Swiss surrealist artist H. R. Giger was contracted to do these designs, after O'Bannon had discovered his visions of bizarre, nightmarish (but oddly sexual and strangely beautiful) alien creatures in Giger's book *Necronomicon.* The results have become almost legendary, and Giger's design of the alien craft is not only effectively weird but also makes a nice contrast to the down-to-earth, engineering-oriented design of the *Nostromo*, clearly establishing that this ship was constructed by a culture very different from our own. Giger's alien (the adult version of which was constructed by creature master Carlo Rambaldi) is among the most effective in all of SF film, especially given that it is actually a rather low-tech creation (though it would be gradually supplemented by computer-generated imagery in the sequels). The main adult alien, in fact, was literally a man (7' 2" Bolaji Badejo) in a rubber suit, much like the famed monsters of low-budget films such as those made by Roger Corman—which was, incidentally, precisely the kind of film originally envisioned by O'Bannon and Shusett, who nearly signed with Corman before taking the project to Fox. Aided by Giger's design and Rambaldi's technical skills, this monster went far beyond its predecessors, however, achieving a combination of strangeness, scariness, beauty, and sexuality never before seen in a movie monster. Scott greatly enhanced the effectiveness of the alien by keeping it somewhat mysterious and never really giving us a very good look at it, somewhat in the vein of the fleeting shots of the aliens in *It Came from Outer Space* (1953).

Of course, the aliens of *It Came from Outer Space* were benevolent, hated and misunderstood by xenophobic humans largely because they looked different. The title figure of *Alien* is a genuine monster, seemingly driven only by the dual urge to kill and to propagate—it is a dark and lurking monster of the kind found in horror films rather than a classic movie monster in the mold of King Kong or Godzilla. Indeed, Scott has suggested that his major inspiration for the horror elements of the film came from Tobe Hooper's *The Texas Chainsaw Massacre* (1974), and it is certainly the case that *Alien* has more in common with slasher films than with classic monster movies or alien-invasion films.

The gleaming spaceships of most SF films open up outer space, allowing their inhabitants to range the galaxy. In contrast, the dark, spooky *Nostromo* has a great deal in common with the isolated and claustrophobic country houses of numerous slasher films, which enclose a small group of victims in a small space as a demonic killer slowly picks them off one after another. Interestingly, one of the most common distinctions made by critics between the horror film and the science fiction film is that the former usually involves violence and terror visited upon a few individuals in a small enclosed space, while the latter often involves cataclyms that threaten to destroy a large city or even an entire society or planet. In this sense, *Alien* would seem more horror film than science fiction. On the other hand, the makers of *Alien* and its sequels seem to go out of their way to suggest that their central monster represents a threat that goes far beyond the *Nostromo* and the ships of the sequels and that, if it ever manages to escape the confined spaces of the films, it might sweep across the galaxy like some sort of contagion, destroying everything in its path.

This aspect of the *Alien* sequence is not necessarily convincing: it requires the assumption that the alien eggs found in the first *Alien* film are the only ones of their kind and that the creatures that spring from them are the only members of their species. Yet there is no real reason to believe this to be the case, other than the fact that the alien craft on which the eggs are discovered apparently crashed so long ago that its dead pilot is now fossilized and that no other aliens have been encountered in the intervening time. This problem aside, the suggestion that the aliens threaten the entire galaxy joins with the film's outer-space setting and extensive SF hardware to make *Alien* quite clearly a science fiction film first and foremost, with horror elements that are only secondary.

Of course, by this distinction, science fiction will almost always dominate horror as a genre: a combined threat to both individuals and society is no different from a threat to an entire society. In the case of *Alien*, the dominance of SF over horror is furthered by the fact that the monster is entirely natural and that the film contains no elements of the supernatural or of evil in the metaphysical sense. (The alien is not evil; it is simply unable by its nature to coexist with humans.) The same might be said for a film like Roger Donaldson's *Species* (1995) or Christian Nyby's prototype for such combinations, *The Thing from Another World* (1951). Nevertheless, it might be interesting to consider the proposition that this phenomenon is a general one and that science fiction, when combined with horror—even Gothic and supernatural horror, as in Hooper's vampires-from-space flick *Lifeforce* (1985, co-scripted by O'Bannon) or Paul W. S. Anderson's *Event Horizon* (1997) and *Resident Evil* (2002)—virtually always comes out as the dominant genre. One could even say, in fact, that science fiction tends to dominate when combined with *any* other genre, as in Scott's own hybrid of SF and the film noir detective story in *Blade Runner* (1982) or Peter Hyams's combination of SF with the Western in *Outland* (1981).

Alien, of course, presents us with a number of hybrid forms, a tendency that combines with its multigeneric nature to make it the subject of much critical discussion of postmodernism in film. For one thing, the film's seemingly simple opposition between human and alien is gradually dismantled in the course of the film, producing a typically postmodern challenge to dualistic thinking. After all, the crew of the *Nostromo* encounters not one, but two different alien species if one counts the fossilized alien pilot, reminding us that humans are not the only bearers of advanced technological civilization ever to have graced the galaxy. In addition, the living alien of the film is so mutable and goes through so many transformations in the film that it seems like several different species in itself. Finally, this alien life form is not the only sentient Other to which humanity is contrasted in the film, Mother and Ash providing still another image of a distinctive mode of intelligent existence that seems alien to our own.

Of the thematic hybridizations and boundary-crossings that are so central to the film's effects, the most extensive critical attention has been devoted to the film's trangression of traditional gender boundaries. The strong, tough Ridley, who contrasts so dramatically with the typical film heroine, represents the most obvious of these streotype-shattering transgressions, and it is certainly the case that her character paved the way not only for her increasingly strong characterization in the later *Alien* films, but also such later SF film heroines as the much-threatened but highly resilient Sarah Connor (Linda Hamilton) of James Cameron's *The Terminator* (1984), who emerges in *Terminator 2* (1991) as a muscular, gun-toting guerrilla fighter. Ridley also paved the way for non-SF heroines, such as Nikita (Anne

Parillaud), the deadly, ass-kicking title character of Luc Besson's *La Femme Nikita* (1990).

The transgressive representation of Ripley in *Alien* reaches its peak in the final confrontation with the alien on the shuttle. As Ripley strips to her underwear, leaving her vulnerable and exposed (to both the audience and the alien, both of whom become voyeurs at this point), she seems to become the classic female victim of the horror/slasher film, only to turn the tables when she still proves capable of defending herself and of blasting her alien rapist/attacker out into space. Here, not only does Ripley violate the conventions of the film heroine (in almost any genre), but *Alien* itself almost playfully mocks the conventions of the horror film genre (as when it continually teases us with the unfulfilled expectation that Jones the cat will surely become host to one of the aliens). Indeed, *Alien*'s relative lack of respect for the conventions of the horror film is another of the ways in which it signals its greater allegiance to the SF genre.

The gender transgressions of *Alien*, however, go far beyond the characterization of Ripley. The attack on Kane by the alien in its "face-hugger" incarnation clearly functions as a sort of rape, leading to the explosive appearance of the "chest-burster" alien in an obscene parody of childbirth. This whole motif thus involves a sort of sexual encounter between an alien and a human, a boldly transgressive move made all the more so by the fact that Kane, a human male, plays the female role in this relationship. Further, the adult alien tends to take its victims by impaling them on its thrusting claw, a gesture of penetration that has sexual implications made all the more obvious by the sinuous, sensuous, and phallic nature of the alien itself.

From a psychoanalytical point of view, the alien is clearly something like a beast from a Freudian nightmare. However, the beast is a sort of capitalist nightmare as well. The film openly invites readings within the context of capitalism with its portrayal of the greedy, grasping Company, willing to risk not only the crew of the *Nostromo* but all of humanity in its quest for increased corporate profits. This aspect of the film (which links it to the themes of the Joseph Conrad novel from which the ship takes its name) suggests a dystopian future in which the socioeconomic woes of the twentieth century have been far from solved. But it also, like all of the best science fiction, provides a commentary on the contemporary context in which the film itself was produced.

On the other hand, while the portrayal of the brutal Company in *Alien* is particularly striking and effective, the motif may suffer for contemporary viewers from being all too familiar. Greedy, unprincipled corporations are a stock image of American film, SF or otherwise, a phenomenon that allows audiences to congratulate themselves on understanding the ruthless power of corporate capitalism, while producing the illusion that, armed with this knowledge, we are equipped to resist this power. *Alien*, however, was one of the first important films to establish this motif. In addition, it supplements its portrayal of the Company itself with other motifs that significantly enhance the film's critique of capitalism. For one thing, the portrayal of social relations on the *Nostromo*, in which gender and racial differences seem to matter very little, but in which class differences are still quite important, can be taken as a verification of the Marxist point that class differences are the most fundamental social distinctions under capitalism and as a rejection of the tendency of contemporary American society to obscure the reality of class difference by concentrating instead on the categories of race and gender. For another thing, the suggested spread of capitalism into deep space seems to verify the insight of Marx and Engels in *The Communist Manifesto* about the inherently expansionist tendencies of capitalism, which for them by its nature must continually mutate and grow like a contagion in order to survive, gobbling up everything in its path.

Ultimately, however, the film's most interesting commentary on capitalism may reside in the alien itself. Gleaming and beautiful, but deadly and unstoppable, the alien in many ways functions as a clear allegorical embodiment of the workings of the capitalist system. Indeed, the portrayal of the alien as predatory, unstoppable, constantly changing, and endlessly adaptable, resembles nothing more than the characterization of capitalism in *The Communist Manifesto*. Similarly, the ruthless single-mindedness of the alien, which is driven only by the desire to propagate, resembles the relentless expansionism of capitalism. Even the horrifying use of humans as disposable hosts for the production of alien offspring invites allegorical comparison with capitalism, which similarly uses human beings as tools in the never-ending quest to produce more capital.

In this sense, *Alien* may be a far more radical film than it first appears to be—or than its makers themselves intended for it to be. On the other hand, by including an overt critique of capitalism in their portrayal of the predatory Company, *Alien* seems to invite comparisons between the alien and the Company and, by extension, capitalism as a whole. In any case, whether one sees the alien itself as an emblem of capitalism, the success of the *Alien* series of films suggests that it taps into the fears and anxieties of its audience at a profound level and that the predicament of the crew of the *Nostromo*—regarded as disposable tools by their own employer while trapped and terrorized by irresistible inhuman forces they can neither understand nor control—reflects the experience of numerous individuals in our contemporary world.

NOTE ON ALTERNATIVE VERSIONS

Several slightly different versions of *Alien* have been released in different video formats and in different countries over the years. The two principal versions, both available in the nine–disc "Alien Quadrilogy" DVD Box Set, are the original theatrical version and the 2003 Director's Cut. The 2003 version may be slightly superior, though Scott himself has oddly expressed a preference for the original version over the thusly misnamed "Director's Cut." Some added footage (most importantly that involving the cocooned Dallas and Brett) actually changes the implications of some parts of the film, while the slight trimming of other scenes makes them a bit tauter. Overall, the Director's Cut is actually one minute shorter than the theatrical version. In addition to the theatrical versions of all three sequels, the DVD set includes Special Editions of those films as well, most of which are changed simply to add footage (the Special Edition of the third sequel, *Alien: Resurrection*, is thirty minutes longer than the original version).

SLIMY ALIENS AND ASS-KICKING WOMEN: THE LEGACY OF *ALIEN*

Alien was a truly groundbreaking film that changed the face of science fiction film forever. Visually, it helped Scott to refine the noir look that he perfected in *Blade Runner* three years later and that appears in any number of science fiction films of the last quarter of a century, perhaps most effectively in Alex Proyas's *Dark City* (1998). The industrial look of *Alien* was quickly adopted by films such as *Outland* and also appears in later films such as *Event Horizon*. *Alien*'s particular vision of an alien enemy also influenced any number of subsequent alien-invasion films, such as the three films in the *Species* series, the second of which even employed Giger to design its alien creatures. Countless low-budget efforts have been clearly influenced by *Alien*, including the baleful 1996 production *Alien Terminator*, interesting because it is so directly modeled on *Alien* and because it was executive produced by Roger Corman, giving us a glimpse of what *Alien* might have been like had it in fact gone into production with Corman's company.

The films most obviously and directly linked to *Alien* are its three sequels. *Aliens* (1986) is a direct sequel to *Alien*, based on the same premises as the first film and directly continuing its action. However, under the direction of James Cameron, *Aliens* is a very different film, something like a combination of the original *Alien* with *The Terminator* (which Cameron had directed in 1984) and *Rambo: First Blood Part II* (which Cameron had written in 1985). Cameron was a logical choice to direct the first sequel: *Terminator*, with its seemingly unstoppable villain and its resilient female protagonist, was clearly influenced by the original *Alien* film. Compared to that first film, *Aliens* is even scarier, much more violent, and more overt in its criticism of the willingness of the "Company" (now identified as the Weyland–Yutani Corporation) to endanger human beings in the interest of extending its own profit. Here, Ripley and Jones have been recovered after drifting in space for fifty-seven years while in hypersleep. Company officials do not appear to believe Ripley's story of the destruction of the *Nostromo* (a valuable piece of hardware), but they nevertheless coerce her into going along as a consultant when they send a military expedition of "colonial marines" back to the planet where the alien was originally discovered to investigate the sudden cessation of communications from a human colony that has been placed there to terraform the dismal world.

The resultant gory battle (featuring numerous spattering alien bodies, blown apart by the considerable firepower toted by the marines) between the humans and multiple aliens makes the film as much a war movie as it is science fiction or horror, perhaps in tune with the tastes of the Reagan era in which the film was made. This film significantly extends our knowledge of the biology of the alien species, especially through the introduction of an alien queen, who has laid thousands of eggs on the planet, somewhat in the mold of a queen bee or ant. Also along on the mission is the company stooge Carter Burke (Paul Reiser), who endangers all of the humans in his quest to garner a live alien specimen for study by the company's weapon's division. Another twist is that the android on this mission, Bishop (Lance Henriksen), is one of the good guys. Though he is torn in half by the alien queen, he manages to use his barely functioning upper half to rescue young "Newt" (Carrie Henn) as the queen is once again blown out into space by Ripley, who in this film gets a first name (Ellen) and becomes much more of an action hero—as well as a mother figure for Newt. As the film ends, Ripley, Newt, and Hicks (Michael Biehn), one of the marines, the only survivors of the expedition, head for home in hypersleep, secure in the notion that they have nuked the planet, which should presumably wipe out the aliens once and for all.

Alien³ (1992) is a dark, brooding film that turns away from the frantic action of *Aliens*, depending more on atmosphere for its effects. Here, it turns out that an alien (now described as a "xenomorph") has once again stowed away aboard the vessel that is presumably taking Ripley to earth and safety. This time, the creature plants the embryo of a new queen inside Ripley herself, meanwhile causing Ripley, Hicks, and Newt to crash land in an emergency evacuation vehicle on what turns out to be a prison planet (run, of course, by the Weyland–Yutani Corporation, though essentially abandoned). In the crash, Hicks and Newt are killed, but Ripley survives and is taken back to the prison infirmary, where she is nursed back to health by Clemens (Charles Dance), the prison doctor, himself a former inmate of the hellish prison.

The alien that caused the crash (a somewhat different version of the aliens in the earlier films) escapes into the prison, where it slowly begins eradicating the prison population, which consists of a handful of ragged leftovers who actually asked to be left behind when the Company ceased full operations on the planet. Most of them have adopted an apocalyptic Christian faith (though few seem very committed to it), and indeed the entire decaying prison has an apocalyptic look to it, like something from the *Mad Max* movies. Most of the prisoners are "Double-Y chromosome" rapists and murderers, which makes them the ultimate nightmare for a stranded woman like Ripley—though she may be their nightmare as well. When their leader, Dillon (Charles S. Dutton) explains that he is a "murderer and rapist of women," she calmly replies, "Well, I guess I must make you nervous."

This line indicates the way in which Ripley's tough character might make some men a bit uncomfortable. Indeed, numerous other aspects of this film make it perhaps the most interesting of the entire sequence in terms of its treatment of gender, as Ripley finally reveals herself as a woman with sexual needs, but adopts a unisex look by shaving her head and dressing like the prisoners, presumably to cause less of a disturbance among them. However, this film's xenomorph is less interesting than in the other films (looking a bit like a large, mechanical rat), while its treatment of the greedy and potentially murderous Company adds nothing of substance to what we have seen before. The film does have a shocking ending: after Ripley and the few surviving inmates have managed to kill the xenomorph that has been stalking them, she throws herself into a furnace full of molten led, thus killing herself and the gestating queen—and apparently ending the sequence once and for all.

Neither Ripley nor the xenomorph is all that easy to kill off, however. Both return in *Alien: Resurrection* (1997), though in modified form. In this film, set 200 years after *Alien³*, Weaver returns as a rebuilt Ripley, constructed from a hybrid combination of the DNA of the original Ripley and the aliens—and only then after a series of ghoulish failed experiments have produced a series of monstrosities. This new Ripley is a dark and brooding character, her personality (and superhuman physical prowess) heavily influenced by her alien genes, though much of her new bitterness and hostility can be attributed to her resentment at having been created in the first place. Meanwhile, the government scientists who have created her (in a special lab on a craft in deep space, for added security) are also working to produce more xenomorphs, again for use as weapons, though this time they apparently plan to use them for "urban pacification" back on Earth.

Importantly, these *are* government scientists. In fact, Weyland–Yutani no longer exists, though we find out only in the Special Edition that the predatory corporation has itself fallen prey to a takeover by a more powerful and ruthless competitor: Wal-Mart. This twist indicates the extent to which this film (especially in the Special Edition, with its comic opening credits replacing the horror-oriented credits of the theatrical version), while in some ways the darkest of the entire series, differs from its predecessors in its tendency toward quirky humor and one-liners. Moreover, the film is largely a postmodern pastiche of references to earlier films, from *Frankenstein*, to *Blade Runner*, to the other *Alien* films themselves. It is also a gorgeous looking film, clearly showing the touch of director Jean-Pierre Jeunet, who had established his elaborate, offbeat visual style in such earlier works as *Delicatessen* (1991) and *The City of Lost Children* (1995). Nevertheless, the over-the-top visual style combines with the strange mixture of darkness and almost campy silliness to make this by far the weirdest of all the *Alien* films. As the film ends, Ripley and her new robot sidekick, Call (Winona Ryder), have just landed on what seems to be a postapocalyptic Earth (with a ruined Eiffel Tower in the background, recalling the half-buried Statue of Liberty at the end of *Planet of the Apes*), very much leaving open the possibility of still another sequel. However, the only subsequent *Alien* film to appear as of this writing is *AVP: Alien vs. Predator* (2004), which dispenses with Ripley and Call and pits the xenomorphs against the warrior aliens of the *Predator* films, with largely uninteresting results.

9

E.T. the Extra-Terrestrial

Released 1982; Director Steven Spielberg

E.T. the Extra-Terrestrial was Spielberg's follow-up to *Close Encounters of the Third Kind,* made in lieu of a sequel to that earlier film. *E.T.* was largely conceived as a children's film and is thus in some ways somewhat simpler than its predecessor. It was, however, even more commercially successful, and its lovable title character became a major icon of American popular culture. Indeed, the film is widely regarded as one of the great works of children's cinema, often mentioned alongside such classics as *The Wizard of Oz* (1939) and the classic Disney films. *E.T.* was also the first commercially and critically successful science fiction film to be made primarily for children, though it also proved popular with adult audiences.

THE STORY: CUDDLY ALIENS AND TRUSTING CHILDREN

E.T. begins as an alien craft lands in the forest. Shadowy figures waddle about, exploring what is to them an alien world. Suddenly vehicles arrive at the scene, seemingly intent on intercepting the aliens. Flashlights glaring, the silhouetted human figures chase a screaming, terrified alien through the dark woods. As they approach the ship, it takes off; however, the alien that has been chased through the woods (the film's title character) is left behind, whimpering with loneliness and fear, clearly identified as an object of sympathy. The humans remain unidentified in the scene, and their dark forms combined with their bright flashlights, make them seem sinister. It is thus clear already that, in this film, we should expect a reversal of the typical good human vs. bad alien scenario so familiar to science fiction film fans. Meanwhile, it is barely possible to make out one of the men, played by actor Peter Coyote, a character we will later learn is a government agent charged with investigating UFO incidents. This character, never named in the film, is identified as "Keys" in the credits, a name derived from the jangling key ring we see on his belt as he chases E.T. through the woods.

Cut to a scene of some boys at a table, immersed in a role-playing game. A younger boy, ten-year-old Elliott (Henry Thomas), tries to join the group, which includes Michael (Robert MacNaughton), his big brother. However, the younger boy is rebuffed and instead sent out to meet the pizza delivery man, establishing his status as a lonely outsider. While outside, he hears a noise and goes to investigate. There is a rattling coming from a shed in the back yard. Startled, Elliott drops the pizza. The older boys go out to check the scene, accompanied by Mary (Dee Wallace), the mother of Mike and Elliott. The older boys mockingly hum the theme from the *Twilight Zone* as they approach the shed. There, they find strange footprints, concluding that the noise must be caused by coyotes. The dropped pizza is a mess, and Elliott is now even further from acceptance by the older boys.

That night, Elliott goes back outside with a flashlight and comes upon E.T. in a cornfield, frightening both himself and the alien. Their joint scream as they come face-to-face provides one of the film's classic moments. It also suggests that Elliott and E.T. have much in common, a notion that will be steadily solidified as they establish a closer and closer connection during the remainder of the film. The next evening, at the family dinner table, we are introduced to the fourth member of the family, little sister Gertie (Drew Barrymore). None of the others believe Elliott's story that he has seen an alien, and Mike makes fun of him. Mary suggests that Elliott call his father and tell him about it, but the boy says he can't, because the father is "in Mexico with Sally." The mother, nearing tears, rushes from the table, making it clear that the family has recently broken up, the father leaving them to be with his new girlfriend. From the kitchen Mary urges Elliott to tell her if he sees the creature again so she can call someone to come take it away. But the boy, even at his young age, has learned to expect sinister things from those in authority: "But they'll give it a lobotomy or do experiments on it, or something," he moans.

That night, Elliott lies outside in a chair, flashlight on. E.T. emerges from the light of the shed, barely visible. The alien waddles toward the frightened boy and slowly reaches out a hand, returning some Reese's Pieces that the boy had left in the woods, apparently as an offering to the alien. Elliott then gets a bag of the candy and uses it to lure E.T. into the house and, eventually, into his room. Inside the room, the alien begins to mimic the boy's gestures, thus showing signs of intelligence. The sleepy boy then suddenly backs into a chair and falls asleep, indicating (though it is not clear at the time) the psychic connection that allows him to experience E.T.'s feelings: his sudden sleepiness, so seemingly odd in the midst of such excitement, may be a reaction to the alien's exhaustion. Meanwhile, out in the night, the men with flashlights are still scouring the area, providing an ominous warning that, however harmless E.T. might be, there are other forces afoot that might not be so friendly.

The next day, Elliott feigns illness in order to stay home from school with his new friend. He shows E.T. his various toys, including action figures of Lando Calrissian and Boba Fett from *The Empire Strikes Back* (1980), providing the first of several direct references to the *Star Wars* franchise in the film. He also attempts to explain the fish food chain, placing sharks (as in Spielberg's 1975 film *Jaws*) at the top. Elliott shows E.T. how to eat Pez, after which the hungry E.T. tries to eat a toy car. Elliott goes into the kitchen to prepare some real food, dropping it when E.T., back in the bedroom, is startled by the opening of an umbrella, further indicating their connection.

Big brother Mike returns from school, still in his football uniform. He takes off the jersey to reveal that he is wearing a "Space Invaders" tee shirt underneath. Mocking Elliott, who announces that he has discovered the alien, Mike starts doing an imitation of Yoda from *Star Wars*, but when E.T. walks in, Mike is stunned into silence. Then Gertie arrives, and soon all three children have befriended E.T. Back outside, the anonymous men continue their search, this time with metal detectors and other equipment.

As the children try to communicate with E.T., he demonstrates the power of telekinesis, levitating a makeshift model of his solar system in the air to indicate that he is from outer space. Later, he begins to learn to read. When he notes that a pot of geraniums has wilted, he restores them to bloom, once again suggesting that he has superhuman psychic powers.

On the way to school the next day, Elliott is mocked by other children, again demonstrating his status as an outsider. At school, Elliott's science class is dissecting frogs. The teacher is totally insensitive to the plight of the animals, treating them merely as objects for study: adult authority figures in this film (and other Spielberg films, such as *Close Encounters*) generally lack the ability of children to empathize with the Other. Meanwhile, E.T., home alone with the dog Harvey, goes into the kitchen to try to get some food. He begins to drink a beer and Elliott belches at school just as E.T. burps at home, further indicating the powerful bond between them. Both E.T. and the boy become intoxicated as E.T. downs a six pack. The alien then watches TV, trying to learn about the strange planet on which he has landed. He becomes upset by the violence of a *Tom and Jerry* cartoon, then watches in amazement as a flying saucer snares a small plane in a tractor beam in the 1954 alien–invasion film *This Island Earth*. He then reads, with alarm, a Buck Rogers comic strip in which an alien gets zapped and cries for help, while a commercial promoting long-distance phone calling plays on the TV in the background, introducing the "E.T. phone home" theme that will become so important later in the film. E.T. begins to tinker with the electronics of a Speak 'n' Spell game, for the first time suggesting that he may have advanced scientific and technical knowledge. The TV is now showing a scene from John Ford's *The Quiet Man* (1952), in which John Wayne passionately grabs and kisses Maureen O'Hara.

Back at school, Elliott, apparently inspired by E.T.'s desire for the alien in the comic strip to be saved, releases his frog to prevent it from being killed, then starts to release the other frogs as well. His fellow students join in, and soon the entire classroom is swarming with frogs. Then, as E.T. watches the scene from *The Quiet Man*, Elliott reenacts the same scene, grabbing and kissing a pretty blonde girl (future *Playboy* centerfold and *Baywatch* babe Erika Eleniak)—possibly his dream girl, by whom he has hitherto been too intimidated to take such an action. Inspired by the film E.T. is watching, Elliott thus lives out a fantasy, reminding us how important the movies are to the collective fantasy life of modern America. The other students are inspired as well, tossing frogs out the window, while the angry teacher leads Elliott away, presumably to the principal's office.

In the next scene, Mary and Gertie come home. The little girl repeatedly tries to introduce "the man from the moon" to her mother, who is so busy and distracted putting away groceries (and complaining about soaring prices) that she doesn't notice, even when she knocks the poor alien in the head with the refrigerator door. Gertie watches a TV show teaching her about the letter "B," and E.T. suddenly says "B." He is learning to speak English! Then a call comes in from the school to tell Mary that she needs to pick up the intoxicated Elliott. Apparently not thinking clearly, the frazzled mother leaves Gertie home alone, as she rushes off to the school. The girl teaches E.T. to say "phone" and asks if he wants to call somebody. When Elliot arrives, he finds that Gertie has dressed E.T. in a hilarious hat, dress, and wig. He calls Elliot by name, and learns to say "E.T." as well. As Mike arrives, the alien, pointing skyward, repeats one of the film's signature lines: "E.T. phone home."

As the boys gather items that E.T. will use to build a communication device to contact his home, Mike notices that Elliott is increasingly using the first-person plural to refer to himself and the alien. Back in the house, Mary reads James Barrie's *Peter and Wendy* to Gertie, introducing the story of Peter Pan (which, among other things, emphasizes the greater imaginative power of children as opposed to adults) as an important parallel to that of E.T. When Elliott cuts his finger on a saw blade found in the garage, E.T., his own fingertip glowing, touches the boy's wound and it is healed instantly, just as Mary reads that an ailing Tinkerbell thinks she can get well if only children believe in fairies. E.T. (as he showed earlier with the geraniums) seems to have the power to transfer life-giving energies to others. He himself, however, seems (like Tinkerbell) to be declining in health, perhaps because Earth's environment and gravity are inhospitable to his kind. Other forces may be inhospitable as well: We see a van idling in the street outside the house, clearly part of the surveillance apparatus that is closing in on the home.

E.T., again demonstrating his technological knowhow, works to construct a sophisticated interstellar communication device from the bits and pieces of junk brought to him by the children. Meanwhile, the geraniums again start to wilt, indicating the decline in E.T.'s energies. It is Halloween, and the boys go out trick-or-treating, taking the opportunity to disguise E.T. as a ghost by covering him with a sheet so they can take him with them, under the pretense that Gertie is under the sheet. Out in the street, E.T. observes with wonderment the bizarrely costumed neightborhood children. In a key moment, he comes face to face with a reveler dressed as Yoda. "Home, home," E.T. cries, apparently recognizing Yoda as a fellow alien. Finally, the boys manage to get E.T. out into the woods. He rides in a basket on the handlebars of Elliott's bike, but the road gets too bumpy, so E.T. lifts it soaring into the air (accompanied by John Williams's soaring theme music), in what can be taken as a visual echo of the flying car in the 1968 classic film *Chitty Chitty Bang Bang* (1968). In the film's signature shot, Elliott and E.T. fly across the sky, silhouetted against a full moon—though this shot also echoes an early episode of *The Flintstones* television series ("The Flintstones Flyer"), in which Barney invents a flying pedal-car and takes Fred for a ride, at one point flying across a background provided by a full moon.

A costumed Mary waits, worried, back at the house, for the overdue children, finally stalking angrily out to the car to go look for them. As she drives away, mysterious men mobilize, onloading equipment from their own vehicles and carrying it into the now-empty house, which they start scanning with Geiger counters. Back in the woods, E.T. and Elliot set up the makeshift communication device to send a signal to E.T.'s home. Unfortunately, they receive no immediate response, and Elliot, still linked to the declining E.T., is obviously falling ill as well. The next morning, a bedraggled and ill-looking Elliot staggers back home, E.T. having disappeared in the night. When Mike goes out on his bicycle to look for the alien, he eventually discovers a fallen E.T. at the edge of a stream, near death. He takes him back home and shows him, ashen and dying, to the mother, who spills her coffee in shock, especially after the alien calls her "Mom." "We're sick," says Elliott. "I think we're dying." Afraid of the strange-looking alien, Mary rushes the kids downstairs, leaving E.T. alone. As they are about to leave the house, men in what appear to be spacesuits (with respirators that sound like Darth Vader breathing) appear at the house, surrounding the family.

Suited men pour into the area, quarantining the house by covering it in plastic and erecting a plastic tunnel from the home to a special ambulance, which they apparently intend eventually to use to take E.T. away. They isolate E.T. and Elliot in a plastic-lined makeshift emergency room as the two lie side-by-side on hospital beds. One of the men asks Mike if Elliott thinks "its" thoughts, but Mike responds that Elliott "feels his feelings," indicating the way in which this film (like most of Spielberg's work) privileges the emotions over the intellect. Keys, who seems to be in a position of authority, interrogates Elliott about the communicator, which he has located in the forest. "I've been wishing for this since I was ten years old," he tells the boy, thereby suggesting that he is not merely a heartless government functionary, but a true enthusiast, sharing some of Elliott's childlike wonder. He also serves as a substitute for the missing father, understanding Elliott in a way that the biological father presumably could not. Keys seems genuinely concerned about E.T. and asks what they can do to keep the alien from dying. "He needs to go home," Elliott says. Keys, in a line that points toward the many religious resonances of the film, responds by saying that E.T.'s presence on Earth is "a miracle."

As the medical team works on E.T., they discover that he has DNA, which means that even such an alien creature has many biological similarities to humans. In a poignant scene, Elliott revives completely as E.T. dies, seeming to sacrifice himself to save the boy. The doctors are unable to revive the alien, despite their best efforts. Gertie and the mother look on and tearfully wish for E.T. to come back, repeating the theme of wishing and the power of belief that runs throughout the film. Keys is genuinely touched by the alien's death, but the doctors go about their tasks in a businesslike manner, going through the motions of documenting E.T.'s death and preparing to take his body away for further study. To them, he is a scientific specimen; to Elliott, he is a fallen friend. Keys explains to Elliott that they have to take E.T. away. "They're just gonna cut him all up," Elliott tearfully (and no doubt accurately) responds. First, however, they give Elliott a moment to be alone with the refrigerated, bagged body. Elliott tells E.T. he loves him and will always remember him, then closes the case that holds the body. As Elliott prepares to leave, the geraniums suddenly spring back to life. E.T.'s chest begins to glow, indicating communication from others of his species. He then revives, possibly because he has received a transmission from the ship that is returning to Earth to retrieve him. Perhaps E.T.'s species is so communal that one of them alone cannot survive, but the presence of others can restore them to life. He begins to repeat "E.T. phone home" over and over. "Does this mean they're coming?" asks Elliott. "Yes," says the alien. Elliott tries to silence him, closing the case and faking a crying fit, so the doctors and scientists won't know E.T. is still alive.

Mike and Elliott hijack the special ambulance and take off with E.T. in the back. An army of police and government agents pursues them, as Mike manages to drive to a playground where three neighborhood boys, Mike's friends, wait with bikes. A glowing E.T. emerges from the ambulance, and Elliott explains that they have to take him to his spaceship. One of the boys, Greg (K. C. Martel), asks, "Can't he just beam up?" Elliott impatiently scoffs at the *Star Trek* reference and replies, "This is reality, Greg."

The five boys lead the police on a spirited chase on their bikes, with E.T. again riding in the basket on Elliott's handle bars. With the way finally blocked by government cars (and agents with shotguns), E.T. lifts all the bikes into the air. (In the Anniversary Edition, apparently to tone down the film's critique of adult authority, the shotguns have been digitally removed and replaced with walkie-talkies). The boys and bicycles soar through the sky and across the face of the setting sun, then back down onto the ground in the forest near the communicator. The alien ship descends, its glimmering circumferential lights looking like shark's teeth, in another apparent nod to *Jaws*. E.T. happily says "Home." Mary and Gertie arrive in the car, as a landing ramp is lowered from the ship.

Next comes the extended goodbye scene, one of the classic examples (along with the scenes of E.T.'s death and resurrection) of the overt sentimentalism that tends to characterize Spielberg films. "Be good," E.T. tells Gertie as she tearfully bids him farewell. She gives him a kiss on the forehead. Mike strokes E.T.'s head as another alien appears from the craft. "Thank you," says E.T. to Mike. Mary and Keys arrive as Elliott approaches for his final goodbye. E.T. invites the boy to come along with him, but he says he must stay. They hug as the others look on. "Ouch," says E.T., expressing the pain of leaving in his limited English. E.T. points to Elliott's forehead with his lighted fingertip: "I'll be right here," he says, echoing the reassurance given him earlier by the boy, while leaving open the possibility that he might some day return and that his psychic connection to the boy might remain in place even after he leaves Earth. E.T. lifts his favorite pot of geraniums and heads up the ramp into the ship. The ramp is raised, and the ship lifts off, now clearly looking like a giant Christmas tree ornament—an effect that is somewhat diminished in the digitally retouched ship of the Anniversary Edition. The ship leaves behind a symbolic rainbow trail as the children, Mary, and Keys look on; the background music turns to a percussion sequence reminiscent of Richard Strauss's *Also Sprach Zarathustra*, providing one last film allusion, this time to Kubrick's *2001: A Space Odyssey*.

THE SOURCES OF THE MOVIE

E.T. is based on an original screenplay written by Melissa Mathison at Spielberg's request, based on his own conception. Spielberg has said that many aspects of the film are based on his own suburban childhood, while numerous other films (in addition to *Close Encounters*) clearly exert an influence. Critics Donald R. Mott and Cheryl McAllister Saunders, in their book *Steven Spielberg* (New York: Twayne Publishers, 1986), call it a "cross between *The Greatest Story Ever Told* (1965) and *Old Yeller* (1957), with a bit of *Peter Pan*" (116). Other films could be mentioned as well, but this list nicely captures the combination of Disney, religion, and sentimentality that provides the texture of the film.

MOVIE MAGIC IN *E.T. THE EXTRA-TERRESTRIAL*: THE POWER OF BELIEF

Though its sentimentalism was sometimes criticized (some accused the film of "infantilizing" its audiences), *E.T.* was even more successful than *Close Encounters*—with both critics and fans. As Andrew Britton put it in a 1987 article in *Movie* (No. 31/32, pp. 1–42), the film "garnered *Gone with the Wind* grosses in tandem with *Citizen Kane* reviews." After its twentieth anniversary re-release to theaters in 2002, it had accumulated $435 million in domestic box-office receipts, placing it third on the all-time list, just behind *Star Wars* and well ahead of *Close Encounters*, which had taken in $156 million and wasn't even in the top 100 in all-time box office. *E.T.* was ranked 25th on the 1998 American Film Institute's Top 100 Films list, as opposed to a 64th-place ranking for *Close Encounters*. *E.T.* also won more awards than its predecessor, including Oscars for Best Original Musical Score, Best Sound, Best Sound Effects Editing, and Best Visual Effects (especially for Carlo Rambaldi's design of the alien, who is very much the star of the film).

Rambaldi was engaged to design the alien star of *E.T.* after Spielberg's initial work on the project with famed creature-maker Rick Baker had come to nought—thus linking E.T. to his alien predecessor, the "Puck" figure of *Close Encounters*, also designed by Rambaldi. Actually, the E.T.s designed and built by Rambaldi and his team (they used three different models, depending on the function required in a given scene) do not look particularly realistic, though they are tremendously effective, creating one of the most beloved characters in all of American cinema. Rambaldi's mechanical E.T. (voiced by the uncredited Pat Welsh, a woman whose unusual voice seemed perfect for the role) was remarkably expressive, given the available technology, though a number of digital enhancements were added in the Anniversary Edition to make the face seem more lifelike.

That E.T. turned out to resemble Puck was entirely appropriate, given that *E.T.* is so clearly a companion film to *Close Encounters*. Indeed, one could almost describe *E.T.* as a children's version of *Close Encounters*. Thus, the later film includes some of the same suggestions that we should be open to new experiences and to those who are different from ourselves, but the aliens of *E.T.* are even less threatening than those of *Close Encounters*. Through most of the film, in fact, E.T. seems more like a lovable pet than an alien intelligence. Similarly, the alien ship is far smaller, more fragile looking, and less imposing than the mother ship of *Close Encounters*, suggesting that we have even less to fear from the advanced civilization that built it.

E.T. also repeats some of *Close Encounters'* critique of American society, but in a considerably reduced form that perhaps signals its aim at a children's audience, but that might also represent a bow to the increasing intolerance of dissent in the Reaganite America of the 1980s. (Significantly, this critique is diminished even further in the 2002 Anniversary Edition, released at a time when this intolerance had reached levels not seen since the McCarthyite years of the 1950s.) In fact, *E.T.* contains virtually no direct commentary on American capitalism, and the biting critique of television in *Close Encounters* as a mind-numbing force in American society is essentially absent as well. In *E.T.* we see a dysfunctional suburban family again, but this one is only mildly dysfunctional, apparently more from the father's mid-life search for adventure than from any basic structural defect. Indeed, the family in *E.T.* (they are never given a last name) could almost be the obverse of the Neary family in *Close Encounters* with the focus (and sympathy) aimed at the mother and children, rather than the wayward father.

In any case, the members of the *E.T.* family (except for the absent father) all genuinely care about each other and ultimately come to each other's aid, presenting a basically positive message about the American family, and we see none of the suggestion of *Close Encounters* that the nuclear family structure itself can be stifling to individual creativity. Indeed, the only problem with the family in *E.T.* is the loss of a strong father figure, an idea very much in tune with the prevailing ideas of the United States under the Reagan administration. That the government official Keys to some extent provides a substitute father figure seems even more of a Reaganesque idea, though Keys does seem to be the sort of kinder and gentler government official who might have been more at home in the preceding Carter administration.

Similarly, *E.T.*'s representation of rebellion against authority (and routine) is considerably muted relative to that in *Close Encounters*. The principal rebellions we see are relatively harmless, involving Elliott's freeing of the frogs in his science class and the "conspiracy" of neighborhood children to help E.T. escape captivity and return to his home. It is worth noting that the escape is facilitated by a gang of teenagers, but these are "good" teenagers (a far cry from the threatening youth gangs so often seen elsewhere in American popular culture), doing the right thing even if it means they must break a few rules. In Spielberg's world, of course, children tend to be basically good, while adults are generally good only to the extent that they have been able to stay in touch with their inner children.

Probably the most frequently discussed aspect of *E.T.* is the film's status as religious allegory, which again links it to *Close Encounters*. In fact, *E.T.* may invite religious readings even more than did its predecessor. For example, E.T. comes to Earth from on high, is misunderstood on Earth, then dies and is resurrected, after which he ascends to the heavens. This sequence of events has led numerous observers (including Ted Koppel during a high-profile episode of ABC television's *Nightline*) to conclude that the alien is a Christ figure, a fact that would link him to science fiction film predecessors such as Klaatu of *The Day the Earth Stood Still* (or even the interventionist aliens of *2001: A Space Odyssey*). On the other hand, both Spielberg (who is Jewish) and screenwriter Mathison have stated that they did not intend E.T. as a Christ figure. Indeed, Spielberg's evocation of savior-like aliens in both *Close Encounters* and *E.T.* can easily be interpreted not as Christian allegory but as an attempt to provide a secular alternative to the Christ story. Douglas Brode, in *The Films of Steven Spielberg* (Citadel Press, 1995), seems to accept this interpretation when he notes that "E.T. provided an alternative to conventional religion" and that, in the film, "Spielberg addressed our collective need for spiritual reassurance, but did so in the context of seemingly secular entertainment" (127). Making no commitment to either side, Mott and Saunders simply conclude that *E.T.* demonstrates the extent to which "science fiction, popular myth, and religion are intertwined" (127).

Whatever *E.T.*'s relationship with conventional organized religion, one thing clear about the film (and one thing it clearly shares with *Close Encounters*) is its loving acceptance of the central role played by the movies in the popular imagination. As Brode notes, *E.T.* is in this sense typical of Spielberg's films, which "are, essentially, movies about movies" (126). The link to *Close Encounters* is particularly strong, both thematically and visually. Indeed, as Brode further notes, the most obvious visual parallel between *E.T.* and *Close Encounters* is the heavy use of bright backlighting in both films, a technique that is itself suggestive of the light produced by a film projector. The prominent use of the Peter Pan motif links *E.T.* not only to the Disney film, but to an entire tradition of films that celebrate the creative imagination of the childlike mind. Moreover, the numerous references to *Star Wars* help not only to place *E.T.* in the company of other recent science fiction films, but to identify *E.T.* as a film that is proud of its status as a work of American popular culture. *E.T.* seems intentionally designed to rejoice in the power of the cinema to stimulate the imagination, even if, in a more subtle way, it also demonstrates a potentially less positive ability of film to manipulate the emotions by virtually forcing audiences to fall in love with its rather hideous central character.

NOTE ON ALTERNATIVE VERSIONS

Both the original 1982 release and the 2002 20th Anniversary Edition of *E.T.* (which differs from the original in some slight digital retouching and a small amount of added material, as indicated above) are contained in the currently available "Limited Collector's Edition" of the film, available on DVD from Universal Studios. This edition is available in either widescreen or full-screen versions. The same material (plus a few more special features and some fancier packaging) is also available in a pricey three–disc widescreen "Ultimate Edition." The film is still available on VHS as well.

CHILDREN AND THE OTHER: THE MOVIE'S LEGACY

As noted above, *E.T.* enters into direct dialogue with any number of films, from *Peter Pan* (1953) and *Chitty Chitty Bang Bang* to *Jaws* and *Star Wars*. The particularly direct connection to *Close Encounters* helps *E.T.* to join in that film's dialogue with the entire alien-invasion genre, including *This Island Earth*, which is specifically "quoted" in *E.T.* Of particular interest in the case of *E.T.*, however, is the connection to the classic horror film *Poltergeist*, released just one week before *E.T.* in June of 1982. Though *Poltergeist* was directed by Tobe Hooper, it was written and produced by Spielberg and shows a number of typical Spielberg touches (such as the frequent allusions to *Star Wars* and the suggestion of something sinister inside our TV sets). Yet *Poltergeist* is a sort of evil twin to *E.T.*; more along the lines of *Jaws*, it is a film that emphasizes the dangerous threat posed by the Other, especially to gullible and trusting children. *Poltergeist* also returns to the critique of American capitalism that was so central to *Close Encounters*. (Recall that the ghosts of *Poltergeist* are angry because a greedy real estate developer built a housing tract over their burial site, opting to save a few dollars by not moving the bodies first.) One might suggest that *Poltergeist* enacts the darker side of Spielberg's imagination, even as *E.T.* dramatizes the lighter side. In this context, it is interesting to note that Hooper later directed the 1986 remake of 1953's *Invaders from Mars*, an "old style" story of sinister alien invaders (and of a child-protagonist who helps to defeat them). One might also note Michael Laughlin's *Strange Invaders* (1983), which is an intentional throwback to the alien–invasion films of the 1950s. In fact, though it is set primarily in 1983, its aliens actually arrive in a small midwestern town in 1958—then take over the town and preserve it in its 1950s form. The film also nods toward Spielberg's recent "pro-alien" films: when a government investigator (played by Louise Fletcher) shows mug shots of aliens recently spotted on Earth, one of them is a picture of Spielberg.

10

Blade Runner

Released 1982; Director Ridley Scott

Though not a huge commercial success on its initial release, *Blade Runner* has gone on to become one of the most important and influential science fiction films ever released. The distinctive *noir* look of the film has combined with its complex and sophisticated exploration of the boundary between human beings and their technology to make *Blade Runner* a favorite topic of academic film critics, who have seen it as a prime example of postmodernism in SF film. *Blade Runner* is a dark and brooding film that couldn't be more different from *E.T. the Extra-Terrestrial*, released only two weeks earlier in June 1982. Together, these two films topped off a five-year explosion in science fiction film production from 1977 to 1982 and provided a reminder of the tremendous range of material that could be encompassed by the genre.

THE STORY: THE OTHER AS REPLICA

Blade Runner begins as on-screen text explains the basic scenario of the film. Early in the twenty-first century, the Tyrell Corporation has advanced robot production into the "Nexus" phase of genetically engineered "replicants" that are virtually identical to humans but superior in strength and agility. The replicants are intended for use off-world as slave labor in hazardous environments. After a bloody rebellion against their human masters in an off-world colony, replicants have been declared illegal on Earth on penalty of "retirement," execution by special police agents known as blade runners.

The film is set, we are told, in Los Angeles, in November 2019. It begins with a panoramic shot of a hellish nighttime cityscape in which flames burst into the air from towering smokestacks while a flying car jets across the screen. The distinctive look of the city, combining high-tech vehicles and huge, brilliant video billboards with an overall air of darkness and decay, is established early-on. At this point, we as viewers are not at all certain what kind of city, what kind of future world, we are about to encounter. In fact, we're not quite sure what we're seeing at all. A close-up shot of an eyeball reflects the flames from the smokestacks, echoing our own situation as viewers. Then a flying car approaches the monumental headquarters of the Tyrell Corporation, which seem ultramodern, yet also look more like an ancient temple than a modern research and manufacturing facility, further emphasizing the incongruous mixture of architectural styles from various periods that marks the landscape of the film's Los Angeles.

With all of these motifs already in place within a few brief seconds, the actual action begins as new Tyrell employee Leon Kowalski (Brion James) is about to be given the Voight-Kampff test, designed to detect whether he might actually be one of a group of recently escaped replicants. Fearful of being detected, Leon blasts the interviewer, Holden (Morgan Paull), with a powerful weapon that he holds beneath the table.

The film cuts back to the cityscape with a huge videoscreen on the side of a building showing a Japanese woman in some kind of advertisement, perhaps for a drug. A loudspeaker from a floating advertising platform encourages individuals to sign up for emigration to the off-world colonies to seek a "new life." The presence of these off-world colonies hovers in the margins of the entire film, though we never actually learn much about them. Down on street level, milling crowds carry umbrellas against the incessant rain, suggesting that something, perhaps some sort of environ-mental disaster or nuclear holocaust, has occurred to change the normally dry climate of Los Angeles in a radical fashion. Protagonist Rick Deckard (Harrison Ford) orders some food from a Chinese counterman. As he sits to eat, he is approached by the mysterious police agent Gaff (Edward James Olmos), who seems to be of indeterminate ethnicity, perhaps a mixture of Hispanic and Asian, much like the city's street-level population. Gaff has been sent to bring Deckard to see police captain Bryant.

In the station, Bryant (M. Emmett Walsh) informs Deckard that a group of four highly advanced Nexus 6 replicants are loose on Earth and that the ace "blade runner" Deckard is needed to hunt them down, even though he has officially retired from the force. When Deckard declines the invitation and starts to leave, Bryant reminds him that, in this society, "If you're not a cop, you're little people," suggesting that this future world might be a dystopian police state. Meanwhile, Gaff makes an origami figure of a chicken and places it on the desk, announcing a motif that runs throughout the film, in which Gaff tends to leave origami figures everywhere he goes. Deckard realizes that he is not being given a choice, so he grudgingly agrees to the assignment. Bryant then shows him a video of the interview with Leon while he explains the background of the current crisis: six replicants escaped from an off-world colony, killing twenty-three humans and hijacking a shuttle to Earth. One replicant has been killed as they tried to break into the Tyrell Corporation. Five are still on the loose. Bryant shows Deckard a profile of Roy Batty (Rutger Hauer), a combat model replicant designed for optimum self-sufficiency, who is suspected of being the leader of the group. In addition, Deckard is briefed on the other escaped "skin-jobs" (a common racist slur for the replicants) including Zhora (Joanna Cassidy), "trained for an off-world kick murder squad," and Pris (Daryl Hannah), a "basic pleasure model," designed for service in military clubs in the outer colonies. Attentive viewers, of course, will notice that, including Leon, Deckard has been briefed on only four escaped replicants, which matches Bryant's initial count, though the detailed briefing has indicated that there are five.

Replicants, we learn, have been designed to have a life span of only four years to prevent them from having time to develop independent emotional responses. To begin his investigation Deckard is sent to the headquarters of the Tyrell Corporation to examine a Nexus 6 replicant there. He is greeted by Rachael (Sean Young), who is introduced as the niece of Doctor Eldon Tyrell (Joe Turkel), the head of the corporation and chief designer of the replicants. However, Deckard's administration of the Voight-Kampff test identifies Rachael as a replicant. Tyrell explains that Rachael is an experiment: She herself thinks she is human and has been given artificial memories to create a "cushion" for her emotions and thus make her easier to control. Tyrell, meanwhile, seems unconcerned with any ethical dilemmas that might arise from this sort of manipulation. For him, it's all a matter of business. "Commerce is our goal here at Tyrell," he tells Deckard.

Deckard and Gaff go to Leon's hotel room in an attempt to track him down. Deckard discovers some sort of scale, perhaps reptilian, in the bathtub. He also finds a collection of photographs (some seemingly old) that seem to suggest that Leon, like Rachael, might have been given an artificial past. Meanwhile, Batty and Leon call on genetic engineer Hannibal Chew (James Hong), who designs eyes for Tyrell's replicants. Batty quotes poetry, then questions Chew about the expected expiration dates of the Nexus 6 replicants, but Chew tells him that only Tyrell himself has such information. He also suggests that one J. F. Sebastian (William Sanderson) might be able to get them in to see Tyrell.

Deckard returns to his own apartment and finds Rachael waiting for him outside his door. She shows him an old photo of herself as a little girl with her mother, trying to convince him that she isn't a replicant. When he reveals that he knows some of her secret memories, she tearfully realizes that they have been implanted. In the meantime, Pris goes to the building in which Sebastian lives, pretending to be lost, hungry, and homeless, so that he will invite her to come in with him to the abandoned building where he has taken up residence with his numerous genetically engineered creatures, or "toys." Back at his apartment, Deckard sits at an old piano and experiences a reverie involving a unicorn running through the woods. The piano is decorated with his own old photos, echoing the old photos of Rachael and Leon and providing a subtle hint that Deckard himself could be a replicant.

Deckard then looks at one of Leon's photos (apparently of the hotel room) and decides to examine it more closely with an electronic image scanner, identified in the film's credits as an "Esper." Eventually, Deckard realizes that there is a sleeping woman in the room, her reflection barely visible in a mirror on the wall. He zooms in on her face and prints out a hardcopy: the woman is Zhora. Continuing his detective work, Deckard takes the scale found in Leon's room to an old Asian woman on the street, who uses an incongruously high-tech microscope to identify the scale as coming from a high-quality artificial snake made by one Abdul Ben Hassan. Deckard locates Hassan in the city's Arab sector and there learns that the snake was sold to Taffey Lewis in Chinatown, still another component of the city's multicultural identity—and a signal of the importance of the film *Chinatown* (1974) as background to *Blade Runner*.

Deckard goes to Chinatown and interviews Lewis (Hy Pyke) in a decadent, Oriental-looking bar. Lewis refuses to identify the woman in the picture from the Esper, but, when, a dancer identified as "Miss Salome" takes the stage in the bar, dancing with a snake, Deckard recognizes her as Zhora. He follows her to her dressing room, where she nearly kills him with her bare hands, but some other dancers arrive, interrupting her. Zhora rushes out into the street. Deckard chases after her, past some Hari Krishnas, and eventually guns her down, sending her crashing though plate glass store windows. She struggles back to her feet; he shoots her again, sending her crashing through still another window. This time she's down for good. Leon looks on as Deckard views the body.

Deckard goes to get something to drink, and Gaff again shows up, with Bryant in tow. Bryant reminds him that there are four replicants to go, including Rachael, who has now disappeared from the Tyrell Corporation. However, the fact that Bryant had initially said that there were five replicants raises the question of whether Rachael had actually been one of the escapees all along, perhaps having taken refuge in the Tyrell Corporation. After Bryant leaves, Deckard spots Rachael in the crowded street and tries to go after her but is accosted by Leon, who demands to know how long he will live, stating that his birthday is April 10, 2017. He uses his superhuman strength to begin to beat Deckard to death, toying with him like a cat with a mouse. As Deckard drifts out of consciousness, Leon rouses him: "Wake up! Time to die!" he announces. He prepares to drive his thumbs into Deckard's eye sockets, when suddenly Leon is shot and killed by Rachael, who has apparently found Deckard's gun lying on the street. Leon falls dead.

Afterward, back at Deckard's apartment, Rachael is badly shaken. Deckard says that he sometimes gets the shakes, too. "It's part of the business," he says. "I'm not in the business," she says. "I *am* the business." Later, when she begins to leave, he stops her and roughly begins to make love to her. She begins to respond.

In Sebastian's apartment, Pris asks Sebastian his age. He says he is twenty-five, though he looks much older because of "Methusaleh syndrome," which causes him to age at an accelerated pace. He is thus unable to pass the medical to emigrate to the off-world colonies. Sebastian takes Batty to Tyrell's headquarters, where Tyrell is in bed in his private quarters, trading stocks over the phone. Batty confronts Tyrell and demands to have his longevity extended. "I want more life, *fucker*," he says threateningly. Tyrell says it can't be done. Batty embraces and kisses Tyrell, then kills him by pressing his thumbs into his eye sockets. This moment, of course, has numerous resonances. For example, if Tyrell is seen as Batty's godlike creator, then Batty becomes a Satanic figure, rebelling against his god. On the other hand, the moment also has the Freudian implications of a son killing his father—the Oedipal suggestions of which are reinforced, though complicated, by the manner of Tyrell's death, which recalls Oedipus's putting out of his own eyes after realizing that he killed his father.

After the police find both Tyrell and Sebastian dead, Deckard is dispatched to Sebastian's building, where he shoots and kills Pris. Batty arrives, and Deckard shoots at him (and misses) as he bends over the prone Pris. Batty excoriates Deckard for his unsporting attempt at an ambush, asking him, "Aren't you the good man?" Then follows an extended duel between the two of a sort that might be a classic film climax, except that, as Batty's question indicates, the usual moral terms of the hero vs. villain confrontation are seriously complicated here. Of course, such confusion is rampant in film noir, which provides so much visual inspiration for this film. Batty's far superior strength and agility give him a clear upper hand in the battle (especially after he cripples Deckard's right hand by breaking two of his fingers—one for Zhora and one for Pris), and he eventually has Deckard at his mercy, dangling from the edge of the building and about to fall to his death.

However, Batty, who realizes that he himself is on the verge of death due to his built-in expiration date, decides to show mercy by pulling Deckard up to safety. Indeed, fighting to retain consciousness, Batty has driven a nail through his own hand to revive himself with pain, but also marking him symbolically as a Christ figure. The good-bad opposition is thus further confused: Batty is both Christ and Satan. As Batty slowly fades, he muses, "I've seen things you people wouldn't believe. Attack ships on fire off the shoulder of Orion. I watched C-beams glitter in the dark near the Tannhäuser Gate. All those moments will be lost in time, like tears in the rain. Time to die." He slumps forward, releasing the white dove that he holds in his hand.

Suddenly, Gaff yells up from the street, congratulating Deckard on a job well done. "It's too bad she won't live," he yells. "But then again who does?" Gaff's remark ostensibly provides a reminder that human beings, too, have a limited life expectancy, though it can also be taken as still another hint that Deckard might be a replicant.

Back at his apartment, Deckard again finds Rachael waiting for him. In response to his questions, she says she loves him and trusts him. As they leave the apartment, planning to run away together, Deckard discovers an origami unicorn on the floor and recalls Gaff's last remark. The unicorn suggests that Gaff has been to the apartment, but also that Deckard's early unicorn reverie might have been an implanted memory, providing the film's strongest signal that Deckard might be a replicant. Deckard and Rachael leave the apartment, closing the door behind them as the film ends, but bringing very little closure to their own story.

THE SOURCES OF THE MOVIE

Blade Runner is based on the 1968 novel *Do Androids Dream of Electric Sheep?*, by SF legend Philip K. Dick. In many ways, the film is a relatively faithful adaptation of the novel, which features protagonist Rick Deckard as a hunter of runaway androids, though the terms "blade runner" and "replicant" are not used in the novel. However, as detailed in such places as Paul M. Sammon's *Future Noir: The Making of Blade Runner* (HarperPrism, 1996), the adaptation of the book was a long and arduous process. Some of the resultant changes from novel to film include the fact that the film's Deckard is single, while Dick's Deckard is married. Several character names are changed, as well. In addition, some of the more interesting aspects of the novel are missing from the film. For example, the title of the book refers to the fact that a nuclear holocaust has virtually wiped out all animal life on Earth, so that most "animals" on the planet are now manmade simulations of animals. Other changes include the presence of technologies such as "mood organs" that Dick's characters can use to generate artificially induced moods and "empathy boxes" that they can use to experience technologically enhanced empathy with one Wilbur Mercer, part of a bogus religion that allows devotees to share Mercer's Christlike suffering. It turns out, however, that Mercer is merely an actor whose experiences have been staged. This fact is revealed on the air by media star Buster Friendly, another major presence in the novel (and a key part of the novel's satire of the media) who is missing from the film. That Friendly himself turns out (apparently) to be an android also enriches the novel's blurring of the boundary between human and android.

In short, many of the most interesting and effective aspects of the novel are missing from the film. On the other hand, many of the most important aspects of the film—especially its powerful overall visual impression—are missing from the novel. Ultimately, the differences between *Do Androids Dream of Electric Sheep?* and *Blade Runner* provide some of the most fascinating examples in American culture of the differences in the resources

available to the two media of book and film. The book and film comple-
ment one another in an unusually effective way, bearing out Dick's remark
that his novel and the film are two halves of a single "meta-artwork."

FUTURE NOIR: SCIENCE FICTION AND POSTMODERN CINEMA IN *BLADE RUNNER*

On its initial release, *Blade Runner* barely made back its $28 million
budget (more than twice the budget of *E.T.*) at the box office. The film
also won few awards. It was nominated for only two Oscars (in the typical
SF categories of art direction and special effects) and won neither. Nevertheless, the film's special visual effects, though relatively simple by today's
standards, remain some of the most remarkable in SF film—not so much
for their technical virtuosity as for their effectiveness in reinforcing the
film's thematic content. The effects were produced by Entertainment Effects Group, a partnership between legendary effects man Douglas Trumbull and Richard Yuricich, who also had an impressive dossier of special
visual effects credits, going all the way back to work on *2001: A Space
Odyssey* and Trumbull's *Silent Running* (1972) and including work on such
films as *Close Encounters of the Third Kind* (1977) and *Star Trek: The Motion
Picture* (1979). More recently Yuricich has helped to produce the effects for
such films as *Event Horizon* (1997) and *Resident Evil* (2002).

Blade Runner has proved to have an ongoing appeal in the more than
twenty years since its initial release, buoyed by the 1992 theatrical release
of a Director's Cut version of the film, which has subsequently become
the standard version in video release. *Blade Runner* is one of the most
respected—and certainly one of the most influential—SF films in history. It
has probably received more attention from academic critics than any other
SF film. Most of this attention has to do with the complex look of the film,
which many critics have felt to be a quintessential example of postmodern
cinema. The film invites this attention to its visual dimension with its own
self-conscious (and postmodern) commentaries on vision and photographic
representation. Other aspects of the film (its mixture of genres, its numerous interpretive uncertainties) are postmodern as well. Finally, *Blade
Runner* is important for its serious exploration of numerous political and
social issues, making it one of the most politically engaged of all SF films, a
genre typically noted for its lack of political content.

Blade Runner represents one of the best examples of mixed genre in all of American film. The film's use of what is essentially a detective-story plot within a basic science fiction framework was not in itself new, of course, and can be found as early as the robot detective stories and novels of Isaac Asimov in the 1940s and 1950s. This generic combination was, however, relatively new to American film, though elements of this mix can be found in such works as Richard Fleischer's *Soylent Green* (1973), while the combination of science fiction and detective story had already emerged fully formed in French film as early as Jean-Luc Godard's *Alphaville* (1965). What is particularly effective about the generic hybridity of *Blade Runner*, however, is the unique extent to which the complex visual texture of the film reinforces the mixture of genres. Thus, the film's juxtaposition of ultramodern, high-technology devices with images of seedy urban decay visually echoes the combination of science fiction and noir detective fiction.

The effectiveness of this visual mix is enhanced by the fact that the images of an old, rotten (both physically and morally) city are so recognizably filmic, given that they are drawn not simply from detective fiction but directly from the tradition of film noir, one of the central repositories of film imagery in the catalog of American culture. And these generically charged images go well beyond the architecture of the city, to include elements such as clothing and hairstyles, especially in the case of Rachael, who spends most of the time looking as if she has stepped directly out of a noir film from the 1940s. Meanwhile, the video billboards, replicants, and flying cars of *Blade Runner* are easily recognized as iconic images of science fiction cinema, so that the mixture of science fiction and detective story is inherently embedded in the complex, hybrid look of the film.

The thematic significance of the visual images in *Blade Runner* is reinforced by the film's incessant focus on eyes and vision, which also helps to direct attention toward the crucial importance of seeing to the medium of film. The replicants seem to have been programmed with an inherent respect for eyes and the visual, perhaps because their "maker," Tyrell has poor vision, at least on the evidence of his huge eyeglasses, which can also be taken as a symbol of his shortsightedness in designing the replicants to be "more human than human" but to be treated as less than human. Both Rachael and Pris wear exaggerated eye makeup, calling special attention to their eyes. Meanwhile, the replicants seem to regard the eyes as a particular site of human vulnerability, as can be seen from their particular choice of a method for inflicting death by plunging their thumbs into the eye sockets of their victims and in their choice of the eye designer Chew as a weak link through which they can begin their penetration of the defenses of the Tyrell Corporation. Finally, as Batty fades into death, his strongest regret seems to be the fact that the memory of all he has seen will now fade into nothingness.

The fact that so much of the film's content and look are taken from the "private eye" genre reinforces all of this eye imagery, just as it is no coincidence that so many of the detective-story motifs in the film refer specifically to eyes and/or vision. Thus, in the Voight-Kampff test that plays such an important role in the detection of replicants, the examiner looks at a screen that shows a closeup of the eyeball of the subject, seeking to gauge emotional response by looking for "fluctuation of the pupil" and "involuntary dilation of the iris."

This focus on the eyes of subjects under interrogation resonates with the motif of surveillance that runs throughout *Blade Runner*. Indeed, one of the central reasons that this Los Angeles seems so disturbingly dystopian is the strong sense that anyone and everyone in the future city is apt to be under official surveillance at any given time, especially by the flying police cars that seem constantly to scan the city's streets for signs of inappropriate activity. Deckard himself is subject to such surveillance: at one point he is stopped and interrogated by one of the flying police cars as he works undercover on a surface street, while he seems constantly to be shadowed by the enigmatic Gaff as he goes about his work.

Granted, this constant surveillance (consistent with Bryant's contrast between "cop" and "little people") does not seem to be particularly effective at keeping order: gangs of apparent mutants roam the street making mischief, while the city has the decadent air of being seeped in crime, much in the manner of the typical urban film noir environment. Of course, it may well be that the police have no desire to eradicate crime. After all, the presence of crime gives them the perfect excuse to operate relatively free of oversight, while their extensive program of surveillance ensures that the crime can be managed so that it will not get out of control and become a genuine threat to official power.

On the other hand, the contrast between the seeming omnipotence of the police and the seeming ubiquity of crime is perfectly consistent with the contradictory nature of the film, in which so many elements defy explanation and complete understanding. The very title of the film defies explanation. We never learn why the replicant hunters are called blade runners, and indeed there is no logical explanation. Screenwriter Hampton Fancher discovered the term in an unproduced screenplay (about smugglers of medical supplies) by the legendary William S. Burroughs. The term was then adopted for the movie simply because Fancher and Scott liked the sound of it.

One of the most interesting (and yet nonsensical) motifs in the film involves the Esper sequence, a bit of science fiction detective work that enacts the hybrid genre of *Blade Runner*, while at the same time commenting upon the medium of film itself, in which high-tech image manipulation has so much to do with what the viewer sees. Via the computerized scanning capabilities of the Esper machine, Deckard is able to tease out an image of Zhora that could never have been seen with the naked eye. On the other hand, fascinating though this sequence might be as an example of self-reflexive cinema, it is absolutely pointless as detective work. The police already have photographs of Zhora on file, and they already know that Leon and Zhora are associated with one another. In short, Deckard learns little from his extraction of the picture of Zhora in this sequence, though it does link her to the snake scale.

The representation of *Blade Runner*'s city serves as still another example of the film's overall interpretive uncertainty. Depicted as an embodiment of postmodern plurality and hybridity, the city is a virtual world's fair of cultures and styles, and its population is a complex multiethnic stew, making it impossible to reach any final conclusion about the character of the city. The city is clearly identified as Los Angeles in the not too distant future, yet the architecture, climate, and other elements of the city seem to have virtually nothing in common with the Los Angeles that we know. Meanwhile, if the city seems simultaneously ultra-modern and old fashioned, it also seems simultaneously crowded and nearly deserted. Teeming crowds of people mill about in the streets, yet Sebastian lives all alone in a large building, explaining that he can do so because there is no "housing shortage around here."

Deckard's movement through the city from one neighborhood to the next is almost like a simulated world tour, except that there is no clear path from one ethnic neighborhood to the next and the viewer (like, one suspects, most of the "little people" who inhabit the city) is never able to map his or her position within the vast urban maze that is the city. This inability to map one's position within the overall system of the city is a perfect example of what the prominent cultural critic Fredric Jameson has identified as the typical disorientation of the individual subject within postmodern society. Indeed, drawing upon the work of urban theorist Kevin Lynch, Jameson specifically compares the difficulty of getting one's cognitive bearings within the world system of late capitalism to the difficulty of finding one's way about in the postmodern city—or within individual postmodern buildings, for that matter.

The layout of the city also reinforces the postmodern mixture of styles and genres for which *Blade Runner* is so well known, though this mixture is not entirely random. In terms of genre, science fiction clearly takes precedence over the detective story. In terms of style, the city is laid out via a process Scott referred to as "layering"; the more modern aspects of the city are built on top of an older, decaying base, as when huge, brilliant video billboards are built upon the sides of dark, looming buildings. Even when the new and the old are thoroughly intermixed, as in the Tyrell complex, they remain hierarchical, the new maintaining a sort of imperialistic power over the old. Moreover, as critic David Desser points out in his essay in the collection *Retrofitting* Blade Runner (edited by Judith B. Kerman, second edition, University of Wisconsin Press, 1997), the whole city is laid out in terms of a vertical stratification that mirrors the class structure of the society. At the street level, the level of the working classes, the city is crowded, old, dirty, and impoverished (images from detective fiction or film noir). Higher up, in the realm of flying cars and penthouses, the city is affluent, ultra-modern, and sparsely populated, filled with images from science fiction.

The city's mixture of architectural styles from different periods can occur even within individual buildings. The Tyrell corporate complex (which seems to house the company's business offices, research laboratories, and manufacturing facilities, as well as Tyrell's own home all in a single location) is probably the most modern, high-tech setting in the entire film. Yet its pyramid-like architectural style seems to be modeled on that of ancient Mayan or Aztec temples, almost as if to announce that the corporation has gained power over the past, which becomes a cafeteria menu of styles and images from which those with sufficient power and wealth can pick and choose. According to theorists of the postmodern, this kind of incorporation of an older style into a new building is a key characteristic of postmodern architecture, as is the fact that it is often difficult to distinguish the interior from the exterior of the Tyrell building. Thus, when Deckard first encounters Rachael and Tyrell in the corporate complex, they seem to be in a sort of open courtyard, yet Tyrell is then able to darken the room electronically when Deckard says that he needs lower light in order to administer the Voight-Kampff test.

This confusion between old and new and between inside and outside in the Tyrell Building is, of course, entirely appropriate given that the Tyrell Corporation is the focal point for the film's central interpretive uncertainty—the extreme difficulty of telling the difference between humans and replicants. This central uncertainty, meanwhile, has ramifications that go beyond mere postmodern play. It challenges the very definition of what it means to be human and, among other things, resonates with the legacy of racism, historically based on the argument that nonwhite peoples (like the replicants of *Blade Runner*) are not fully human and therefore do not have the same rights as fully human whites.

To an extent, that the replicants are visually indistinguishable from their masters places them in the tradition of SF films such as *Invasion of the Body Snatchers*, in which the alien Others seem all the more sinister because they are so hard to identify. In *Blade Runner*, however, the uncertainties go much farther. For one thing, there is the strong possibility that even the protagonist Deckard might be a replicant. For another, even if one could distinguish between the humans and replicants in *Blade Runner*, the replicants are at least as much victims as evil Others, and it is impossible to identify either side in the human-replicant opposition as unequivocally good or unequivocally evil.

In terms of the film's political significance, that the replicants are manufactured as property for use as slaves would seem to link them to the legacy of African American slavery, though this connection is also complicated by the fact that all of the replicants we see are white, including the ultra-white Batty, who looks something like a Nazi dream of an Aryan superman. The fact that the replicants seem racially indistinguishable from their masters suggests that the difference between human and replicant is really one of class, rather than race, while the obvious parallel between the white replicants and African American slaves thus asks us to consider whether many of the inequities that we attribute to racism in our society are also really more a matter of class than of race.

Class difference, in fact, is a powerful subtext that underlies virtually every motif in *Blade Runner*. The future society of the *Blade Runner* is intensely hierarchical, and in ways for which class difference serves as the crucial model. Thematically, the human-replicant opposition is the most important of such hierarchies in the film, though it is clear that class hierarchies operate within the human population as well. For example, emigration to the space colonies is clearly a privilege, and most of those left on Earth seem to be among those who, for reasons of race, economics, or genetic inferiority, are not able to qualify for emigration. Among those left on Earth, there are clear hierarchies as well, as can be seen in Bryant's description of the society as divided into "cop" and "little people." This suggestion seems to suggest the operation of a police state in which the hierarchies are matters of raw physical power, rather than the more subtle class-based hierarchies of capitalism. However, it is also clear that Bryant's statement applies only to a certain working-class segment of the population (including Deckard), for whom joining the police is a means to rise in social stature. This rise occurs largely because those who become cops have agreed to act in defense of the real upper classes (such as the wealthy Tyrell) and thus indirectly to gain some of the advantages of upper-class status.

The thematic and visual hierarchies of *Blade Runner* suggest that a crucial theme of the film is capitalism itself, which inherently creates class differences and in fact depends upon their continuation for its survival. Indeed, the film goes out of its way to call attention to the theme of capitalism, particularly in its portrayal of Tyrell, who participates in the long SF film tradition of the mad scientist (Victor Frankenstein is a particularly obvious predecessor), but who (by his own declaration, at least) is far less interested in advancing scientific knowledge than he is in turning a tidy profit. Thus he states that the main goal of his company is "commerce," while the only scene in the film in which we see him in a private moment shows him engaged not in speculation about the nature of universe but in trading stocks. All of the mind-boggling scientific achievements of Tyrell and his minions, such scenes tell us, are harnessed strictly in the interests of business, a suggestion that, by extension, reminds us of the centrality of profit-making to virtually every aspect of life in our own world. Then again, all of the major questions raised by *Blade Runner* really pertain more to our own world than to its fictional world of the future—a characteristic the film shares with most of the best literary science fiction.

NOTE ON ALTERNATIVE VERSIONS

The above discussion refers principally to the 1992 Director's Cut of *Blade Runner*. The original theatrical version of the film differs most obviously in its use of voiceover narration (by Harrison as Deckard), a technique that was designed to make the events of the film less confusing and that also linked it further to the tradition of film noir, in which such voiceovers are common. The original version of the film also includes a rather contrived happy ending, in which it is discovered that Rachael has no built-in termination date, making it possible for her and Deckard to live together happily ever after.

DARK CITIES: THE LEGACY OF *BLADE RUNNER*

Though strikingly innovative, especially in its representation of the urban future, *Blade Runner* does have predecessors, the most important of which is probably *Metropolis*, a film that also uses its portrayal of the city of the future to comment on class conflict. Meanwhile, *Blade Runner* has exerted a powerful influence on virtually all subsequent film visions of the urban future. This influence has been particularly strong on films such as Alex Proyas's *Dark City* (1998), which includes both the darkness and the retro film noir feel of *Blade Runner*'s Los Angeles. *Blade Runner*'s aesthetics and its vision of the future are also widely acknowledged to have been a major influence on the important SF literary phenomenon of cyberpunk, and the film's impact on cyberpunk-influenced films such as *Johnny Mnemonic* (1995, scripted by cyberpunk maven William Gibson based on his own short story) and *The Matrix* (1999) is obvious.

Numerous films involving cyborgs or androids can claim *Blade Runner* as an important predecessor. Michael Crichton's *Runaway* (1984), which features Tom Selleck as a cop assigned to the task of hunting down runaway robots, seems especially derivative of *Blade Runner*. The *Terminator* films, beginning with the first installment in 1984, have essentially reversed the terms of *Blade Runner* by featuring cyborg bounty hunters assigned to track down and kill human subjects; other cyborg films include the *Robocop* series. A pair of turn-of-the-century films carried on (in much less interesting ways) *Blade Runner*'s interrogation of the boundary between human being and technological object. Chris Columbus's *Bicentennial Man* (1999) also challenges this boundary with its portrayal of an android (played by Robin Williams) who unexpectedly begins to develop human emotions, then struggles to become human. Steven Spielberg's *A.I. Artificial Intelligence* (2001) is a more promising and ambitious effort that was originally slated to be directed by Stanley Kubrick. It involves a variety of classic SF motifs, from the central focus on humanoid robots, to environmental disaster, to dystopian nightmares of future society, to the arrival of benevolent aliens on a future Earth already devoid of human life. Unfortunately, the central *Pinocchio*-inspired focus on the emotional travails of the little boy robot (played by Haley Joel Osment) who wants to be human never allows any of these other themes fully to develop, and the film is ultimately a disappointment.

Films that continue some of the social and critique of *Blade Runner* include Paul Verhoeven's *Total Recall* (1990) and Spielberg's *Minority Report* (2002), both—perhaps not coincidentally—based on stories by Philip K. Dick. Much of the media critique (including the giant video displays that dominate the cityscape) embedded in *Blade Runner* is repeated (though in a campier vein) in Paul Michael Glaser's *The Running Man* (1987), while *Blade Runner*'s focus on capitalism as the root of all social evil is also repeated in a campier (and more overt) form in John Carpenter's underrated *They Live* (1988).

11

The Terminator

Released 1984; Director James Cameron

The Terminator was a relatively low-budget film made by an essentially unknown director who received most of his training working for schlock-meister Roger Corman. It did feature a central actor who had a developing reputation, but that reputation was mainly negative, involving his lack of acting skills and inability to speak English without an almost indecipherable accent. Its plot was straight out of the science fiction pulps. Little wonder, then, that the film did not seem very promising or that the production company, Hemdale Film Corporation, upped its budget to $6.4 million (less than one-fourth that of the then-recent *Blade Runner*, a film with which it is now often compared) only with reluctance. The film more than made back that investment in its first two weekends in release, though it never became a huge box-office hit. It did, however, become one of the most influential and widely-discussed films of the 1980s—and one of the most important SF films of all time. It propelled its laconic star, Arnold Schwarzenegger into superstardom, and put its director, James Cameron, on the road to being one of the most commercially successful directors of all time.

THE STORY: KILLER CYBORGS FROM THE FUTURE

The Terminator begins as a high-tech flying car zooms over a ruined urban landscape; on-screen text identifies the setting as Los Angeles in the year 2029. We are also informed through text that, by this time, machines have been engaged in a decades-long war with humans, but that this war, surprisingly will end with a final battle fought back in our own time.

The film then cuts back to May 12, 1984, where two naked men (played by Arnold Schwarzenegger and Michael Biehn) separately appear amid flashes of electrical energy in urban Los Angeles, then go about the task of acquiring clothing and weapons. The one played by Schwarzenegger seems particularly formidable, displaying superhuman strength and toughness. However, both seem to be engaged in the same task—hunting down one Sarah Connor, which both of them proceed to do by the rather unreliable method of looking up the name in the L.A. phone book. Meanwhile, we are introduced to Sarah Connor herself (played by Linda Hamilton), a completely ordinary young woman who lives with her roommate Ginger Ventura (Bess Motta) and works as a waitress in a fast-food restaurant.

When the character played by Schwarzenegger shoots down a gun-store owner while acquiring weapons and then proceeds to gun down the first Sarah Connor from the phone book, his murderous intentions become clear. After a second Sarah Connor is killed, the police, led by Lieutenant Ed Traxler (Paul Winfield) and Detective Vukovich (Lance Henriksen), realize that something odd is going on. Meanwhile, the character played by Biehn is shown apparently stalking Hamilton's Connor, who has by now become terrified by the murders of her two namesakes. Schwarzenegger's character goes to Sarah's apartment, where (in the high tradition of the slasher film) he kills Ginger and Ginger's boyfriend, Matt (Rick Rossovich), immediately after they have had sex. Then he tracks Sarah herself to a bar with the interesting SF name of "Tech-Noir." He and Biehn's character converge on Sarah and pull their weapons, both seemingly intent on killing her. However, Biehn's character instead opens fire on Schwarzenegger's, eventually getting Sarah out of the bar unhurt (though scared out of her wits), with the police and Schwarzenegger's character in pursuit.

Biehn's character reveals to Sarah that he is Kyle Reese, a man from the future who has time-traveled back to 1984 in an effort to protect her from Schwarzenegger's character, the Terminator of the title, a Cyberdyne Systems Model 101 cyborg—an armored, computer controlled machine wrapped in living human tissue so that it looks entirely human. The cyborg has been sent back to 1984 specifically to kill Sarah to prevent her from giving birth to one John Connor, who in the future has led humanity in an ultimately successful revolt against the machines, who had driven humans to the brink of extermination in Nazi-style death camps.

Both the Terminator and the police pursue Reese and Sarah in a rather ordinary action-movie car chase, leading to Reese's arrest by the police, who think him insane after hearing his fantastic story. The chase also results in a crash in which the Terminator is damaged, leading to a memorable scene in which it goes back to a motel room and performs "surgery" to repair itself. First, it opens up its arm with an X-acto knife, revealing the mechanical workings inside (no explanation of why its armored exoskeleton does not protect the workings of the arm). Then, in a moment that has reminded numerous film critics of a notorious scene in Luis Buñuel's surrealist classic *Un chien andalou* (1929), the Terminator cuts out its damaged human left eye with the knife and plops it into the sink. It then covers the exposed mechanism of its electronic eye by donning sunglasses.

In one of the film's bloodiest scenes (and one that many have seen as an anti-authoritarian fantasy of violent retribution against the police), the Terminator goes to the police station seeking Sarah. It blasts it way through the halls, mowing down cops (including Vukovich and Traxler) as it goes. Reese, however, manages to get free and once again to make off with Sarah, escaping the station in a stolen car. On the run, Reese tells Sarah more about the future, eventually confessing that he had come to love her from afar (*really* afar), partly via a photograph of her given him by her son John.

The two take refuge in a cheap motel, where they make love—and pipe bombs. Sarah calls her mother to assure her that she is okay, but instead gets the Terminator, impersonating the mother's voice over the phone (it has apparently killed Sarah's real mother). The Terminator manages to get Sarah to give it the number where she can be reached, then uses that information to locate the motel. Its arrival at the motel begins much like a run-of-the-mill action sequence (the clichéd background music doesn't help), as the Terminator bursts into their room, spraying it with machine-gun fire. However, having been alerted of the Terminator's approach by barking dogs, Reese and Sarah manage to escape the room. What follows is a completely formulaic, yet utterly effective chase scene, part action film, part science fiction, and part horror movie.

The virtual unstoppability of the Terminator in this scene has reminded some critics of the murderous central figures in the *Halloween* and *Friday the Thirteenth* films), though it also may owe something to the remarkably robust title creature from *Alien*. Sarah Connor also begins to blossom in this sequence. With Reese badly wounded early on, she has to display a level of courage and capability far beyond anything she has shown up to this point. Driving the getaway car, she is able to slam into the Terminator's motorcycle, sending it skidding along the highway and into the path of a gasoline tank truck that runs it over then drags it along underneath. However, the Terminator surprisingly survives (though with a limp), then commandeers the tank truck to continue the chase. Reese manages to blow up the truck with one of the pipe bombs, and all seems well as we see the Terminator, fully engulfed in flames, collapse onto the pavement in the midst of a fiery holocaust.

Next, however, the cyborg's robot torso suddenly arises from the flames, limping forward to continue the pursuit. It chases Sarah and Reese (she practically drags him along with her) into an automated factory, into which the Terminator itself soon staggers, looking about almost as if it appreciates the irony that it now finds itself among its own ancestors, the robotic devices in the factory. Reese manages to insert a pipe bomb into the frame of the Terminator, blowing off its legs and seeming to stop it once and for all. Reese himself is killed in the explosion, and Sarah is badly wounded by a piece of shrapnel that strikes her leg. Unable to walk, she suddenly realizes that the Terminator is still in pursuit, dragging itself along by its arms. She herself is able only to crawl, but she manages to crush the Terminator inside a heavy machine press, the red light indicating its continuing brain function flickering out at last. Police and emergency personnel then arrive, taking Sarah away in an ambulance.

In the final scene, six months later, a pregnant Sarah Connor drives through the desert in her jeep (accompanied by a gun and a guard dog), recording a message for her unborn son. She explains, rather sentimentally, that, though she knew the boy's father only briefly, "We loved a lifetime's worth." At this point it becomes clear that Reese is the father of John Connor, triggering a chain of mind-teasing time-travel paradoxes. When she stops for gas, a small Mexican boy snaps a Polaroid picture of her in order to offer it to her for cash, she buys the photo, and we realize that it is the one given to Reese in the future by John Connor. "There's a storm coming," the boy says in Spanish, indicating the weather. "I know," responds Sarah. She then drives away, looking for a remote site from which to await the coming nuclear holocaust.

THE SOURCES OF THE MOVIE

The Terminator is based on an original screenplay by Cameron and his then future wife Gale Anne Hurd, though it shows the influence of numerous predecessors, including *Metropolis, Westworld* (1973), the *Mad Max* films, *Blade Runner*, and any number of slasher films. Perhaps the most important immediate predecessor was *Alien*, and perhaps it should come as no surprise that Cameron, coming off the success of *The Terminator*, was selected to direct the first *Alien* sequel. Many aspects of *The Terminator* are also reminiscent of well known science fiction television series such as *The Twilight Zone, The Outer Limits*, and *Star Trek*. Controversy arose after the original release of the film, when SF legend Harlan Ellison filed suit, charging that the film drew heavily upon several of his works, especially his classic story "I Have No Mouth and I Must Scream" and the script for "Soldier," a 1964 episode of the television series *The Outer Limits*. As a result of the suit, an on-screen credit reading "Acknowledgment to the Works of Harlan Ellison" was inserted in subsequent versions of the film for television and video release.

MAN VS. MACHINE: TECHNOLOGY AS THREAT IN *THE TERMINATOR*

Though only a moderate success at the box office in its initial theatrical release, *The Terminator* soon gained a strong following in the then relatively young video rental market and was arguably one of the first films to become an important work of cinema largely because of video rentals. It won the Saturn Award (given by the Academy of Science Fiction, Fantasy, and Horror Films) for the year's best science fiction film on its initial release. However, it received no Oscar nominations and little else in the way of immediate critical recognition. Yet it would eventually be named by *Esquire* magazine as "the film of the eighties" and has now received attention from academic film critics exceeded by that accorded only a handful of SF films.

The Terminator is, on the surface, little more than standard pulp science fiction fare, along the lines of any number of films produced by Cameron's mentor, Roger Corman. On the other hand, the film clearly has something special. Most of the acting in the film is competent, but unmemorable, but Schwarzenegger's performance is stunningly memorable, if not really all that competent by classical standards. Schwarzenegger's robotic acting style makes him a perfect cyborg, and there can be little doubt that his portrayal of the Terminator in this film was the key role in his career, the one role that best allowed him to convey his own unique form of charisma on the screen—even more so than in the two sequels, in which his performances progressively turned more and more into parodies of the original. Cameron's perfect pacing was crucial to the ultimate success of the film as well.

The special effects in the film are minimal, clearly reflecting the limited budget. We see only a couple of brief scenes from the world of the future, and those are quite simplistic, giving us only very limited views. The scene in which the Terminator's robotic skeleton arises from the flames and limps after its prey is the most impressive effect in the film, yet even that effect (accomplished through a combination of a model created by famed monster maker Stan Winston and a puppet built by Doug Beswick) is unimpressive, the skeleton's jerky movements reminding many of the low-budget stop-motion animation of the legendary Ray Harryhausen in the 1950s.

Yet the link to Harryhausen almost makes the scene better, evoking a special kind of nostalgia that frequently occurs in *The Terminator*, offering a special pleasure to viewers who have sat through endless really bad science fiction films only to discover that they have now come upon one that is clearly in the same family but that is somehow, almost miraculously, actually *good*. Thus, *The Terminator*'s refreshing refusal to make any attempt to obscure its roots in pulp science fiction (or, to put it differently, Cameron's deft handling of the collection of science fiction and horror film clichés that provides the basic material of the film) is one of the secrets to its surprising success, one of the reasons why it is far better as a film than it seems to have any right to be.

Among other things, the pulp clichés that abound in *The Terminator* tend to lower audience expectations from the very beginning, making it easy for the film to exceed those expectations. The brief opening shot of a wasted, post-apocalyptic 2029 Los Angeles, with its obviously low-budget special effects, seems to identify this film as run-of-the-mill SF fare from which we should not demand very much thoughtfulness. Indeed, this basic situation has not changed very much, even by the end of the film, in which the background of this opening scene has (at least to some extent) been explained. For one thing, we've seen it all before, even if we have rarely seen so *many* clichés collected in one place. For another thing, the film's description of the coming nuclear war and subsequent rise of the machines (the major motif that seems to add "seriousness" to the film) seems a bit hasty and confused, which is partly due to the fact that Reese, who delivers the explanation to Sarah, doesn't know "tech stuff," and so is unable to describe the exact mechanism by which the defense network computers "got smart" and then decided to try to exterminate humanity by starting a nuclear war. Still, it is almost as if this whole scenario were a mere after-thought, a throwaway concocted just to let the film get quickly to its real material, which is gun battles, explosions, and car chases.

The idea of an artificially intelligent computer system rebelling against its human makers has numerous precedents in science fiction, including the human-hating computer of Ellison's "I Have No Mouth and I Must Scream," as well as such obvious film examples as HAL in *2001: A Space Odyssey*. On the other hand, for a film released in 1984, the cautionary story of a runaway computer-controlled defense network (known as "Skynet") has special significance because of its relevance to the "Star Wars" Strategic Defense Initiative then being touted by the Reagan administration. While a recognition of this fact does little to explain the ongoing appeal of the film well beyond the Reagan years, it does serve as an example of the way in which *The Terminator* continually repays close examination, yielding up tidbits of significance for those willing to look beneath its pulp surface.

In fact, one might suggest that *The Terminator*'s numerous pulp motifs (whether derived from science fiction, horror, or just action films in general) function as a sort of disguise for the unusual thematic richness of the film, which is thus able to address an astonishing variety of social and political concerns (and to introduce an amazing number of science fiction conceits) without seeming preachy or pretentious—though it is also the case that the film avoids any sort of overt didacticism by the simple ex-pedient of raising issues without, in general, taking any clear stand with respect to them. In addition, the film raises various issues with a very light touch and a slight wink, suggesting that any greater significance that might be found in the film shouldn't be taken all that seriously.

For example, *The Terminator* is a film with a number of mythic res-onances, the most obvious of which is the clear parallel between John Connor and Jesus Christ, that other savior of humanity whose initials he shares. Of course, James Cameron shares these same initials as well, so it might be a mistake to take this alphabetical correspondence too seriously. Nevertheless, the Connor/Christ parallel is there and does add something to the film, because the evocation of the Christ story reinforces the film's suggestion that humanity has reached a weak and fallen state and is thus very much in need of redemption. In *The Terminator*, whatever its warnings about technology run amok, the fault lies not in our machines but in ourselves, even if the film never quite explains what that fault is or how it might be corrected. Still, the main effect of this parallel is probably the brief moment of self-congratulation afforded to viewers when they first recognize the link between Connor and Christ.

Among other things, the overarching theme of the dangers of technology (a science fiction commonplace) is ironized by the fact that *The Terminator*, like all films, is itself a product of technology, though its relative lack of reliance on high-tech special effects means that *The Terminator* is less technologically driven than most SF films. But this is surely a product of budget rather than ideology, as can be seen by the unusually high level of technological effects in the much more expensive sequels. Meanwhile, the film's presentation of technology as a threat to humanity is rather low key, even if it drives the entire plot. The war machines of 2029 are menacing but not very realistic, while the nuclear war theme evokes a realistic threat but is not pursued with any real interest. For example, while the film's future Los Angeles looks ravaged and wasted, it is not clear whether the destruction we see was caused by the nuclear war of the 1990s or the subsequent war between humans and machines. There seems to be no problem with radiation, nuclear winter, or other lasting side effects that would be expected of a nuclear war.

The film's warning against dangerous future technologies is enhanced by its depiction of technology in 1984, reminding us that the technologies that might prove our undoing in the future are already in development. However, the parallels drawn by the film between technologies of the present and the future are more witty than chilling, as in robot skeleton's entry into the robotized factory near the end of the film or in the visual rhyme that occurs when the film's first post-credit sequence begins with a shot of a mechanized garbage truck that at first looks like one of the sinister war machines shown before the credits.

In any case, the technology of 1984 is generally shown more as dysfunctional than as too sophisticated for human control. For example, disaster (comic or real) strikes whenever poor Sarah picks up a telephone in the film, beginning with her accidental interception of a mock obscene phone call from Matt, who mistakes her for his girlfriend Ginger. Soon afterward, Sarah receives a call on her machine from a man breaking their Friday night date. Later, Sarah is at first unable to get through when she attempts to place an emergency call to the police from the Tech-Noir club; is also unable to get through to Ginger to warn her to leave the apartment, instead succeeding only in informing the Terminator that she is at the club. Finally, Sarah's attempted call to her mother once again inadvertently informs the Terminator of her location.

Perhaps the most interesting example of excessive human reliance on unreliable telephone technology in *The Terminator* occurs when both Sarah and the police unsuccessfully attempt to call her home with warnings that might have saved Matt and Ginger. For one thing, Ginger can't hear the phone ring because she is listening to music on a portable device (a machine) with headphones. For another, the calls are repeatedly answered by Sarah and Ginger's machine, including one witty moment when Sarah's call is picked up by the machine just after the brutal murder of Ginger (the Terminator's most unattractive moment in the film). Apologizing for being a mere machine, Ginger's recorded greeting ironically reminds Sarah that "Machines need love, too."

These examples of telephone disasters include a certain amount of social commentary, given that, in 1984, the "telephone company" was still a central image of big-business manipulation of technology for profit. (The federally-mandated breakup of Ma Bell went into effect only in January 1984.) The other social commentary embedded in *The Terminator* is presented with a light touch as well. Thus, when the Terminator first appears in a slummy, garbage-strewn Los Angeles, quickly to be confronted by a gang of switchblade-toting street punks, it would be perfectly appropriate to take the scene as a commentary on contemporary urban violence and decay—and perhaps even as a criticism of the Reagan administration's lack of emphasis on aid to cities. But the film offers very little support for the latter interpretation, while most viewers are more likely to focus on the self-consciously over-the-top nature of the scene as an example of film art. In the scene, a totally naked Schwarzenegger approaches the outrageously done-up punks, then plunges his fist into the chest of one, withdrawing it with the still-beating heart in his grasp. It is hard to take such a scene seriously as social commentary—or seriously at all, and the scene is essentially comic, its violence more cartoonish than shocking, partly because Schwarzenegger himself is so cartoonish.

This scene also offers a key to one of the most interesting complexities of *The Terminator*, the fact that the title character, a heartless machine engaged throughout the film in the indiscriminate slaughter of human beings does not really seem all that detestable. After all, we really don't care about the punks, and they seem to get what they deserve. The same might be said for the gun store owner, who is more than happy to distribute deadly assault weapons to the general population in the interest of his own profits, but now pays the ultimate price himself. (This scene also satirizes inadequate gun laws by noting that customers can take rifles and assault weapons with them when they buy, but must wait fifteen days for handguns.) Indeed, one of the film's high comic moments occurs with Schwarzenegger's deadpan delivery of the one word riposte, "Wrong," after the store-owner tells him he can't load his purchased weapon in the store—and just as he blasts the store-owner with the newly acquired weapon. However, if this scene can be taken as a call for stronger gun control laws, much of the film seems almost to glorify the gun culture of the United States.

Similarly, the film's bloodiest and most violent scene, the shootup of the police station, is prepared by an extended portrayal of the cops as unprofessional, insensitive, and incompetent. Thus, we see them smirking and leering as they secretly watch the interview of the captive Reese by the police psychiatrist, Dr. Silberman (Earl Boen). The cops then joke with Silberman, who salivates over the boost that his career might receive from his work with Reese, whom he inappropriately refers to as a loon. Viewers are thus authorized by the film not to be all that appalled by the carnage at the police station, even though the more politically correct sequel, *Terminator 2* (1991, also directed by Cameron), will attempt to convince us that the massacre was a terrible tragedy, involving the deaths of seventeen policemen, many with wives and children.

Certainly, most viewers do not root for the Terminator to succeed in its mission to assassinate Sarah Connor and thus prevent the future human rebellion against machine domination. But there is a certain guilty pleasure in identifying with this powerful killing machine that fears no man and respects no human authority. It is certainly the case that Schwarzenegger is far more pleasurable to watch on the screen during this film than either Hamilton or Biehn, despite the fact that the latter are both more talented and better looking. After all, Biehn's character may be heroic, but he seems a bit dull, not to mention dumb. For her part, Sarah Connor does not really blossom until late in the film (and does not become a *really* interesting character until the first sequel), becoming truly heroic only after Schwarzenegger has exited the stage in favor of the robotic skeleton. Most of the film's highlight moments are those in which the viewer roots for or even identifies with the Terminator, as when it rips the heart out of the punk or when it rebuffs a nosey janitor with "Fuck you, asshole"—a line it learned from the punks at the beginning of the film and now amusingly retrieves from its data bank of useful phrases.

The pleasure of such moments is, of course, retroactively increased by Schwarzenegger's subsequent superstardom. Thus, for later viewers of *The Terminator* on video, the Terminator's terse "I'll be back," uttered to the desk sergeant who first turns him away at the police station, becomes a key moment in the film not just because of the spectacular way he does come back (crashing through the front of the building in a pickup truck) because it has become familiar as a catch-phrase repeatedly used by Schwarzenegger in any number of other films. For viewers in 2004 and later, there is a special amusement (or horror?) in seeing the governor of California in any number of unlikely situations, from strutting butt-naked across the screen in the opening confrontation with the punks, to blasting his way through the Tech-Noir club, to blowing up a police station.

Schwarzenegger's personal appeal is such that the final destruction of the Terminator is made enjoyable only by the fact that he has by that point been removed from the character, which is now merely a mechanical puppet with none of Schwarzenegger's charm. Thus, as it is not Schwarzenegger that is being crushed in the machine press, but merely a prop, we need feel no sympathy or regret at its demise. We can also enjoy Hamilton's parting zinger ("You're terminated, fucker"), the only memorable line in the film *not* spoken by Schwarzenegger.

Schwarzenegger's weirdly appealing screen presence helps to explain the odd attractiveness of the Terminator as a film character, though the character itself is part of the attraction as well, enacting as it does any number of fantasies shared by frustrated viewers of the 1980s, who would very much have liked to be able to say "fuck you" to anyone they pleased and then to blast to smithereens anyone who didn't like it, damn the consequences. At the same time, the fact that the Terminator is a mere machine, carrying out its programming, makes its behavior more excusable. It is not evil or even malevolent: it is just what it is, doing what it was designed to do. Yet, in many ways, even before it turns benevolent in *Terminator 2*, Schwarzenegger's cyborg Terminator seems far more human than such superslashers as Jason Voorhees or Michael Myers, even as it is also superhuman, a sort of Superman unrestrained by the spotless goody-goody ethics of the classic superhero.

Film theorists have argued that American film tends to be constructed from a masculine perspective in which audiences are urged to experience a fantasy identification with the central male character and a fantasy desire for the central female character. In *The Terminator* this situation is significantly complicated by the fact that Schwarzenegger's Terminator, rather than Biehn's Reese, is clearly the central object of masculine identification. Meanwhile, the central female character, Hamilton's Sarah Connor, is certainly attractive, but her evolution in the course of the film from seemingly helpless girl to strong, capable woman (an evolution that goes much farther in the sequel) makes her far more than a conventional object of masculine desire. In particular, she provides a potential alternative object for *feminine* identification in the film. At the same time, if Schwarzenegger's villain, however deadly, is in many ways more fascinating than threatening, Hamilton's evolved Sarah is not really the kind of feminist icon that might seem threatening to some male egos. In a sense, in fact, she remains a prototypical wife and mother. Even in the sequel, she remains sentimentally, devotedly, in love with Reese, and she becomes a sleekly muscled killing machine primarily in order to protect her son.

Sarah is also made less threatening (and the Terminator more attractive) by the fact that the whole film is a bit tongue in cheek, a clever entertainment that never pretends to be anything else. Part of this cleverness again comes directly from Schwarzenegger, who delivers his deadpan lines with just enough of a twinkle in the eye to let us know that it's all in fun. But *The Terminator* is a clever and witty film in ways that go well beyond Schwarzenegger's ironic delivery of his very few lines of dialogue. It is also well structured. For example, the introduction of Reese in such a way that he first appears to be a second Terminator is a nice touch, while the handling of the time-travel twist in which Reese becomes the father of John Connor is also handled well. All in all, *Terminator* demonstrates that science fiction films need not choose between action and thoughtfulness, even if its thoughtfulness is a bit superficial and formulaic.

CELLULOID CYBORGS: THE LEGACY OF *THE TERMINATOR*

Terminator and its sequels are among the central time-travel films of American SF cinema. Other films in this mode go back to George Pal's *The*

Time Machine (1960), based on the classic novel by H. G. Wells and featuring Wells himself (played by Rod Taylor) as a time traveler. This film was remade by Simon Wells in 2002, while Nicholas Meyer's *Time After Time* (1979) was a sort of spin-off of *The Time Machine*, again with Wells himself (this time played by Malcolm MacDowell) as a time traveling protagonist. One of the most interesting and entertaining (though dark and disturbing) time-travel films is Terry Gilliam's *Twelve Monkeys* (1995), while the Jean-Claude Van Damme vehicle *Timecop* (1994) is in many ways particularly reminiscent of the *Terminator* films.

The title figure of *The Terminator* spawned numerous imitations of one kind or another, most of them somewhat unfortunate. Among these, one might mention films starring Arnold wannabes, including the Van Damme vehicles *Cyborg* (1989) and *Universal Soldier* (1992) and the Sylvester Stallone vehicles *Demolition Man* (1993) and *Judge Dredd* (1995), the first of which is not all that bad, thanks to its quirky humor. In the same category are the cyborg films starring French kickboxer Olivier Gruner, incuding *Nemesis* (1993) and *Automatic* (1994), the first of which directly alludes to *Terminator* several times, as when its chief cyborg villain occasionally lapses into Schwarzenegger impressions. More interesting films, such as the *Robocop* movies (beginning with the first installment in 1987) also owed a great deal to *Terminator*. Meanwhile, *Terminator* helped establish action SF films as an important genre, especially for Schwarzenegger himself, as he went on to play action-hero protagonists in a string of subsequent SF films, including *Predator* (1987), *The Running Man* (1987), *Total Recall* (1990), and *The 6th Day* (2000).

Of course, the Schwarzenegger vehicles most directly influenced by *The Terminator* were the film's own sequels. By the time of *Terminator 2: Judgment Day* in 1991, both Cameron and Schwarzenegger had become major forces in Hollywood, so that the sequel was able to command a budget of approximately $100 million, more than fifteen times that of the original. In a motif that makes little sense but that facilitates the scenario of the sequel, it turns out that, in addition to the Terminator from the first film, a second (more advanced) Terminator (played by Robert Patrick) has been sent back from 2029 to the year 1994 as a backup—programmed to kill a ten-year-old John Connor (Edward Furlong) should the first Terminator fail to prevent his birth. (Interestingly, per the first film, John should be ten in 1995, not 1994, but no matter). Meanwhile, the humans of 2029 have gotten their hands on a second Model 101 Terminator (now described as a T–800, Model 101), reprogrammed it, and sent it back to 1994 to protect John. This expedient allows Schwarzenegger to play the good guy this time, and much of the charm of *Terminator 2* lies in the evolving relationship between this kinder, gentler Terminator and young John. Meanwhile, Hamilton's Sarah Connor (following in the footsteps of Sigourney Weaver's Ripley from the *Alien* films) has evolved significantly as well, and appears here as a tough, well muscled, and slightly unbalanced guerrilla fighter who bears little resemblance to the sweet, soft girl we saw at the beginning of the first film.

Terminator 2 is full of visual and verbal echoes of the first film, many of them with comic touches that help to make the sequel altogether lighter and more optimistic. Schwarzenegger also delivers far more of his trade-mark one-liners. On the other hand, the film does have its dark moments, especially in its portrayal of the mental health system. Sarah, having attempted to blow up the headquarters of Cyberdyne Systems hoping to prevent them from developing the technology that will lead to the apocalypse, has been arrested and then (because of her crazy stories about the coming disaster and killer cyborgs from the future) committed to an asylum, where she is brutalized by the staff and incompetently treated by Silberman, the bumbling police psychiatrist from the first film.

Terminator 2 fills in a significant number of details about the coming nuclear apocalypse, including the date on which it is to occur: August 29, 1997. It even shows us scenes of a nuclear explosion in an attempt to remind us of just how horrifying a nuclear attack can be. The time travel narrative of the *Terminator* series is significantly expanded when it becomes clear that the advanced computer technology that will enable the im-plementation of Skynet (and thus lead to the nuclear apocalypse) will actually be based on studies of the few remaining pieces (including the central processor) found after the destruction of the first Terminator.

Patrick's advanced Model T–1000 has been enhanced with liquid metal technology, which is to say that Cameron, coming off his experience with *The Abyss* (1989), now has at his disposal the sophisticated morphing technology that becomes the hallmark of the impressive special effects of *Terminator 2*. The shape-shifting abilities of the T–1000 give it a significant advantage over the clunky old T–800, but the older Terminator rises to the occasion and manages finally to destroy the T–1000 by dumping it into a vat of molten steel. The remaining pieces of the first Terminator, retrieved from the Cyberdyne vaults after a spectacular shootout with the still-in-competent LAPD, are also tossed in the vat. Then the human-friendly T–800 insists on being lowered into the molten metal as well. The film thus ends on a sad and sentimental note, as did the first. However, the focus on the heroic sacrifice of the Terminator virtually obscures the fact that humanity may now have been saved. It also obscures the delicious explosion of time-travel paradoxes that this ending produces. After all, with all the Terminator technology destroyed, Skynet may never be developed, and the war with the machines will be averted. Moreover, thanks to the intervention of the Terminator, Terminators will never exist and none of the events of the preceding two films will ever occur!

In *Terminator 3* (2003, directed by Jonathan Mostow), however, it turns out that the nuclear holocaust has not been prevented, just delayed. Here the heavy use of computer animation provides a significantly stepped-up level of special effects action, and *Terminator 3* is, in fact, a competent action film. It also adds a new twist in the form of a female Terminator, the T–X (Kristanna Loken), once again sent back in time to kill John Connor (now played by Nick Stahl). Of course, the T–X, like the T–1000, can assume any shape or any gender it likes, and it is a measure of our commitment to gender as a category of identity that we consistently think of the T–1000 as male and the T–X as female, despite overt evidence that gender is in this case a pure artifice. In any case, Schwarzenegger returns as the "good" Terminator (now labeled the T–101) sent back to protect Connor, this time by Connor's future wife after Connor himself has been killed by the T–101 in the year 2032. All in all, however, *Terminator 3* is a bit confused (it can't even get simple facts straight, as when it is stated that the T–1000 had tried to kill Connor when he was thirteen, rather than ten). It also relies a bit too much on amusing references to the first two films to try to provide a bit of humor, while Schwarzenegger seems largely uninterested in the T–101's heroic battle against the more advanced T–X Terminator, his old twinkle having been converted into a struggle to keep a straight face. *Terminator 3* is also uninteresting as a film of ideas, especially when compared to the first two *Terminator* films. In fact, the major new idea of the third film is to cancel out the "no fate but what you make" theme of the first two films by showing that certain historical developments apparently really are inevitable, despite the best efforts of humans and machines. Thus, the film ends as Skynet goes online and launches its deadly nuclear strike against humanity, though the T–101 has seen to it that Connor and the woman who will eventually become his wife, Kate Brewster (Claire Danes), are safely sequestered in a hardened bunker so that they can survive the attack and begin to lead the resistance.

12

Robocop

Released 1987; Director Paul Verhoeven

Robocop was one of the surprise hits of the late 1980s. When initially proposed, it was a film that no director wanted to direct and no actor wanted to appear in. Eventually, though, director Paul Verhoeven was imported from Holland for his first American film, and a suitable cast was assembled. The result was a film that not only became a box office hit but, in its title hero, produced one of the iconic figures of American science fiction film. This hero lived on in two film sequels, two television series, and a series of comic books, while serving as a central inspiration for the spate of SF films in the 1990s that also featured robots or cyborgs as central characters. *Robocop* was also an effective work of political satire that produced one of the definitive film critiques of late–Reagan era America.

THE STORY: MACHINES, MEDIA, AND MAYHEM IN THE MOTOR CITY

Robocop begins with a broadcast of the mock television news program *Media Break*, immediately announcing the motif of media satire that is crucial to the film. This *Headline News*–style broadcast begins with the promise, "Give us three minutes and we'll give you the world," indicating the way in which contemporary news programs break the news into quick packets of superficial information, with little background or analysis. The program then begins with a report of unrest in the "city-state" of Pretoria, where the government has just announced the acquisition of a French-made neutron bomb for use as a last resort defense against protestors. This suggestion of excessive force in the interest of the restoration of order sets the stage for a similar development closer to home, as the program moves (after a commercial break) to introduce us to the urban problems plaguing Old Detroit, where a recent rise in crime has been accompanied by a wave of cop killings, many attributed to criminal kingpin Clarence Boddicker (Kurtwood Smith) and his gang. We soon learn that the Detroit police force has recently been privatized and is now being run by the giant conglomerate Omni Consumer Products (OCP) through its subsidiary Security Concepts.

OCP, it becomes evident, has far bigger plans for Detroit than the meager profits it might make from running the police force. Indeed, it plans to wipe out the entire inner city, replacing it with Delta City, a sparkling new, ultramodern urban complex designed as a perfect corporate business environment. However, the crime rate is so high in Old Detroit that it is unsafe for workers to go into the area, so the company must first attempt to wipe out crime in the city. To do so, they are developing automated police robots, especially the Series 209 Enforcement Droid—ED–209 for short—which they hope eventually to market to the military for use in combat. ED–209 is the favorite project of the corporation's second in command Dick Jones (Ronny Cox), the Senior President of Security Concepts. Unfortunately, the machine goes berserk in its initial demo in the OCP boardroom, riddling a junior executive with high-caliber bullets in an extremely bloody scene that is nevertheless grimly comic and perfectly in tune with the campy air of the film thus far. Ambitious executive Bob Morton (Miguel Ferrer) is then able to convince the corporation head, simply identified as the Old Man (Dan O'Herlihy), to put the company's resources behind his pet project, the Robocop, a robot policeman driven by a human brain.

The problem, of course, is to find a human brain. OCP approaches that problem in an efficient, but ruthless way—by transferring cops with histories of recklessness to the most dangerous precincts in the hope that one will be killed, thus becoming a potential brain donor. Officer Alex J. Murphy (Peter Weller), newly assigned via this program to the high-crime Metro West precinct, is on patrol with his new partner, Officer Anne Lewis (Nancy Allen), when they spot Boddicker and his gang fleeing from a bank they have just robbed. They track the gang back to an old, abandoned steel mill (sign of the decay of industrial America) that they are using as a hideout. Murphy and Lewis, rather than waiting for backup, split up and go into the mill, looking for the culprits. Once inside the mill, Lewis is quickly knocked senseless by one of the gang members, while Murphy is captured by the gang. Then, in a scene of truly shocking and viscerally powerful violence (very much *not* in accord with the otherwise campy nature of the film), he is literally shot to pieces (including a bullet to the head). The gang flees, and Lewis arrives to call for help. Murphy is rushed to a hospital, where he is soon pronounced dead. Morton's team then manages to retrieve what is left of the head, as well as the left arm, attaching them to a robot body. Morton, however, wants an all-robot body, so he has them remove and discard the arm, demonstrating just how heartless he really is.

In a variation on Isaac Asimov's famous Three Laws of Robotics, the newly assembled Robocop is programmed with four prime directives. These include: to serve the public trust, to protect the innocent, and to uphold the law. The fourth directive, however, is classified and undisclosed. Robocop is soon put into service, driving about the city interceding (with little subtlety and much violence) in a series of crimes, including one in which the mayor and other officials are being held hostage by a deranged former city councilman, upset over losing his bid for re-election. This particular scene, clearly based on the 1978 assassination of San Francisco Mayor George Mosconi, along with gay city councilman Harvey Milk, indicates the tendency of *Robocop* to draw upon specific historical events.

The news media make a big deal of the exploits of the new robotic policeman, and Robocop becomes an instant celebrity. Morton is made a vice president of OCP and seems to be riding high, but then Robocop begins to experience dreams of his former life and his human personality, supposedly extinguished, begins to re-emerge, making him harder to control. This comes to the fore when, in a computerized search of Boddicker's criminal activity, he uncovers the record of Murphy's murder. Robocop then goes to Murphy's old home, but discovers it now abandoned, the family moved away; walking through the house he begins to experience flashbacks of his former life.

Robocop then sets his sights on Boddicker and his gang. Meanwhile, Morton is living it up with women and drugs, until Boddicker, working on orders from Jones, bursts into his home and shoots him in the kneecaps, then shows him a gloating farewell video of Jones before blowing him and his home up with a grenade. Soon afterward, Robocop bursts into a drug factory where Boddicker and some of his gang members are negotiating to buy cocaine for distribution in the city. In a spectacular shootout (modeled on those in the spaghetti Westerns of Sergio Leone), Robocop shoots up the factory, killing many of the workers there, including the boss. He arrests Boddicker (whom he refrains from killing only because of his Third Directive, to uphold the law), despite the latter's arrogant insistence that he works directly for Jones and is thus immune from police interference. It becomes clear at this point that the crime wave in Old Detroit has in fact been instigated by Jones and OCP (probably without the knowledge of the Old Man), both to justify the leveling of the old city and to produce an excuse to try out their robotized police officers, opening the way for huge defense contracts. Robocop records Boddicker's statement, then takes him to precinct headquarters, where he drops him off, identifying him as a cop killer.

Robocop then goes after Jones, who he now realizes is the real mastermind behind the crime spree in Old Detroit. He confronts Jones in his posh office at OCP, only to discover that he is unable to arrest him because his secret fourth directive (programmed at the insistence of Jones himself) prevents him from taking such action against a senior officer of OCP. Paralyzed, Robocop is then confronted by the revamped ED–209, which launches a barrage of weaponry at him but is soon disabled when it tumbles down a stairway in an attempt to follow the more nimble Robocop.

Having won that battle, Robocop prepares to leave the building, only to find himself confronted by a large contingent of police, who have been ordered to destroy him. He is badly damaged in the ensuing melée, but escapes with the help of Lewis, who also helps him to hide out and to repair himself. She then helps him to begin to recover his memories of being Alex Murphy. Meanwhile, Jones has gotten Boddicker out of jail and ordered him to kill Robocop in order to prevent him from revealing Boddicker's connection to Jones. In compensation, Jones offers Boddicker the vice concession for the two million workers who will be employed in constructing Delta City.

Upset with their treatment by OCP, the Detroit police go out on strike, leading to chaos in the streets. Boddicker and his gang go after Murphy, armed with advanced weapons acquired for them by Jones through OCP's extensive connections with the military. Both Murphy and Lewis are wounded in a subsequent shootout at the blighted site of the old steel mill, but Boddicker and his gang are all killed. Murphy is ready to go after Jones, despite his fourth directive. He bursts into the OCP boardroom and presents the evidence of Jones's crimes. In response, the Old Man fires Jones, which means that he is no longer an officer of OCP and no longer protected by the directive. Murphy blasts Jones with a hail of bullets, sending him crashing through the window and plummeting to the ground far below. As Murphy begins to leave, the Old Man asks him his name. "Murphy," he says, indicating that he has recovered his sense of his human identity.

THE SOURCES OF THE MOVIE

Robocop is based on an original screenplay by Edward Neumeier and Michael Miner.

CYBORGS 'R' US: CONFRONTING TECHNOLOGY IN *ROBOCOP*

Robocop actually received two Academy Award nominations (for best sound and best film editing), though it seems, at least on a superficial examination, to be little more than a pulp SF thriller. On the other hand, its director, Paul Verhoeven, had established a reputation as the director of quirky, complex, hard-to-categorize films during his work in Holland before coming to the United States to do *Robocop* as his first American feature. Thus, one might expect to find more substance in the film than first appearances might indicate—and one would not be disappointed. *Robocop* combines science fiction with the cop action genre and mixes taut thriller elements with moments of hilarious (if dark) comedy to produce a complex hybridity that helps it to join films such as *Blade Runner* and *The Terminator* as key examples of postmodernism in science fiction film. Moreover, its satirical engagement with any number of social and political issues relevant to its late–Reagan era context make it one of the most topical SF films in the history of American cinema.

Robocop can also be read in a number of mythic and allegorical ways that go beyond specific political contexts. For example, Murphy, like so many other characters in SF film, can clearly be read as a Christ figure. After all, he dies and is resurrected, while he clearly serves as a savior for the people of Detroit, defending them from the secular power of OCP, which is thus figured as a sort of latter-day Roman Empire. Meanwhile, director Verhoeven has suggested that he himself saw the film as a sort of "Paradise Lost" with Murphy's loss of his human self (and his seemingly idyllic family life) taking on universal dimensions. Whether or not one sees *Robocop* in this way, it is clear that the film can be read as a sort of quest for identity in which Murphy's struggle to recover his selfhood serves as a allegorization of the general difficulty of finding and maintaining a stable identity amid the constant, dehumanizing flux of modern life.

Of course, this latter interpretation becomes less universal and more particular as soon as one realizes that the tribulations of the self explored in *Robocop* are specific to life under late capitalism and even more specific to working-class life in Detroit and other embattled bastions of working-class America, as more and more Rust-Belt jobs are either lost to automation or shifted overseas. Thus, even allegorical interpretations of the film ultimately tend toward topicality. Indeed, the overt topicality of *Robocop* is announced early on, in the initial *Media Break* broadcast. The *Media Break* broadcasts satirize television news programming itself, as bright, attractive anchors report all events (no matter how serious or complex) with the same seriousness and superficiality. This satire was enhanced by the casting of well-known *Entertainment Tonight* co-host Leeza Gibbons as one of the co-anchors (along with longtime television news anchor, consumer news reporter, and sports commentator Mario Machado), indicating the conversion of television news into pop-cultural entertainment. But these news broadcasts also provide the film itself with a quick and convenient method for introducing topical issues. In this opening broadcast, the anchors report on a presidential news conference being held aboard the "Star Wars Orbiting Peace Platform," which adds an immediate futuristic touch to the film. Unfortunately, a power failure has caused a loss of artificial gravity on the platform, setting the President and his staff comically afloat, much to the obvious amusement of the newscasters, who present the event as light entertainment.

While this report helps to establish *Robocop* as a work of science fiction, it also satirizes the contemporary media of the 1980s. Indeed, except for a couple of SF touches the film could easily have been set in the 1980s. For example, apart from Robocop and the ED–209 unit, there is very little in the way of advanced technology presented in the film. Partly, this was a matter of budget; the film dispenses with futuristic vehicles and costuming (which can be quite expensive to produce), opting simply to go with production line automobiles and clothing from the 1980s. A great deal of money was also saved by filming in real city locations, rather than using expensive sets and simulations, though the film was shot in Dallas, rather than Detroit, to give it a slightly more futuristic look. Still, *Robocop* looks pretty much as if it is set in the mid to late 1980s. While this makes its futuristic robots seem a bit out of place, it is not really a shortcoming and does not interfere with the flow of the action. In fact, the look of the film is in many ways an advantage. By minimizing the amount of science fiction hardware on the screen, the film is able to maintain its focus on the human story of Murphy, including the pathos of the loss of his past life and the redemptive triumph of his recovery of his individual identity.

In addition, the contemporary look of *Robocop* reinforces its satirical engagement with so many issues from the 1980s. Much of the satire of *Robocop* is quite clearly aimed at the Reagan administration, including its portrayal of the Old Man, head of Omni Consumer Products, as a sort of Reaganesque executive officer, affable, aging, bumbling, and a bit out of touch. The film's highly critical treatment of OCP and its nefarious operations can be taken not only as a commentary on the lack of humanity in American corporate culture but also on the Reagan administration's support of that corporate culture—and its lack of support for America's urban centers. Indeed, *Robocop* probably addresses the issue of urban decay more directly and effectively than any other American SF film, even though rundown future cities have been a staple of SF film since *Blade Runner*. It is not for nothing that *Robocop* eschews the typical futuristic SF urban landscape (most commonly set in Los Angeles) for a decidedly rundown Detroit, a city whose social and economic problems were emblematic of the woes of American cities in the 1980s.

The Detroit setting is appropriate partly because the city was so closely associated with the automobile industry, the decline of which (especially in relation to Japanese imports) was the central example of the decline of American manufacturing as a whole during the 1980s. Given the iconic status of the American automobile as the worldwide symbol of American capitalism, the decline of the automobile industry has particularly profound implications. Moreover, the Detroit automobile industry is emblematic of an entire phase of capitalist production, typically (and tellingly) labeled by economists as "Fordist" (after Detroit automobile magnate Henry Ford). The decline of Detroit thus potentially signals the decline of Fordism as a whole. Indeed, the important theorist David Harvey, in his book *The Condition of Postmodernity* (Blackwell Publishers, 1990) has argued that a shift from a Fordist mode of production to a mode he refers to as "flexible accumulation" was central to the historical movement toward the era of postmodernism. One could argue, then, that *Robocop*, with its central emphasis on the decline of Detroit, also announces the coming of postmodernism—or at least announces an awareness that something fundamental to the texture of life and art seems to have shifted in the years between the end of World War II and the coming of the Reagan administration.

Robocop does little directly to suggest that the Reagan administration was to blame for the troubles of American cities like Detroit in the 1980s, though it does drop in numerous indirect references to the Reagan administration that attentive viewers might see as clues pointing to its culpability. For example, the Detroit police strike not only calls attention to contemporary concerns over the issue of strikes by essential public workers but to the hard, anti-labor line taken by the Reagan administration in relation to such strikes, most famously in the August 1981 air-traffic controllers' strike, to which Reagan responded by firing all of the controllers involved. *Robocop*'s sympathetic presentation of the plight of the Detroit police can thus be taken as a subtle and indirect critique of the heavy-handed attitudes of the Reagan administration, which failed to address the root causes that led groups such as the air-traffic controllers to strike in the first place.

Robocop's most overt references to the Reagan administration are to the Star Wars program, which is featured not only in the opening *Media Break* broadcast but in a later one as well. In this second, more ominous, report, viewers are told of a failed test of the new orbiting platform, referred to here as the Strategic Defense Platform (in an obvious reference to the official name of the Star Wars program, the Strategic Defense Initiative). In the test, a laser cannon has misfired, scorching 10,000 acres of wooded residential land near Santa Barbara and killing 113 people, including two former presidents who have retired there. These two presidents are not named in the film, but they are surely Richard Nixon (who did indeed retire to the Santa Barbara area) and Reagan himself (who spent a great deal of time while in office at the Rancho del Cielo—which came to be known as the Western White House—about thirty miles northwest of Santa Barbara). The film thus offers a sort of comic fantasy fulfillment (for liberals) in which Reagan is hoist on his own technological petard, taking Nixon with him.

That the two reports on the Star Wars system both refer to malfunctions of one sort or another contribute to the overall dystopian tone of *Robocop*, just as the anxieties of the Detroit policemen at being replaced by robots echo a general fear among the American working class that automation might someday lead to the loss of their jobs. On the other hand, the implications of motif are somewhat more complex than a simple fear of being replaced by machines. Robocop is, after all, a human who essentially becomes a machine, then struggles to regain its humanity, a fact that blurs the boundary between human and machine and suggests a more fundamental threat of actually being turned into a machine as part of the general regulation, routinization, and automation of life under capitalism.

A similar concern was voiced by Karl Marx as part of his critique of capitalism as early as the mid-nineteenth century. On the other hand, Marx also saw a positive side to automation, which he hoped might release human beings from the drudgery of repetitive tasks, while creating a general level of affluence that would free up individuals to explore their full human potential. A similar faith in the potential of technology is voiced in a great deal of American science fiction, perhaps most notably in the *Star Trek* sequence of television series and films. *Robocop* itself is far from unequivocal in its warnings of the dangers of technology, at times showing some of this same technological optimism. After all, Murphy, in the final analysis, remains Murphy despite the high-tech hardware that has replaced his physical body.

In this sense, *Robocop* is a relatively conventional, conservative, and uninventive film. Much like the cyberpunk science fiction with which it shared the late 1980s, it posits a strict separation between mind and body, a separation that is itself in the best dualistic tradition of the Enlightenment. Murphy is still the same person, we are told, regardless of the fact that his entire body, below the neck, has been replaced by machinery. By extension, this motif reassures us that we can still remain who we are, regardless of how much our lives are changed by the advent of new technologies. Furthermore, if Robocop embodies the fear of being replaced by technology or even turned into a machine, Murphy's transformation into Robocop also represents a fantasy of empowerment. Equipped with his new high-tech body, Murphy becomes almost invulnerable, ultimately maintaining his identity while meting out just revenge on all of those who have wronged him in the past. Viewers can thus identity with the figure of Robocop, imagining that they, too, might be able to avenge themselves on their enemies. In particular, Robocop's ability to walk into a corporate boardroom and blow away the company's most evil executive surely resonated with a number of working-class fantasies of the 1980s, allowing workers of America's declining industries to imagine revenge against the heartless corporations that were gradually depriving them of their jobs and their lives.

This ambivalence of *Robocop* toward technology can perhaps best be seen in the contrast between Robocop and ED–209. The latter, which is all machine, is ostensibly the more powerful of the two, but it tends to malfunction (with sometimes dire results) and, even when it works well, it is no match for the quick-witted Robocop, whose human brain seems capable of a level of creativity not available to the pure machine. The message here seems fairly clear: technology can be a good thing, but it works best when it maintains a human face and when it is kept under control as a tool to be used for the benefit of human beings, rather than for its own sake (or for the expansion corporate profits). Of course, one can also read into the confrontation between ED–209 and Robocop a clear comment on filmmaking, especially SF film making. From this point of view, ED–209 represents the purely effects-driven SF film that is produced largely as a demonstration of the latest special effects technology. The cyborg Robocop then becomes an emblem of science fiction filmmaking that employs advanced effects technology, but maintains a strong human element at its core. The human story of Murphy, including the pathos of the loss of his past life and the triumph of his recovery of his identiy, remains very much at the heart of this film.

The malfunctioning ED–209 serves as a vehicle for social commentary in other ways as well. When it is first introduced, Jones announces that it is currently programmed for "urban pacification," a term that was widely used to describe certain U.S. strategies during the war in Vietnam, a link that is reinforced by Jones's immediate suggestion that the most important applications for ED–209 will probably be military. In addition, ED–209, in the scene in which it is introduced, is controlled by a scientist by the name of Dr. McNamara (Jerry Haynes), in an obvious reference to Secretary of Defense Robert McNamara, the architect of the failed U.S. strategy in Vietnam. ED–209 thus becomes a symbol for the same kind of technological arrogance that led the United States to become involved in Vietnam in the first place, confident that superior firepower would inevitably lead to victory. By extension, the film suggests that more contemporary developments, such as the Star Wars program, were driven by a similar arrogance, enabling a belief that the United States could be rendered impervious to attack by the sheer power of its technology. That this technology malfunctions more often than not in the film can thus be taken not as a rejection of technology itself but as a critique of this kind of arrogance.

Robocop, through its representation of the predatory OCP, is also specifically critical of the American tendency to invest more in the development of military technologies, designed to destroy, rather than to improve the quality of human life. This critique is clear in the satirical focus on the Star Wars program and on the intention of OCP to market its robotic policemen as military killing machines. On the other hand, the characterization of OCP as willing to do anything and everything in the quest for larger corporate profits seems aimed more at capitalism than militarism. Meanwhile, that OCP seeks profits in "service" industries such as health care and law enforcement, but does so in a ruthlessly self-serving fashion, with no regard for actually serving the public, can be taken as a rejoinder to the Reagan administration's privatization policies, suggesting that certain crucial public services should not be left up to profit-seeking corporations.

Though *Robocop* ultimately identifies corrupt individuals such as Jones, Morton, and Boddicker as the agents of villainy, one can easily infer from the film that they become the villains they are as a result of the corporate environment in which they function, an environment that rewards ambition and backstabbing and leaves little room for cooperation or altruism. That the drug-dealer Boddicker essentially works for OCP is no accident, either. After all, the corporate environment at OCP is essentially the same as the criminal environment of Boddicker's gang, while *Robocop* is quite clear in its identification of capitalism as a form of legalized robbery. In one of the film's most pointed moments of political commentary, we see two of Boddicker's henchmen discussing the gang's business. When one explains that they are robbing banks in order to get capital to finance their drug dealing operation, the other asks why they even bother to try to make money buying and selling drugs when they can just steal it. The other answers succinctly: "No better way to steal money than free enterprise."

Robocop's portrayal of the baleful condition of downtown Detroit is made all the more striking by the stark contrast, within the same city, of the poverty and squalor of the cirty's streets with the gleaming luxury of the OCP headquarters. This contrast suggests that a major reason for the poverty of the people of Detroit is that the resources of the city have been sucked up by the corporation, draining the city of its very life and making its people poorer and poorer, while the company grows richer and richer. Finally, despite the Old Man's claim that the company hopes to "give something back" (echoing the Reagan administration's vision that increased corporate wealth would somehow trickle down to the general population), it is quite clear that OCP as an organization is entirely unconcerned with the suffering its activities are causing among the people of Detroit.

The company's lack of regard for human life is signaled most openly in its willingness to convert Murphy into a machine, sacrificing his humanity, while making him into a commodity, a product designed to be marketed for profit. This same tendency is announced at the beginning of the film, in the commercial for mechanical hearts (from the "Family Heart Center") that interrupts the first *Media Break* broadcast. For one thing, the very presence of a commercial reminds us that *Media Break* is designed not to serve the needs of the public, but to make money. For another, that human hearts in this dystopian future can be routinely replaced by mechanical ones marketed like any other commodity foreshadows the mechanization of Murphy by suggesting the penetration of capitalist business practices into every aspect of human life, including the human body itself.

The media of this future world—like the media of our own world—are saturated with commercials. In the course of the film, we observe a commercial for the latest high-end automobile, the SUX–6000, reminding us of the way in which automobiles have long functioned as the central emblem of American consumerism, while also calling attention to the centrality of the automobile industry to the economic fortunes of Detroit. At the same time, the self-parodic name of this product reminds us of the tendency of the American automobile industry to be more interested in flashy marketing than in manufacturing quality products. Meanwhile, the later commercial for the utterly tasteless "Nuke 'Em" nuclear war game indicates the willingness of American corporations to manufacture, market, and sell any product that they believe will make them money, regardless of the values (in this case acceptance of nuclear war as a source of fun) it might promote.

The constant flow of commercials in this future world—as in our own—serves not merely to further the marketing of specific products but to promote the general acceptance of consumerism as a way of life. The same can be said for the programming that this advertising finances. Indeed, other than the fluffy news program *Media Break*, the main television programming that we see in the film consists of a few brief snippets of a program apparently entitled *I'll Buy That for a Dollar*. The nature of this program is not entirely clear. All we know is that at certain key moments, a mustachioed and bespectacled host mugs into the camera and leeringly proclaims "I'll buy that for a dollar"—generally while flanked by two scantily clad beauties. While this clearly implies that the dollar in question would be used to purchase the sexual favors of these two women, it also suggests that, in this society, anything desirable can be purchased for cash. Of course this program also suggests the culpability of television in the reduction of everyday language to a string of TV–induced catch-phrases. It also lampoons the silliness and venality of real-world television programming in the 1980s (especially the game shows that serve so clearly as enactments of the consumerist fantasies of the society at large), thus suggesting that this same universal drive toward commodification holds sway in our own contemporary American society.

Although this satire is most specifically aimed at Reaganite America, its diagnoses of the ills of American society remain relevant enough in the early twenty-first century. Indeed, the effectiveness of such satirical moments goes a long way toward explaining the ongoing appeal of *Robocop* and the continuing sense that this is a special film that stands apart from run-of-the-mill science fiction fare. Ultimately, however, the core of this film is the story of Murphy's struggle to retain his sense of his individual human identity despite all the corporate and technological forces that seem determined to turn him into a machine. In this sense, he becomes the perfect hero for the postmodern age, in which a similar struggle to maintain a coherent identity is perhaps the central human experience.

CYBORG VIOLENCE: THE LEGACY OF *ROBOCOP*

Robocop draws in obvious ways upon predecessors such as *Blade Runner* and *The Terminator*—not to mention the Japanese *8 Man*, which became a live-action film in 1992, but which aired as a cartoon on American television as early as the 1960s. *Robocop* itself exerted a strong influence on the proliferation of robot/android/cyborg films that were so crucial to American film in the 1990s. Such films include *Cyborg* (1989), *The Guyver* (1991), *Nemesis* (1993), *Death Machine* (1994), and *Solo* (1996). Verhoeven's own *Total Recall*, an Arnold Schwarzenegger vehicle from 1990, is a highly interesting film that recalls *Robocop* in a number of ways, including the casting of Ronnie Cox as the central villain, an exploitative capitalist on Mars who controls the colonists there through his monopoly on the very air they breathe. Meanwhile, Schwarzenegger's Douglas Quaid loses his life somewhat in the same manner as Murphy when he discovers that his entire life has been fabricated, his memories implanted in his brain, his beautiful wife a secret agent planted to keep an eye on him.

The most obvious influence of *Robocop*, however, was on its own two sequels of the 1990s. *Robocop 2* (1990, directed by Irvin Kershner) picks up directly where the original *Robocop* ended. With the city of Detroit in arrears on its payments to OCP, the corporation (still led by the Old Man, who seems significantly tougher and meaner in this film) seeks to foreclose on the entire city. In the meantime, the corporation continues to work to develop a more advanced Robocop model, leading to their development of Robocop 2, who is given the brain of a drug dealer/cult leader (1990). Not surprisingly, this Robocop is evil, leading to a cataclysmic battle with the original Robocop, still played by Weller. In this sense, the film anticipates the battle between the T–800 and T–1000 models in *Terminator 2* (1991). The good Robocop ultimately wins, of course, though OCP escapes relatively unscathed, managing to blame the damage done by Robocop 2 on the psychologist who had been in charge of its programming. *Robocop 2* includes much of the same sorts of satire as the original *Robocop*, but it is a relatively lackluster film that never quite captures the unique energy of the original film.

In *Robocop 3* (1993, directed by Fred Dekker), OCP (now referred to in graffiti as "Oppressive Capitalist Pigs") is again up to no good, pressing its plans for Delta City by employing a paramilitary force (referred to as Rehabilitation Troops) to evict the residents of Old Detroit so they can tear it down. However, in an added twist, OCP has now been taken over by the larger (and possibly even more evil) Japanese conglomerate, Kanemitsu. Meanwhile, the residents of Detroit have organized their own guerrilla force to battle against the corporate takeover of their city. Predictably, Robocop (now played by Robert Burke) ends up siding with the rebels, especially after Anne Lewis (still played by Nancy Allen) is shot and killed by the Rehabilitation Troops. Eventually, tired of their treatment by corporate management, the regular Detroit police join the rebels as well. This basic scenario seems promising and even offers the prospect of one of the few genuinely radical political films in American cinema. Unfortunately, this prospect doesn't really play out. For one thing, the Rehab troops get out of control, and the film ultimately becomes more antimilitary than anticapitalist. For another, the film ultimately descends into silliness, with Robocop (now able to fly thanks to an add-on jet pack) battling both the Rehabs and a group of Japanese android ninjas built by Kanemitsu. The good guys win (of course), OCP stock plummets, and the *Robocop* film series comes to a merciful end, though a short-lived television series (with the anticapitalist politics significantly watered down) did appear in 1994. The franchise then continued with a TV miniseries (*Robocop: Prime Directives*) in 2000, set ten years after the original film, when Delta City has become a reality, but has nearly bankrupted OCP.

13

The Abyss

Released 1989; Director James Cameron

Coming off of his success with the major science fiction films *The Ter-minator* and *Aliens*, director James Cameron had enough clout in Holly-wood to secure a gigantic budget for his next project, in which he turned his attention to his lifelong fascination with the world beneath the sea. The result was *The Abyss*, perhaps the most technically complex and challenging filmmaking effort that had been attempted up to that time. It was also a science fiction epic that combined an ocean-floor exploration narrative with the story of an encounter with advanced, but benevolent, aliens, while at the same time providing a political commentary on the Cold War arms race. Ultimately, however, the real focus of *The Abyss* is on the personal emotional experiences of its central characters, an aspect of the film that clearly anticipates the sentimental turn taken by Cameron's work in *Terminator 2*, which culminated in his *Titanic*, one of the most senti-mental (and commercially successful) films of all time.

THE STORY: ALIENS FROM THE DEEP

As *The Abyss* begins, the crew of the U.S.S. *Montana*, an American nuclear submarine cruising in the Caribbean near the Cayman Trough, detects a mysterious and impossibly fast-moving underwater object. After a close encounter with this object, the submarine crashes into an underwater outcropping of rock and then slides over a cliff and sinks into a deep pit at the bottom of the ocean. The military quickly moves to mount a rescue/ salvage operation, but is hampered by the fact that a hurricane is rapidly moving into the area. To save time, they call on the *Explorer*, a ship (owned by Benthic Petroleum Corporation) with a submersible oil-drilling rig ("*Deepcore 2*") that happens already to be in the area. We see no details, but we can probably surmise that Benthic will make a tidy profit from the deal with the military, while Benthic offers the crew members of *Deepcore 2* triple the usual dive pay for the mission, emphasizing their status as workers rather than heroic crusaders.

The rig is commanded by Virgil "Bud" Brigman (Ed Harris) and includes a crew of seasoned oil workers, though they are not trained to handle an operation of this sort. The military sends a team of Navy Seals, led by Lieutenant Hiram Coffey (Michael Biehn), to lead the actual "rescue" operation ("Operation Salvo"), though it soon becomes clear that the American military is more concerned about the wrecked sub and its warheads falling into Russian hands than about any potential survivors. The Seals are accompanied by Lindsey Brigman (Mary Elizabeth Mastrantonio), Bud's estranged wife and the designer of *Deepcore 2*. The strain between Bud and Lindsey combines with friction between the Seals and the oil riggers to create an immediate air of tension aboard *Deepcore* as it proceeds on its dangerous mission. Tension mounts as the hurricane approaches and as Russian and Cuban ships circle the area of the wreck, which is only eighty miles from Cuba.

Deepcore quickly locates the submarine, which is carrying 192 nuclear warheads, each five times the power of the bomb dropped on Hiroshima. "It's World War III in a can," remarks Lindsey. Indeed, World War III seems to be a real possibility after an American ship collides with a Russian one in the area, leading to a sudden deterioration of United States–Soviet relations, with both sides placing their militaries on full alert. Back beneath the surface, an initial exploration of the *Montana* finds no survivors. Lindsey, piloting a small submarine, observes a strange, fast-moving ball of light zipping about in the water, momentarily looking like some sort of translucent craft. Another member of the oil crew, Jammer Willis (John Bedford Lloyd), already distraught after seeing a crab emerge from the mouth of a drowned sailor aboard the submarine, also sees something strange that causes him to panic, damaging his air regulator and sending him into a coma. (Later, he suggests that he saw an angel, and thus thought he was dead.)

Rough weather conditions on the surface cause *Explorer* to come unmoored, dragging *Deepcore 2* along the ocean floor toward the abyss and causing considerable damage to the drilling rig, which cannot be unhooked from the ship in time because the Seals commandeer the equipment needed in order to retrieve a warhead from the *Montana*. Then the crane that connects *Explorer* to *Deepcore* buckles and collapses into the sea, hurtling downward and narrowly missing the drilling rig as it lands on the edge of the abyss. The crane topples into the pit and nearly drags the platform in after it. In all of this extended commotion, several on *Deepcore* are killed and much of the platform is flooded. All contact with the surface is lost. The survivors are left low on oxygen, forcing Lindsey to go outside *Deepcore 2* to hook into some auxiliary storage tanks. While she is outside, she observes some strange, graceful, transparent objects, filled with dancing and flashing lights. She returns to report the sighting to her colleagues, convinced that she has seen some sort of living machines, perhaps from another planet. "Something not us," Lindsey calls the objects, then suggests that they might represent some form of "NTI," or "non-terrestrial intelligence"—a term the filmmakers chose to use instead of "extra-terrestrial intelligence" to avoid suggesting a link to the film *E.T. the Extra-Terrestrial*.

In the meantime, one of the oil men, Alan "Hippy Carnes" (played by Todd Graff and notable for the pet white rat that he carries through the film), discovers that the Seals have brought a nuclear warhead from the *Montana* aboard the platform. He concludes that they plan to use it to destroy the sunken sub to prevent it from falling into Russian hands—an action that would destroy *Deepcore* and all aboard as well. His finding leads to a taut confrontation between the oil men and two of the surviving Seals, including Coffey, who now seems on the verge of complete insanity, apparently from High Pressure Nervous Syndrome. Soon afterward, a strange tentacle of water enters the platform, apparently as a sort of probe from the aliens. Often identified as the first completely computer-generated film "character," this pseudopod of water approaches Lindsey and Bud and attempts to communicate with them. It then leads the crew to the warhead that Coffey and his men brought on board, as if to warn them. However, it recedes after Coffey slams a hatch shut on it, cutting it in half. Bud conjectures that the ability to control and manipulate water might be the key to the entire alien technology.

After another violent confrontation between the Seals and the oil drillers, Coffey locks the oil crew in a compartment on the drilling rig. However, Jammer, having regained consciousness and overcome the Seal who was left guarding the compartment, appears and lets them out. Coffey, meanwhile, has strapped the warhead onto a small remote-controlled sub, planning to send it into the abyss, though he now seems more intent on destroying the aliens than destroying the *Montana*. Bud attempts to stop him and escapes being shot only because one of the other Seals, realizing Coffey's condition, has removed the ammunition clip from Coffey's gun. Bud is then nearly killed in a hand–to–hand battle, though he is saved by the intercession of the burly Catfish De Vries (Leo Burmester), one of his crewmen, a former Marine and boxer. Coffey takes off in one of the miniature subs to deliver the warhead and its remote vehicle into the trench. Bud and Lindsey follow him in the other miniature sub, leading to an underwater battle in which the two subs collide, sending Coffey's sub sinking into the abyss. Structurally damaged from its battle with the other sub, it is soon crushed by the increasing pressure. Unfortunately, the warhead is also sent into the trench, while the sub containing Bud and Lindsey is disabled and leaking badly.

Bud is wearing a diving suit that will enable him to get back to *Deepcore 2*, but Lindsey has none. This situation leads to one of the film's most memorable sequences, in which Lindsey insists that Bud let her drown, then tow her back to the platform in the near-freezing water, which she hopes will allow her to be revived. The plan works, and Lindsey is indeed revived, though with great difficulty and only because Bud, now realizing how much he still loves her, simply refuses to let her go, virtually willing her back to life after the others in the crew have given up.

The moment of joy at Lindsey's recovery is short-lived, however, because there is still the matter of the nuclear warhead in the trench. Bud resolves to go down into the trench to try to disarm it, using a special diving suit filled with a special fluid (earlier demonstrated on Beany the rat in a scene that provoked numerous complaints from animal rights activists) that will allow him to breathe liquid and help him to resist the tremendous pressures in the deep trench. In still another tense scene, Bud manages to survive the descent and disarm the bomb, helped by Lindsey's encouragement via radio. Then he learns that he doesn't have enough oxyen left to get back to the platform. It appears that he is doomed, and he admits that he never expected to return alive from this mission. Lindsey realizing how much she still loves him, begs him not to leave her alone. Suddenly, another of the strange, angel-like undersea aliens appears. This one extends a three-fingered hand to Bud and then leads him further down the trench to its huge mother ship, though these aliens seem almost indistinguishable from their hardware, which also appears to be alive.

Using their water-manipulation technology, the aliens create a room in which Bud can breathe. They begin to communicate with him by creating a video wall that displays a series of images, making it clear that they have been observing earth for some time. They then allow Bud to watch television news reports as they use their technology to create huge walls of water that approach coastal areas around the world. Just as the walls of water are about to crash down on the helpless people below them, the aliens stop the water short and allow it to recede harmlessly into the ocean. But they have made clear that they have great destructive power should they so wish. They convey to Bud that this display is meant as a warning for Earth's military powers to cease their confrontational Cold War tactics, else the aliens will be forced to intercede. This time, however, the aliens have decided to give humanity one more chance, because they have also observed a great deal that is good in the race, as epitomized by Bud's willingness to sacrifice himself to disarm the bomb, saving his colleagues, and by the tenderness they have seen between Bud and Lindsey as she talked him down during the descent into the trench.

The huge alien ship ascends to the surface, seeming to take on a more solid form as it rises. It lifts the undersea drilling platform with it, and emerges beneath the *Explorer*, lifting it from the water as well. The crew of the platform, apparently because the aliens have "done something" to them, is able to withstand the ascent without the long period of decompression that would normally be required. One is left to wonder, of course, just what sort of physiological modifications the aliens might have made and just how far they might extend. In any case, the crew members descend and walk toward the *Explorer*; Bud suddenly appears from the alien ship and is reunited with Lindsey. They kiss as the screen fades to black, giving the film a classic Hollywood ending. Though the film ends here, the implication (in the Special Edition version of the film, at least) is that the aliens have shown themselves in order to help Bud deliver their message and that this message might well lead to an end to the Cold War tensions between the United States and the Soviet Union.

THE SOURCES OF THE MOVIE

The Abyss is based on an original screenplay by Cameron, growing out of a short story he wrote while still in high school and his lifelong interest in diving and the undersea world. The novel version of *The Abyss*, written by leading SF writer Orson Scott Card, though published shortly before the release of the film, was based on the film, rather than the other way around.

THE DAY THE OCEAN STOOD STILL: ALIEN INVASION AND THE COLD WAR IN *THE ABYSS*

With a budget ultimately approaching $70 million, *The Abyss* was one of the most expensive films ever made, though it would be far outstripped by the big-budget films of the 1990s. This investment produced an impressive film with the feel of a grand epic. Indeed, Cameron has stated that, with *The Abyss*, he hoped to do for the underwater SF film what *2001: A Space Odyssey* had done for the SF film in outer space. However, competing directly with such blockbusters as *Batman* and *Star Trek V*, *The Abyss* was not a huge hit at the box office, requiring income from international distribution to move it past the break-even point. Nevertheless, it was an important film that still stands up well. The underwater special effects arc convincing, the aliens are genuinely interesting, and even the soundtrack has an air of grandeur. The film also has a serious and important message, even if it was something of a cliché by 1989. It won an Oscar for best visual effects and was nominated for best set direction, best cinematography, and best sound, suggesting that the film was more respected for its technical achievements than for its message. The most important influence of the film was probably its pioneering use of digital morphing technology, as in its representation (produced by George Lucas's Industrial Light and Magic) of the alien probe of water, which moves through the drilling station, then mimics the faces of Lindsey and Bud as it attempts to communicate with them. Many other films would subsequently use this technology, perhaps most notably Cameron's own *Terminator 2* (1991).

The Abyss was also the first film to shoot underwater blue screen elements with live actors and to record underwater dialogue between live actors. Its most impressive engineering achievements involved the actual underwater filming, which was done in two huge tanks of water set up at the never-completed Cherokee Nuclear Reactor Plant near Gaffney, South Carolina. The larger of these, converted from the reactor's main containment vessel, held 7.5 million gallons of water and contained a full-scale model of much of the underwater oil-drilling platform. Simply filling these tanks with water, while keeping the water clear, heated, and otherwise useable for filming, was a major task, not to mention the obvious difficulties of acting and filming under water.

The Abyss deals with large public issues, though its focuses on the private dramas of the people aboard *Deepcore 2*. The motif of a small group of people trapped in an isolated and dangerous environment is, of course, a common one in science fiction film, and in this sense, the underwater drilling platform plays much the same role as the isolated cold-weather research stations of such films as *The Thing from Another World* (1951) or *Alien Hunter* (2003) or the spaceships in films such as the *Alien* series. Indeed, the plight of the crew members of *Deepcore 2* is highly reminiscent of that of the crew of the *Nostromo*: both groups are just doing a job and suddenly find themselves in dangerous situations they had never expected to encounter. Thus, if the crew of the *Nostromo* are sometimes described as truckers in space, the crew of *Deepcore* can be described as truckers under the sea, a characterization that is supported by a scene early in the film when several of them sing along with Linda Ronstadt's recording of the classic trucker song "Willing." (*Deepcore* even has a couple of truck license plates affixed to the front of it.) *The Abyss* is reminiscent of the *Alien* films in other ways as well, especially in the industrial look of the *Deepcore* drilling platform, which was modeled on an actual off-shore drilling platform that the set designers studied before making the film. Indeed, much of the conceptual design of *Deepcore 2* was done by Ron Cobb, who had helped to design the original *Nostromo*. On the other hand, Cameron (who himself directed *Aliens*, the second film in the *Alien* series) has said that he specifically conceived of the highly-evolved aliens in *The Abyss* as the antithesis to the monstrous alien creatures in the *Alien* series.

Of course, *The Abyss*'s motif of ordinary people placed in an extraordinary situation, then responding heroically, is one of the staples of American film in general. In fact, the film makes good use of a number of motifs that are essentially cinematic clichés. For example, Hippy's love for his pet rat (which includes one moment in which he risks his life in order to save the rodent) builds upon the well-known fact that children and animals function well as objects of audience sentiment in film. Here the sentimental attachment normally shown by audiences for dogs and other conventionally loveable animals is shown to extend even to rats.

There are no children in *The Abyss*, though they do come into play in a scene that was added for the expanded Special Edition of the film. Here,

Bud and Lindsey scan television news reports of the worsening global political situation, including one sequence in which reporters conduct person-on-the-street interviews about the crisis. The prevailing view seems to be a fatalistic acceptance of the situation as something ordinary people can simply do nothing about. In one key interview, however, a construction worker sums up his perplexity at the situation: "Hey, they love their kids, too. So why are we doing this?" This evocation of children adds a sentimental twist to the anti–nuclear war element of the film, though it also adds a certain universality. The hardhat in this sequence is clearly referring to the Russians, but he might just as well be referring to the opposite side in any conflict. Indeed, despite its specific Cold War setting, the antiwar message of *The Abyss* remains highly relevant after the fall of the Soviet Union. After all, the level of organized global violence has increased significantly since the end of the Cold War, rather than the opposite, a fact the filmmakers seem to have anticipated by substantially increasing the antiwar emphasis of the film in the 1992 Special Edition.

The love story between Bud and Lindsey is, of course, the most important sentimental element in *The Abyss*, which shows the same combination of impressive technical filmmaking with overtly sentimental romanticism that would later come to mark Cameron's most commercially successful film, *Titanic* (1997). In the case of *The Abyss*, however, the star-crossed lovers are separated by their own history together, rather than class difference, though this motif does vaguely come into play with the suggestion early in the Special Edition version of the film that Lindsey, having left the relatively working-class Bud, has already had a relationship with a new rich, yuppie boyfriend, though that relationship has conveniently ended by the time she and Bud are reunited in the film. Actually, we never really get details about the reason for the breakup between Bud and Lindsey, though the implication seems to be that both are strong, independent people and that Lindsey, in particular, is a radically alienated individual who simply has difficulty sharing her life and her feelings with anyone else.

In another scene added for the Special Edition, as Lindsey attempts to keep Bud focused amid the disorientation that occurs as he descends into the abyss to defuse the bomb, she reminds him of an intimate moment early in their marriage. Even in their togetherness, she had looked at a lit candle and remarked that she felt like that candle, burning alone in the darkness. Bud's response had been to light a second candle and to place it beside the first, saying that the second candle represented him. Lindsey then promises to the descending Bud that she will, in the future, always be with him.

Lindsey provides companionship to Bud not only as he descends into the abyss at the bottom of the ocean, but also as he seeks to ascend from the abyss of personal loneliness. This added scene thus greatly reinforces the multiple allegorical significance of the film's title image. The abyss is not only the physical deep trench in the ocean floor, but the metaphysical abyss of hell, an interpretation particularly suggested by Bud's Christian name, Virgil, which suggests the Roman poet who helped Dante negotiate his way through hell in *The Divine Comedy*. The abyss of the title is also the potential catastrophe of nuclear warfare, as well as a variety of personal abysses, including the abyss of madness into which Coffey descends. Thus, Lindsey helps Bud to survive and return from the abyss at bottom of the ocean, just as he had earlier helped her to return from the abyss of death and as, by the end of the film, both Bud and Lindsey promise to rescue each other from the abyss of personal, existential loneliness—a motif re-inforced by the inclusion of an epigraph, added for the Special Edition, from Friedrich Nietzsche: "When you look long into an abyss, the abyss also looks into you."

In this sense, Lindsey seems to be the one who has particularly learned a lesson, as might be expected of someone who has literally died and been reborn. From the beginning, it seems clear that Bud still wants to be with her, as can be seen from the fact that he still wears his wedding ring. At one point, after an initial row with her when she arrives at *Deepcore 2*, he throws the ring into the toilet in frustration, but then retrieves it, setting up a later scene during the dragging of *Deepcore* across the ocean floor when Bud's hand is caught in a closing hatch but the titanium ring saves his fingers from being crushed.

This moment symbolically suggests that it is better for Bud and Lindsey to be together. But she is apparently a difficult woman to be with. When she first appears in the film, another character describes her as the "queen bitch of the universe," a description that perhaps seems apt after our first few views of her, which include her descending from a helicopter onto the deck of *Explorer* wearing totally impractical high heels. In one scene, just as Bud is being told by radio from the *Explorer* that hurricane Frederick is approaching, he suggests that hurricanes should be named for women, perhaps reflecting his experience with Lindsey. We cut back to the control room on the *Explorer*, where papers start to blow wildly about because

Lindsey has just opened the door to enter. The implication is clear: Lindsey is a force of nature, perhaps akin to a hurricane. In her first encounter with Bud in the film, she excoriates him by radio for allowing the military to appropriate "her" rig for its purposes, as if he had any choice. She insists on addressing Bud as "Virgil," which is apparently her way of establishing emotional distance. She also calls him a "wiener" and complains that he never could stand up to a fight. "God, I hate that bitch," complains Bud.

Lindsey herself, while later talking Bud down into the trench, admits that she has great difficulties with opening up to other people. "It's not easy being a cast-iron bitch," she tells him. "It takes discipline and years of training." Yet, despite the repeated characterization of Lindsey as a bitch in the film, she is generally presented as a positive character, somewhat along the lines of the strong women in other Cameron SF films, including Ripley in *Aliens* and Sarah Connor in *Terminator* and (especially) *Terminator 2*. One could, in fact, read a distinctly feminist message into the portrayal of Lindsey in *The Abyss*, which demonstrates that a strong, independent, intelligent woman like Lindsey is likely to be regarded as a bitch by those around her, no matter how personable she might actually be.

The difficulty of being a successful professional woman in a world that regards such women as bitches also provides at least a partial explanation for Lindsey's alienation from those around her. At the same time, the film ultimately undermines its own feminist message by suggesting that Lindsey has probably concentrated too much on her professional duties and has neglected her feminine side in the interest of appearing tough and avoiding emotional vulnerability. The film clearly suggests that she has learned to overcome this mistake due to her recent experiences, allowing her not only to open up to Bud but to be safely circumscribed within the orbit of their marriage. Thus, as Bud and Lindsey greet each other at the film's close, she calls him "Brigman," and he responds by calling her "Mrs. Brigman," an appellation she happily accepts, though she has earlier made it clear that she has always hated being called that, even when their marriage was going well. The film presents her acceptance of the role of wife as a positive resolution, even though the consequent suggestion that she must accept a secondary role in order for their relationship to function is highly problematic.

Granted, Bud is presented as a sensitive, enlightened type who will presumably support Lindsey in the pursuit of her own interests. The real counter to Lindsey as an independent woman is Coffey, the ultra-masculine

Navy Seal, who finds Lindsey absolutely intolerable, even before his madness. Thus, when she first insists that he stop calling her "Mrs. Brigman" (something he nevertheless continues to do throughout the film, unless he is referring to her as "the Brigman woman"), he suggests that perhaps she would prefer to be called "Sir." For a man like Coffey, Lindsey's refusal to be passive and subservient means that she is not a proper woman. Coffey's hostility to her later peaks in one of his violent post-madness confrontations with the oil workers, when he slams her against a wall and holds her there, while he appears to be ripping her clothing. "This is something I've wanted to do since we first met," he tells her, with the suggestion that he is about to rape her. It turns out, however, that he is actually tearing off a piece of duct tape to place over her mouth. He has no interest in having sex with a woman who is so able to speak for herself: what he has really wanted to do all along is shut her up.

While Coffey's pressure-induced madness (which we are told could happen to anyone) serves as an explanation for much of his most extreme behavior, it is fairly clear that he was a fairly unstable individual to begin with and that his personal madness can be taken as an emblem of the madness of the military in general. Indeed, the fact that the central military figure in the film is mad can be taken as a sort of comment on the fact that the buildup of nuclear weapons in both the United States and the Soviet Union has led to the point appropriately known as "MAD" (mutually assured destruction). *The Abyss* is definitely an anti-military, as well as antiwar film, and its representation of the confrontation between the Navy Seals and the oil riggers clearly favors the point of view of the latter. One message of the film is that, left to themselves, ordinary people will typically do the right thing, and that it is only the self-serving operations of the military-industrial complex that have led the United States to the brink of nuclear war.

This confrontation between civilians and the military is one that often occurs in science fiction film. The confrontation in *The Abyss* is particularly reminiscent of that in Christian Nyby's *The Thing from Another World*, one of the prototypical alien-invasion narratives of the 1950s. Here, opposed groups of scientists and military men encounter an alien ship (and an alien) in the arctic, an isolated setting that serves much the same function as the deep-sea setting of *The Abyss*. From this point, however, the films are almost polar opposites. The alien in *The Thing from Another World* is a vicious killer, set on the destruction of the humans it encounters, while the highly-evolved aliens of *The Abyss* only want to save humans from themselves. Further, while *The Thing* presents its military men as sensible and strong, the scientists who oppose them are excessively devoted to logic and thus cut off from their own humanity. Moreover, the chief scientist, Dr. Arthur Carrington (Robert Cornthwaite), even wears a Russian-style hat, suggesting that his blind devotion to the scientific method aligns him with the cold rationality of communism.

In *The Abyss* it is the military men who are excessively devoted to their own narrow point of view, while the oil riggers who oppose them are aligned with genuine humanity. In short, as a Cold War film, *The Abyss* is much more in the antiwar spirit of *The Day the Earth Stood Still* than the militaristic spirit of *The Thing*, which urges vigilance against enemies, rather than understanding. On the other hand, the sentimentalism of *The Abyss* takes it well beyond *The Day the Earth Stood Still* to reassure its audiences that human beings can often be noble and kind and that the race is thus well worth saving.

This point is especially clear in the Special Edition of the film, which delivers a message entirely missing from the original theatrical version. Here, the aliens make it clear that they have the power to destroy humanity but that their observations of Bud's love for Lindsey and of his willingness to sacrifice himself for her and his fellow oil riggers have convinced them that there is enough good in the human race that they might still be saved. Of course, there is also an implied warning (again reminiscent of *The Day the Earth Stood Still*) that the aliens might still find it advisable to destroy the human race if they do not heed this warning.

This motif of humanity being judged by a superior alien species often appears in science fiction. It provides the central plot of numerous episodes of the *Star Trek* franchise, including the two-part episode "Encounter at Farpoint" that inaugurated *Star Trek: The Next Generation* in 1987, two years before the release of *The Abyss*. In that episode the seemingly omnipotent alien "Q" literally places humanity on trial, but the noble and courageous deeds of Captain Picard and the crew of the starship *Enterprise* convince him that humanity is a species with promise—though he vows to keep a close eye on them in the future. There is even a Cold War twist to this plot: part of Picard's defense is to assure the shape-shifting Q (who at one point appears as a Cold War–era military officer and tries to rally the crew of the *Enterprise* to fight "commies") that humanity has moved well beyond the "nonsense" of the Cold War.

To an extent, then, the Special Edition of *The Abyss* is very much in tune with message of *Star Trek: The Next Generation*, which may not be surprising given that both are late Cold War works in which conciliation toward the *Glasnost/Perestroika*-era Soviet Union was the rule of the day. However, while "Encounter at Farpoint" (in good *Star Trek* fashion) argues that human beings are worth saving because of their capacity for courage and good judgment, *The Abyss* opts for the far more sentimental argument that humanity is worth saving because of the human capacity for love and self-sacrifice.

NOTE ON ALTERNATIVE VERSIONS

The DVD release of *The Abyss* includes both the 1989 theatrical version and an extended "Special Edition" version, originally created for release to laserdisc in 1992 and released to a limited run in theaters in early 1993. The two versions differ primarily in the twenty-eight additional minutes of footage that have been added into the latter. Most of the additions are meant to strengthen the plot line involving the relationship between Bud and Lindsey, but the most important addition involves the scene in which the aliens threaten the world's coastal areas with destruction from towering tidal waves, which adds an entirely new dimension to the film. The above discussion pertains primarily to the Special Edition.

UNDERSEA ADVENTURE: THE LEGACY OF *THE ABYSS*

In addition to its obvious echo of the antiwar warnings of *The Day the Earth Stood Still* (at least in the Special Edition), *The Abyss* follows in the footsteps of a number of undersea SF films that remind us of the existence of an entire alien world beneath the seas of our own planet. Perhaps the most notable of these are Disney's *20,000 Leagues under the Sea* (1954) and Irwin Allen's *Voyage to the Bottom of the Sea* (1961), which formed the basis of a similarly-titled television series that ran in the United States from 1964 to 1966. *The Abyss* certainly gave new credibility to the undersea SF genre, though the difficulty and expense of making such films meant that there was never any danger that *The Abyss* would trigger a spate of imitators. The subsequent film most directly related to *The Abyss* is probably Barry Levinson's *Solaris*-inflected *Sphere* (1998), which also involves the discovery of an alien in a spacecraft deep beneath the ocean. One other relatively major undersea film is George Cosmatos's *Leviathan* (1989), though that film came out five months before *The Abyss* and ultimately becomes a monster picture more reminiscent of *Alien* than of *The Abyss*. Renny Harlin's *Deep Blue Sea* (1999) is also essentially an underwater monster film, with the added SF twist that the monsters in question are sharks made more dangerous by a genetic experiment gone wrong.

14

Independence Day

Released 1996; Director Roland Emmerich

German director Roland Emmerich made his debut in American science fiction film in 1990 with the moderately interesting SF crime thriller *Moon 44*, actually a German production but filmed in English with a mostly American cast, largely for uAmerican distribution. He followed in 1992 with the unremarkable Jean–Claude Van Damme vehicle *Universal Soldier*, then moved into the big time with *Stargate* (1994) a profitable big-budget SF adventure. This success allowed Emmerich to make the expensive *Independence Day* (1996). An alien–invasion film modeled on the disaster films of the 1970s, *Independence Day* employed the more advanced special effects techniques of the 1990s to produce one of the most spectacular SF films of all time. It was also one of the most profitable films of all time, grossing more than $300 million in the United States and nearly $500 million in the rest of the world. The technical and commercial success of *Independence Day* have had a profound impact on American science fiction film ever since.

THE STORY: VICTORY IS OURS

Independence Day begins on July 2 (of an unspecified year) with a shot of the site of the 1969 American landing on the moon. Suddenly, the site is cast into shadow as a huge spaceship passes overhead, announcing the presence of a technology far in advance of that responsible for the earlier moon landing. Soon, it becomes clear that this huge ship is of alien origin, though attempts by those on Earth to contact it come to no avail. When the huge mother ship (more than 550 km in diameter and one-fourth the mass of the moon) approaches the Earth, it releases nearly three dozen smaller ships (themselves more than fifteen miles in diameter), which proceed to station themselves over various major cities around the world. It soon becomes clear that the aliens have hostile intentions, especially after helicopters that approach them to try to communicate are blasted out of the sky.

Following the formula of disaster films such as Irwin Allen's *The Towering Inferno* and Mark Robson's *Earthquake* (both released in 1974), the elaboration of the growing crisis is accompanied by the introduction of a cast of characters who will be affected by the disaster or who will be involved in dealing with it. Given the nature of this particular crisis, it is not surprising that the first major character introduced is U.S. President Thomas J. Whitmore (Bill Pullman), a former war hero who had served as a fighter pilot in the 1991 Gulf War. As the film begins, Whitmore's conciliatory policies have led to a drastic drop in his approval rating, the public perceiving that they have elected a warrior but actually gotten a wimp. Whitmore is first seen with his small daughter Patricia (Mae Whitman), giving his introduction a personal touch. Whitmore's wife is First Lady Marilyn Whitmore (Mary McDonnell), currently away in Los Angeles. We also meet some of Whitmore's top aides, including Press Secretary Constance Spano (Margaret Colin), who will play a particularly important role in the coming confrontation with the alien invaders.

Another key character introduced early on is unambitious electronics genius David Levinson (Jeff Goldblum), who works for a cable television station in New York City. Levinson is the former husband of Spano, their marriage having apparently broken up due to conflicts caused by her dedication to her career—and her devotion to Whitmore, in whom she strongly believes. In keeping with the film's tendency to focus on family relationships, we are also introduced to Levinson's father Julius (Judd Hirsch), who has a close relationship with his son, though he criticizes him for failing to use his genius to become more than a "cable repairman." In addition to remarkable characters such as Whitmore, Spano, and Levinson, we also meet ordinary guy Russell Casse (Randy Quaid), who is himself a former fighter pilot (in Vietnam), but who is now down on his luck. Casse works as a cropduster in Arizona, a job he does very poorly, largely due to his propensity for alcohol. His condition, we learn, may be due to post-traumatic stress syndrome related to his service in Vietnam. He has also suffered a psychic trauma from the death of his wife (leaving him with two stepchildren and one child of his own, who are also important characters in the film) and from his apparent abduction by aliens ten years earlier. Casse is contrasted with the last of the major characters to be introduced, ace fighter pilot Captain Steven Hiller (Will Smith), an ambitious young man who hopes some day to fly the space shuttle. Continuing the film's interest in personal relationships, we also meet Hiller's girlfriend, stripper Jasmine DuBrow (Vivica A. Fox), and her son Dylan (Ross Bagley).

Levinson, investigating interference in his station's communication with its satellite, realizes that the aliens are using Earth's own system of tele-communications satellites to relay signals from the mother ship to the saucers. He also deduces from his study of the signals that the aliens are counting down toward a massive assault on the cities over which the saucers are stationed. Unable to get through by phone, Levinson (himself not a driver) convinces Julius to drive him to Washington so that he can warn the government to evacuate the cities. He manages to do so, and the evacuation orders are issued, but chaos reigns, and many people are still in the cities when the aliens begin their assault, obliterating individual buildings (including the White House, in perhaps the film's best-known shot) with a sort of energy beam. The resultant explosion then radiates outward across the cities in spectacular expanding circles of explosive fire. Large areas are left decimated and in flames.

On July 3, the air force attempts to retaliate, but attacks on the saucers prove ineffective when it becomes clear that they are protected—like the Martians of *War of the Worlds* (1953)—by seemingly impenetrable energy shields. In one such attack, Hiller is nearly killed when alien fighters are launched against his squadron of planes. He manages to eject safely and to cause the alien fighter pursuing him to crash into the desert. He walks to the downed ship, opens the hatch, and punches the tentacled alien pilot in the face, knocking it unconscious and taking it prisoner. He then proceeds to drag it across the desert toward a nearby base he spotted from the air—which turns out to be Area 51, long rumored in UFO lore to be the headquarters of a top-secret government effort to investigate and deal with the possibility of alien visitations.

At this point, the stories of the various characters are rapidly converging. Hiller is picked up by Casse, who is driving his family camper as part of a caravan of such vehicles that has fled into the desert to escape the alien attacks. Hiller directs Casse and the caravan to Area 51, where Whitmore, Spano, and the Levinsons have already gone. The facility, we learn, is so hush-hush that even Whitmore had not previously known about it; he is given a tour by the facility's research director, Dr. Brackish Okun (amusingly—and allusively—played by Brent Spiner, who had played the android Data on television's *Star Trek: The Next Generation*). During this tour we learn that the facility holds three dead aliens, as well as an alien fighter that crashed back in the 1950s, now largely functional after years of repair efforts. The fighter's power has mysteriously reactivated, apparently in response to the arrival of the alien invasion force.

When Hiller arrives with his unconscious prisoner, Okun is excited by the chance to study a live alien. However, when he opens the biomechanical suit that encloses the alien, the alien itself escapes and takes him hostage. Speaking through Okun and also using a form of telepathy, the alien communicates with Whitmore. When Whitmore asks what the aliens want humans to do, it simply replies, "Die." Whitmore learns through his telepathic contact that the aliens are like locusts, their whole civilization traveling from one planet to another, using up each planet's resources, then moving on. By this point, it is clear that the aliens are to be regarded as unequivocally evil, so that audiences need feel no guilt for wishing their total destruction and can give their wholehearted support to Whitmore's immediate decision to "nuke the bastards."

Nuking the bastards, as it turns out, is not so easily done. After some last minute reluctance (because of fallout and other side-effects), Whitmore gives the final go-ahead for the use of nuclear weapons against the saucers, but these weapons also prove unable to penetrate the alien shields. At this point, Earth appears defenseless. We also learn that the injuries suffered by Marilyn Whitmore in one of the alien attacks are inescapably fatal, reinforcing this public calamity with personal tragedy.

As the film moves into July 4, a drunken and despondent Levinson suddenly realizes, during a conversation in which Julius warns him against catching cold, that it may be possible to infect the alien computer system with a virus that will cause the shields to become inoperative. Unfortunately, this plan will require someone to fly the captured alien fighter to the mother ship, interface with its computer system, and upload the virus there. Hiller volunteers to pilot the ship, and Levinson (though he hates flying and gets airsick) volunteers to go along to upload the virus.

Independence Day is a very hawkish film. When Secretary of Defense Albert Nimziki (James Rebhorn) urges caution concerning Levinson's plan, Whitmore responds angrily and fires the man, calling him a sniveling weasel. Audiences are clearly meant to sympathize with Whitmore, though Nimziki has a point given the unlikely nature of the plan. Meanwhile, the United States (using old-fashioned morse-code communication because the satellite system is down) leads a worldwide effort to prepare a massive simultaneous assault on the alien saucers if and when Hiller and Levinson are able to deactivate the shields. Before they leave, however, Hiller and DuBrow have an impromptu wedding, with Levinson and Spano as witnesses.

Pilots around the world line up to join the mission against the saucers, including Casse and Whitmore, who decides personally to lead the attack against an alien saucer that is approaching Area 51 itself. As the pilots there prepare to take off, he gives them a rousing speech, suggesting that, if they prevail, July 4 will no longer be known as an American holiday but as independence day for the whole world, humanity having put aside its "petty differences" in the interest of solidarity against the aliens.

Amazingly, the plan succeeds. Not only are Hiller and Levinson able to deactivate the shields, but they manage to blow up the mother ship and to escape with their lives. The moment is treated as one of joyous celebration despite the carnage it implies: the film suggests that the entire alien civilization, consisting of many millions of individuals, resides on the mother ship, so what we witness in this scene is the total destruction of an alien race. Meanwhile, the saucers at first seem indestructible even with their shields down, but then Casse, his last missile lodged in his plane and unable to launch, flies into the opening through which the saucer over Area 51 is about to fire its weapon. The resultant explosion brings down the saucer and reveals the point of vulnerability that can then be used to down saucers around the world.

The film concludes a crescendo of triumph. People around the world celebrate the victory. Meanwhile, the film ends in classic Hollywood fashion as Hiller and Levinson are passionately greeted by their women, while Whitmore's daughter wishes him a happy fourth of July. Meanwhile, Hiller looks to the sky and asks his new stepson, "Didn't I promise you fireworks?" We then see that the sky is filled with streaks of light as debris (apparently from the destroyed mother ship) plummets through the atmosphere.

THE SOURCES OF THE MOVIE

Independence Day is based on an original screenplay by producer Dean Devlin and director Emmerich, though it clearly draws upon numerous predecessors in SF film (most importantly Byron Haskins's 1953 film adaptation of H. G. Wells's *The War of the Worlds*), as well as the disaster films of the 1970s.

SPECTACULAR CINEMA: SCIENCE FICTION AS AMERICAN FANTASY IN *INDEPENDENCE DAY*

Independence Day is the epitome of the effects-driven science fiction film. Its Oscar for best special effects was well deserved, and its effects are among the most impressive ever put on film. The scenes involving attacks on the alien saucers and dogfights between the alien fighters and Earth fighters are extremely convincing, and the spectacular pyrotechnics associated with the scenes of the alien assaults on cities are particularly effective. The tremendous commercial success of the film was highly influential, pushing SF film even further in the direction of big-budget effects spectacles. *Independence Day* is almost entirely devoid of social or political satire, and it lacks the thoughtfulness that is often associated with the best science fiction. In that sense, it demonstrates why many critics and fans of science fiction have been concerned that improvements in effects technology have actually led to a decline in the quality of science fiction film. In many ways, *Independence Day* is a simple, least-common-denominator film, with us as the good guys pitted against them as the bad guys, which probably helps to account for the fact that, despite its overt Americanism, it was a huge success in the global market. On the other hand, the film is not intended to be thought provoking or to challenge audiences to reexamine their ideas about the world; rather, it represents film as pure entertainment, a Hollywood tradition that goes back at least as far as the Busby Berkeley musicals of the 1930s. In this sense, the film is a great success, as its box-office receipts demonstrate. Audiences clearly regarded it as a feel-good film, despite the fact that it depicts the worst calamity in human history, with millions dead and many major cities destroyed.

Independence Day is entertaining in ways that go well beyond its fancy space ships and big explosions. It is, in fact, a rich and well-made film that is full of human interest elements and effective details, in addition to the big-time special effects. The kind of small, clever touches that make *Independence Day* a special film begin to appear quite early. In one of the first scenes, as a researcher at the S.E.T.I. (Search for Extra Terrestrial Intelligence) Institute in New Mexico first detects the signal from the alien mother ship, the music playing in the background is R.E.M.'s 1987 hit "It's the End of the World as We Know It (And I Feel Fine)." This music perfectly establishes the tone of the film, which deals with the potential end of the human race, yet is intended to make audiences feel good about what they have seen. There are also numerous clever cuts in the film (especially as we move among different story lines early in the film), as when the military decides to call the Secretary of Defense to alert him of the approach of the alien mother ship, then we cut to a ringing phone that happens simply to be Marilyn Whitmore calling her husband from Los Angeles. Similarly, when the President orders the U.S. military to increase its readiness to DEFCON 3 (Defense Condition 3), we cut to urgently blinking warning lights that turn out merely to signal that food has finished heating in the microwave oven in David Levinson's office.

Independence Day also has lots of comic moments that help to lighten the mood and keep the film entertaining, despite its end-of-the-world scenario. Many of the best comic lines belong to Smith, who plays Hiller with wise-cracking movie-hero panache, especially a persona that he would carry over into numerous subsequent films. Several secondary characters are included largely for comic effect, though many of these characters border on the offensive. Quaid's turn as the comic movie drunk obviously ignores the real-life tragedies of alcoholism and post-traumatic stress syndrome, and the supposedly amusing scenes that show him irresponsibly flying his crop-dusting plane while intoxicated, bottle in hand, seem rather inappropriate as sources of comedy. Meanwhile, the film employs the old Hollywood strategy of playing ethnic stereotypes for humor when Hirsch plays Julius Levinson as the stereotypical movie New York Jew, a comic, kvetching immigrant, impressed but unawed by his experiences in the film, which take him into the White House's Oval Office, aboard Air Force One, and into high-echelon top-secret circles in Area 51. Of course, both Quaid's Casse and Hirsch's Levinson ultimately turn out to be positive characters, partly because of their love for their children. On the other hand, there is no such positive figuration for David Levinson's boss, Marty Gilbert, whom Harvey Fierstein plays as the stereotypical limp-wristed, frantic, flitting homosexual. Gilbert shows love, or at least concern, for his mother and brother, but never achieves the status of a genuinely human character. As a result, even his death, squashed beneath a flying car thrown toward him in the alien bombardment of New York, can be treated as an essentially comic moment (his final "oh shit" is his best line in the film) without much fear of alienating most members of the audience.

For science fiction fans, some of the pleasure of watching *Independence Day* comes from its frequent allusion to earlier SF films. For example, when we first meet the Casse children, they are watching *The Day the Earth Stood Still* on television, though the alien signal interferes with their reception. Soon afterward, a reporter at Levinson's television station is shown in the midst of a phone call concerning the aliens and says, "Yes, I like *The X-Files*, too." When we first meet Dylan DuBrow, he is carrying a toy Godzilla, which not only alludes back to the classic Japanese film monster, but anticipates Emmerich's next project, the 1998 megabudget film *Godzilla*. A similar "inside" allusion occurs later when Levinson urges Hiller, "Must go faster!" as they attempt to fly out of the mother ship, a line he had also spoken in *Jurassic Park* (1993). Hiller himself, during the briefing before his first mission against the aliens, announces that he is anxious to "get up there to whup E.T.'s ass." Hiller remains similarly truculent with his allusions when he punches the downed alien pilot, then declares, "Now that's what I call a close encounter." Other allusions visually refer to specific moments in other films, as when a shot of New York City after it has been devastated by the alien assault shows a ruined Statue of Liberty, clearly recalling the chilling ending of *Planet of the Apes*. Still other allusions are simply thematic, as when Levinson's plan to defeat the aliens with a computer virus clearly echoes the destruction of the alien invaders in H. G. Wells's *War of the Worlds* (1898) by airborne microbes (specifically identified as the common cold virus in Byron Haskins's 1953 film version of Wells's novel).

Such allusions help to place *Independence Day* within the genre of science fiction, despite its obvious structural similarity to the disaster films of the 1970s. It is a film with strong science fictional elements. On the other hand, much of the success of the film comes not from its impressive alien ships and other science fiction hardware, but from its focus on human relationships, often in a highly sentimental mode. The wedding of Hiller and DuBrow is a peak sentimental moment in the film, presumably announcing that his love for her has finally overcome his professional ambition, given that he has been warned that marrying a stripper will mean the death of his hopes to join the space program. Then again, he now has no reason for such concern. If his mission fails, humanity will be destroyed and his future ambitions will become irrelevant; if his mission succeeds he will no doubt be able to write his own ticket in the U.S. space program. In any case, the sentimentality of this wedding is greatly enhanced by the presence of Levinson and Spano, who look lovingly at one another, then take each other's hands (after she notices that he is still wearing his wedding ring after three years apart). The implication is that they are being symbolically re-wed as well, and the film's conclusion clearly suggests that the two are now on their way to a new life together—perhaps because Spano now need not be frustrated by Levinson's status as an underachiever.

The film's children, including Casses' kids as well as Patricia Whitmore and Dylan DuBrow, are also good for substantial sentimental mileage, partly because threats to children tend to carry more weight with film audiences—though it is also the case that the filmmakers, in the interest of making a feel-good film, took care to ensure that the children never really seem all that seriously at risk. In the same way, Boomer, Dylan's faithful dog, also survives the film uninjured, though there is one scene in which he does, in fact, barely escape obliteration. Emmerich has reported that test audiences for the film found this scene the most disturbing in the film, and that it was clear to him that the dog had to survive, no matter how many humans died. The children of the film also provide an opportunity for a number of touching parent-child scenes, as does the relationship between the Levinsons. The scene in which Whitmore comforts Patricia after it becomes clear that her mother is dying is perhaps the most powerful and effective of these, though there are numerous images of parent-child communion—up to and including the fact that the film ends not, as it might have, on the classic movie kisses of the two reunited couples, but on moments shared between Whitmore and Patricia and between Dylan and his new daddy, Hiller.

Dylan and Patricia also serve as images of innocent inter-racial and cross-class communication; the film includes an almost obligatory scene in which Dylan and Patricia get together and become friends, despite the differences in their backgrounds. In a similar way, DuBrow and Marilyn Whitmore meet and briefly become friends in the midst of the crisis, during a touching scene in which DuBrow becomes a version of the stereotypical whore-with-a-heart-of-gold as she comforts the injured First Lady and explains to her that she is unashamed of being a stripper because it helps her to provide for her son, who is "worth it." Of course, the filmmakers have also been careful to introduce DuBrow as a sympathetic character well before we even find out that she is a stripper, so that only the meanest of viewers could possibly root against the classic film resolution of her marriage to Hiller.

That marriage, between an upwardly-mobile professional and a stripper, is also an image of cross-class communication, and as a whole the film depicts the realization of the American fantasy of a society in which individuals are judged for who they are and not on the basis of their gender, class, or race. It is no accident, for example, that the main characters together provide a fantasy enactment of the American melting pot, or that a black man and a Jew team up to pilot the most daring and heroic action of the entire film. Nevertheless, the film is careful not to go too far with this motif. For example, it leaves little room for heroic action on the part its one obviously gay character, while it still provides us with a WASP President. Had the filmmakers really wanted to be daring, they might have allowed a woman to pilot the craft that destroys the alien mother ship—and perhaps had her marry a male stripper. They also could have made Du-Brow white, and so on.

Still, the interracial and interclass harmony depicted in *Independence Day* is a sort of Americanist fantasy, as are many other elements of the film. Indeed, despite its European director (and its tremendous box-office success overseas as well as in the United States), *Independence Day*, as its title indicates, is a film unapologetically bursting with American patriotism. For one thing, though the alien invasion is certainly depicted as a global event, the focus of the film is entirely on the United States, and it is the United States that must lead the way in the response to the invasion. The first scene in Washington, in which the Pentagon scrambles to deal with the approach of the alien mother ship, begins with a foreground shot of the well-known Marine Corps War Memorial (a statue depicting the raising of the American flag by a group of Marines after the battle of Iwo Jima in World War II). This shot not only anticipates the importance of the Marine Hiller (whom we have not yet met at this point), but also suggests the patriotic/militaristic tone of the film itself by evoking one of the most famous of all images of American military triumph. As the alien saucer passes over Washington, we see its shadow move across a series of crucial icons of Americanism, including the Washington Monument, the Capitol Building, and the White House. Later, in addition to the destroyed Statue of Liberty, we see the destruction of both the White House and the Capitol Building by the alien saucer.

These shots of the destruction of key American monuments might be almost too alarming for American audiences, especially in the retrospective light of the September 11, 2001, attack on the World Trade Center. Indeed, the World Trade Center is at one point in the film shown as it falls into the shadow of an alien saucer, though the actual destruction of the twin towers is not depicted. However, in keeping with the overall tone of the film, these shots of destruction merely serve to set up the third act of the film, in which the American forces strike back with a vengeance—on July 4, no less. The message is clear: anyone who attacks the United States is likely to suffer swift and terrible retribution. In this sense, though the film was made in the midst of the Clinton years, *Independence Day* almost uncannily anticipates the aggressive response of the Bush administration to the 9/11 attacks, while at the same time providing a clear path to victory that is unavailable in the more nebulous battle against international terrorism.

Especially in the latter part of the film, President Whitmore's rhetoric of defiance strongly anticipates the "bring it on" rhetoric of the Bush administration's "war" on terrorism. Moreover, the film essentially endorses this rhetoric, depicting Whitmore's turn from compromising politician to staunch military commander as a decidedly positive development that makes Whitmore the kind of strong leader that many Americans want. Whitmore—a young, handsome, charismatic former war hero—is a President much more in the mold of John Kennedy than of either Clinton or Bush. Thus, in terms of the film's function as an Americanist fantasy, one might also consider Whitmore as a kind of fantasy President. Not only does he provide strong and dramatic leadership in a terrible national crisis, but he is also depicted (in contrast to the popular perception of politicians in the 1990s) as a figure of absolute virtue, a dedicated family man who is, we are reminded at least twice in the film, virtually incapable of telling a lie. From this point of view, it is even possible to see his initial tendency toward political compromise as a virtue, his shift to a more hawkish attitude in the wake of the alien attacks simply indicating the way in which he is able to change his leadership style to match the situation at hand.

It is also crucial to the film that Whitmore is able to provide strong leadership not only for the United States but for the world. Remarkably, once he gives the go-ahead for David Levinson's plan to lower the alien shields via a computer virus, Whitmore has no trouble at all in eliciting the complete cooperation of military forces around the globe, even with the global communications system on the fritz. In fact, he seems to be able to give instructions directly to troops in the field, even without going through their governments. The American government is, in fact, the only one we see in the film, making it the de facto government of the world. Much of the value of the film as an Americanist fantasy, then, comes from its vision of the United States as the unquestioned leader of the entire world, able to make policies that all other nations will follow without question or resentment. And rightly so, because—in this film, at least—American leadership saves the day, thanks to the all-American combination of Levinson's intellect, Hiller's valiance, and Whitmore's decisiveness.

The immediate response of military forces around the world to Whitmore's call to action is not very realistic, even in such a crisis, but then *Independence Day* is not a film that is much concerned with realism. This is a film designed to entertain with spectacular action and touching moments of human emotional contact; as such, it is not designed to stand up to a great deal of thoughtful scrutiny. Nevertheless, there is one fascinating element of the film that should be closely analyzed, and that is the contradictory nature of its self-conscious effort to serve as an American national allegory. The Americans of the film are completely outgunned, faced with a foe far superior to them in firepower and technological know-how. As such, the film is perfectly in keeping with what is widely regarded as a typical American tendency to root for the underdog. The problem, of course, is that in the global political situation of the real world, the United States is not an underdog, but is the most powerful nation on the planet. In the real world of geopolitics, the United States does not occupy the position of underdog as depicted in the film. Instead, the real United States is in very much the position occupied in the film by the alien invaders, facing numerous smaller nations around the globe from a position of vast military and technological superiority—and often using force to impose its will on smaller and less powerful nations.

Just as the beloved rebels of *Star Wars* bear a striking resemblance to the despised terrorists of our own world, so too do the valiant Earth forces who battle the aliens in *Independence Day* resemble the guerrilla freedom fighters who have struggled against Western colonial and neocolonial domination for the past half century. The title of the film virtually indicates as much, suggesting an anticolonial struggle for independence. Other aspects of the film also tend to support this kind of subversive interpretation of the film as *anti*-American and pro–Third World. It is, for example, almost weirdly appropriate that the first alien saucer is sighted over the desert of Iraq, a country on which death has rained down from the air in two different American assaults in a little more than a decade. Also interesting is the fact that Casse brings down the first alien saucer by acting as a suicide bomber, in a move treated by the film as admirable and heroic, even though suicide bombers have now come to be regarded as despicable (and somehow cowardly) by the American public. Moreover, that Casse performs this suicide bombing by flying a plane into the saucer almost eerily anticipates the mode of the 9/11 bombings, the most striking historical case of Third World retaliatory violence against America. For that matter, the crucial mission flown by Hiller and Levinson resembles those bombings as well, given that they essentially fly a hijacked alien plane into the mother ship in order to blow it up, just as the 9/11 bombers flew hijacked planes into the World Trade Center and the Pentagon—though in the case of the film the hijackers manage to escape with their lives.

This is not, of course, to say that the makers of *Independence Day* somehow anticipated the 9/11 attacks, and it is certainly not meant to imply that the film influenced or even inspired the attackers. Further, it seems clear that *Independence Day* is not in any way *intended* as an allegory of anticolonial resistance to American or other Western domination, even if it can be read that way. If anything, the film supports the ideology of colonialism in the way it depicts the aliens as inhuman Others unworthy of sympathy. Nevertheless, the possibility of reading *Independence Day* as a critique of colonialism demonstrates that even the simplest of political oppositions are sometimes more complex than they appear, especially in the real world, when simple good vs. evil oppositions such as those around which *Independence Day* is structured seldom occur.

NOTE ON ALTERNATIVE VERSIONS

The DVD edition of *Independence Day* includes both the original theatrical version and the 1998 Special Edition produced for Laserdisc. However, the versions do not differ in any substantial way; the Special Edition merely includes about eight minutes of extra footage, including a few new scenes and extended versions of several scenes from the theatrical version. The above discussion applies primarily to the Special Edition.

SCIENCE FICTION AS DISASTER FILM:
THE LEGACY OF *INDEPENDENCE DAY*

Independence Day has much in common with earlier alien-invasion films, especially those, such as *Earth vs. the Flying Saucers* (1956), that show actual combat between Earth forces and invading alien craft. But the film's primary contribution to SF film was its demonstration of the effectiveness with which the disaster-film formula could be applied to science fiction. In this sense, the film is reminiscent of the 1985 alien-invasion novel *Footfall*, by Larry Niven and Jerry Pournelle, which had already used a similar formula. Director Emmerich would go on to apply the disaster-film formula to the monster movie in *Godzilla* (1998), then to apply state-of-the-art effects technology to a more conventional disaster plot (though one with strong science fiction elements) in *The Day after Tomorrow* (2004), an environmental disaster film that became another big box-office hit, though it did not achieve the commercial success of *Independence Day*.

Other big-budget disaster-oriented SF films that followed in the wake of *Independence Day* include Michael Bay's *Armageddon* (1998), a film with nearly twice the budget of *Independence Day*, in which a huge asteroid threatens to strike the Earth with disastrous effects. In Mimi Leder's *Deep Impact* (1998), a film with a budget roughly equal to that of *Independence Day*, it is a comet that threatens to strike the Earth. More recently, Jon Amiel's *The Core* (2003) continued this trend, though this time the threat comes from inside the Earth rather than outer space. A number of other big-budget effects-driven SF films—especially Paul Verhoeven's alien-blasting *Starship Troopers* (1997)—clearly owed something to *Independence Day*, while the success of *Independence Day* also led to a resurgence in the disaster film itself, including such efforts as Mick Jackson's *Volcano* (1997), Roger Donaldson's *Dante's Peak* (1997). In this vein, one might also mention Bay's *Pearl Harbor* (2001), which retold the story of the 1941 Japanese bombing of Pearl Harbor using the effects-driven disaster film format. Steven Spielberg's 2005 remake of *War of the Worlds* essentially employs a disaster film scenario as well, relying for much of its effect on its sentimental focus on a hero (played by Tom Cruise) who is not actively fighting the aliens, but simply trying to get his children to safety.

15

The Matrix

Released 1999; Directors Andy
and Larry Wachowski

The Matrix was written and directed by brothers Andy and Larry Wachowski, virtual newcomers to Hollywood who had previously made only one commercial film, the low-budget (but impressive) crime thriller *Bound* (1996); they had made no science fiction at all. Perhaps this lack of experience accounts for some of the freshness of the film, which may include little in the way of new science fiction concepts but which, in the tradition of the best SF film, genuinely shows viewers things that they have never seen before on the screen. The innovative effects and camera work and extensive use of motifs from Hong Kong martial arts films in a science fiction setting proved both successful and influential, making *The Matrix* one of the most talked about (and imitated) films of the past few years. The film was followed by two sequels, *The Matrix Reloaded* (2003) and *The Matrix Revolutions* (2003), both of which were also box-office successes. The first sequel was an even bigger commercial hit than the original *Matrix* film, grossing over $700 million worldwide. The *Matrix* franchise triggered a huge wave of interpretive response, as critics struggled to come to grips with the philosophical implications of what has proved to be much more than a mere pop cultural spectacle.

THE STORY: HONG KONG COMES TO CYBERSPACE

The fast pace of *The Matrix* is set early on as Trinity (Carrie-Anne Moss) is working at a computer terminal (in her trademark skin-tight black latex) when the police burst in. In a high-energy sequence accompanied by the hard-driving music that will characterize such scenes throughout the film, she dispatches the police easily, employing an array of gravity-defying martial arts techniques. When a group of "agents" (who, like Trinity, seem able to break the laws of physics) arrives, she has to flee, leading to a spectacular rooftop chase and to a narrow escape as she heads into a phone booth and then mysteriously disappears, just before Agent Smith (Hugo Weaving), the film's principal villain, crashes a large truck into it.

At this point, audiences have very little idea what is going on, but it is clear that we should be on the lookout for happenings that differ from our everyday expectations of reality. The next scene introduces us to computer programmer Thomas Anderson (Keanu Reeves), who leads a secret life as Neo, a notorious computer hacker. Trinity (herself a famed hacker who once cracked the IRS database) contacts Anderson with a mysterious message on his computer urging him, like Lewis Carroll's Alice, to "follow the white rabbit." Some hipsters, led by one Choi (Marc Gray), then arrive to purchase an illegal computer disk, which Neo extracts from its hiding place inside a hollowed-out copy of Jean Baudrillard's *Simulacra and Simulation*, the title of which is shown very clearly on the screen as if to alert us to its relevance. Neo then notices that Dujour (Ada Nicodemou), a young woman in the group, bears a tattoo of a white rabbit, so he accepts the group's invitation to go with them to a club, where Trinity manages to approach and warn him that he is being watched, though he does not really understand her warning. Nor does he quite comprehend what is going on the next day when one Morpheus (Laurence Fishburne) calls him at work (on a special cell phone they have just sent him via FedEx) to warn him that "they" are coming after him. Frightened and confused, Anderson is unable to use Morpheus's instructions to escape from the high-rise building and is instead taken into custody, where he is interrogated by Smith, who, like all of the "agents," looks a bit like an FBI man, or perhaps even a Man in Black of UFO lore (or of the 1997 film *Men in Black*), with his conservative business suit and tie, white shirt, and dark sunglasses. In particular, Smith wants Anderson to help him capture Morpheus, whom Smith describes as "the most dangerous man alive."

When Anderson refuses to cooperate with Smith, his mouth mysteriously disappears from his face, perhaps alluding to Harlan Ellison's classic story "I Have No Mouth and I Must Scream," in which intelligent machines subjugate the human race. Anderson is then thrown onto a table, where a weird mechanical bug is dropped onto his abdomen and begins to tunnel into his navel. Suddenly, Anderson awakes in his own bed, his mouth restored. Audiences (and Anderson) can breathe a sigh of relief: the weird happenings we have been observing can now be explained as a mere nightmare on the part of Anderson.

In this film, however, the distinction between reality and dream is not so simple. Called to meet Morpheus, Anderson, generally known as Neo from this point forward in the film, is picked up by Trinity, who uses an electromechanical device to remove the bug from his abdomen—it was "real" after all, though the film will go on to question the definition of reality in fundamental ways. Morpheus greets Neo at the rebel hideout within the Matrix, the interior of which looks a bit like a Gothic haunted house. Continuing the *Alice in Wonderland* motif, Morpheus tells Neo, "I imagine that you are feeling a bit like Alice, tumbling down the rabbit hole." Later, continuing the *Alice* motif, he offers Neo a blue pill and a red pill. The blue pill will return him to his former life. The red pill will allow him to stay in Wonderland and to discover "how deep the rabbit hole goes."

Neo chooses the red pill, and the rebels take him on a bizarre road of discovery in which he learns that it is apparently approximately 200 years later in history than he had thought and that his real physical body—like that of most other humans—is encased in a small womb-like compartment where it is tapped for energy (essentially used as a battery) by the machines that actually dominate the real world. This situation arose after the development of artificial intelligence in the early twenty-first century, leading to all-out war between humans and machines. When humans employed the tactic of "scorching the skies" to block out the sun and deny the machines the solar energy on which they depended, the machines retaliated by developing the human batteries as a power source. Nightmarishly, human beings are grown in fields to be harvested for use as such batteries, while the dead are liquefied to be fed intravenously to the living. The world of 1999 that Neo had thought to be real and the person he had thought himself to be are simply computer-produced simulations, manufactured by the machines to keep the humans unaware of their real plight. However, if one is killed in the Matrix, he apparently dies in the real world as well, lending importance to activities within the simulation.

The only humans living outside this system reside in the underground city of Zion, sending out rebels like Morpheus and his group to conduct a guerrilla campaign against the machines in both the real world and the

Matrix. The rebels rescue Neo's body from the power plant so that he can join them in the real world, taking him aboard their ship, the *Nebuchadnezzar*, a large, industrial-looking hovercraft, apparently (according to a nameplate aboard the ship) manufactured in 2069. Morpheus, meanwhile, reveals his belief that Neo is the reincarnation of "the One," the legendary founder of the resistance movement, a man supposedly born within the Matrix and gifted with almost unlimited powers to change and manipulate it. (Note that "Neo" is an anagram of "One.") Morpheus believes with a religious passion that Neo is the One, though many in the resistance doubt that the story of the One and his Christlike second coming is more than a myth. When Neo begins his training to work as an agent of the resistance in the Matrix, it soon becomes clear that he is an especially gifted student, lending credence to the notion that he may be the One. This training (and his subsequent activity in the Matrix) consists largely of martial arts, which may make little sense as a technique for fighting the massive power of the machines, but certainly makes for numerous scenes of effective cinema.

In the midst of Neo's training, the *Nebuchadnezzar* is attacked by a "sentinel," a tentacled, search-and-destroy killing machine, but the crew manages to disable it by firing off an EMP (electromagnetic pulse), which disables any and all electrical systems within the blast radius. (As a result, they must shut down all of their own systems before firing the device.) Eventually, Morpheus takes Neo to visit the enigmatic "Oracle" (Gloria Foster), an entity within the Matrix who had originally prophesied the second coming of the One. The Oracle, appearing in the guise of a kindly grandmother baking cookies, hints (but does not unequivocally state) that Neo is not the One. In addition, she warns him that there will soon come a time when either he or Morpheus must die and that Neo will have to choose which of them survives. Meanwhile, one of the rebels, Cypher (Joe Pantoliano), tired of the rigors of life as a real-world guerrilla, has sold out to the machines, informing against his fellow rebels so that he can return to the power plant and to the illusion of a comfortable life within the Matrix, living a simulated life as someone rich and important, "like an actor." This treachery leads to a Smith-led ambush of Morpheus, Neo, and those who accompany them on the way back from seeing the Oracle. Neo and Trinity escape, but only because Morpheus stays behind to battle Smith, knowing he cannot win. Morpheus is then taken captive. Meanwhile, Cypher returns to the *Nebuchadnezzar* and seemingly kills two "operators" who are monitoring the group in the Matrix. He then starts unplugging the bodies of the group that is still in the Matrix, killing two of them before he comes to Neo. Then he gloatingly announces that, if Neo were the One, some miracle would occur to save him from being unplugged. At that moment, Tank (Marcus Chong), one of the seemingly dead operators, arises and blasts Cypher, saving Neo and Trinity, whom he then helps to exit the Matrix safely.

Neo and Trinity plan a daring operation to rescue Morpheus, despite the fact that he is being held in a heavily guarded facility. What follows is a spectacular combat and rescue sequence (a sort of stepped-up version of the attack on the police station in *The Terminator*), leading to the successful exit from the Matrix of both Morpheus and Trinity. This time, however, Neo is left behind to battle Smith, who eventually pumps him full of bullets at point-blank range, seemingly leaving him dead. Back on the *Nebuchadnezzar*, Trinity speaks to Neo's physical body and tells him that the Oracle prophesied that she would fall in love with the One and that, since she now loves Neo, he must be the One and cannot therefore be dead. He suddenly revives, finding himself now gifted with greatly enhanced powers. When Smith and a group of agents open fire on him, he simply stops their bullets in mid-air and causes them to drop harmlessly to the floor. He then easily defeats and seemingly destroys Smith in hand-to-hand combat and exits the Matrix just in time to allow the crew of the *Nebuchadnezzar* to use their EMP to shut down a group of sentinels that is assaulting the ship. As the film ends, Neo returns to the Matrix to exercise his new superpowers, presumably in the fight to free humanity from subjugation by the machines.

THE SOURCES OF THE MOVIE

The Matrix is based on an original script by the Wachowski brothers, drawing upon a plethora of sources. There has, however, been considerable controversy (including copyright infringement lawsuits) over the Wachowskis' borrowings from some of these sources. Similarities between *The Matrix* and predecessors such as *The Invisibles* comic books series are particularly strong, but the film has so many influences (including any number of Japanese *animé* films and cyberpunk science fiction such as the novels of William Gibson) that it is probably impossible to identify any single predecessor as a direct source.

BAUDRILLARD FOR BEGINNERS: *THE MATRIX*
AND POSTMODERN "REALITY"

Originally released to relatively little fanfare, *The Matrix* went on to become one of the sensations of 1990s film. It won Saturn Awards (from the Academy of Science Fiction, Fantasy, and Horror Film) for best director and best science fiction film, beating out *Star Wars: Episode One— The Phantom Menace*, which won the award for best special effects of 1999. However, *The Matrix* trounced its *Star Wars* rival in the effects categories of the Oscars; it was nominated for four Oscars and won all four, in the categories of best editing, best sound effects editing, best visual effects, and best sound. It is indeed a technically impressive film, and its look and sound have influenced numerous subsequent films. Its combination of a thoughtful science fiction premise with high action sequences (including the martial arts sequences for which the film is perhaps best known) was a landmark in science fiction film.

Despite the effectiveness of these action sequences and the tremendous success of the film as a work of visual art, it is ultimately the thought-provoking ideas (however superficially they may be pursued) behind the action for which *The Matrix* is most important. These ideas have triggered a staggering amount of serious critical commentary, most of it focusing on the philosophical and religious dimensions of the film. Book-length works on the film include such titles as *Taking the Red Pill: Science, Philosophy, and Religion in The Matrix; The Matrix and Philosophy: Welcome to the Desert of the Real; Like a Splinter in Your Mind: The Philosophy Behind the Matrix Trilogy; Jacking in to the Matrix: Cultural Reception and Interpretation; The Gospel Reloaded: Exploring Spirituality and Faith in The Matrix*; and *The Matrix Cultural Revolution: How Deep Does the Rabbit Hole Go?*

Many commentators have been particularly impressed by the spiritual dimension of *The Matrix*. The Christian aspects of Neo as a savior returning from the dead are rather obvious, but one can also find resonances from Buddhist, Hindu, and other religious sources in the film and its sequels. Indeed, rather than endorsing any particular system of religious belief, *The Matrix* seems to valorize the principal of belief in general, drawing upon a number of different sources to create a pluralistic combination that can be viewed as either a powerful spiritual hybrid or a meaningless pop cultural hodge podge. Still, the overt religious references in the film are primarily Judeo–Christian. For example, in a retelling of the story of the fall from the Garden of Eden, we are told that the machines originally created a utopian Matrix in which all human desires were fulfilled and in which pain and sorrow were unknown, but that humans rejected this "programming," preferring to live instead in a reality that was defined by misery and suffering. Zion, meanwhile, is the name of the heavenly city promised to the Israelites by their God in the Old Testament. Trinity's name also has strong Christian ramifications, though her role is roughly that of a somewhat androgynous Mary Magdalene. Cypher does not have a religious name (though his name may suggest Lucifer), but he clearly plays the role of betrayer that is played in the New Testament by Judas. Finally, while Morpheus is named for the god of dreams in Ovid's *Metamorphosis* (and his name also suggests the morphing technology that is used aplenty in *The Matrix*), he clearly plays the role of precursor to the savior, relating to Neo as John the Baptist relates to Christ.

Neo, though, is a rather problematic savior. For one thing, there is a certain amount of self-conscious irony to his depiction as a Christ figure, which is, after all, by this time a sort of science fiction cliché that recalls predecessors from Klaatu of *The Day the Earth Stood Still* to E.T. Indeed, *The Matrix* shows an awareness of the glib and superficial way in which our culture often makes use of Christ metaphors. Thus, when Neo hands Choi the illicit computer disk, the latter responds with mock-religious joy: "Hallelujah! You're my savior, man. My own personal Jesus Christ." From this point of view, the link between Neo and Christ might be seen more as a postmodern pastiche of Christ imagery than as a genuine parallel, meant to be taken seriously. Meanwhile, as opposed to the peaceful Christ, Neo is a virtual killing machine, blasting his way through the Matrix and leaving a trail of bodies in his wake—most of them law enforcement officers. Many critics, in fact, have criticized *The Matrix* for using its spiritual and religious references in a mere attempt to make its cartoonish violence seem more acceptable.

Numerous technical aspects of the film seem designed for a similar purpose. It is certainly the case that the violence of the film is made more palatable by the fact that it is so unrealistic, its "bullet-time" super slow motion and other effects making the battle scenes seem almost ballet-like. The violence is cartoonish, rather than realistic; more accurately, the violence is reminiscent of a video game, which no doubt adds to its appeal for viewers who are video gamers—but which is also appropriate, given that it occurs within a computer simulation. However, the film suggests that the simulated people in the Matrix are the avatars of real people in the machine power plants, and that the deaths of those avatars bring about the deaths of the real people. Thus, as Neo kills cops and others in the Matrix (except for Smith and other "agents"), he is also killing people in the real world, an implication that many viewers seem to miss entirely.

However problematic its presentation of Neo as a figure of Christ, it is clear that *The Matrix* exemplifies the notion of filmmaking as mythmaking, creating an elaborate mythic structure to underlie its basic plot and scenario. And, if the actual implications of that mythic structure are a bit unclear, *The Matrix* does deliver a fairly clear overall message, perhaps best summed up in Neo's final speech at the end of the film, when he returns to the Matrix with his newfound powers, addressing those who control the system:

> I know you're out there. I can feel you now. I know that you're afraid . . . afraid of us. You're afraid of change. I don't know the future. I didn't come here to tell you how this is going to end. I came here to tell how it's going to begin. I'm going to hang up this phone, and then show these people what you don't want them to see. I'm going to show them a world without you. A world without rules or controls, borders or boundaries. A world where anything is possible. Where we go from there is a choice I leave to you.

Human beings, in short, are enslaved largely because they do not know and understand the nature of their enslavement. Knowing the truth, the film suggests, will set them free. Unfortunately, this message is little more than a cliché, though one that is central to the ideology of modern capitalist society, in which the "truth" is constantly valorized (sometimes to disguise an absence of truth). Thus, much of the popular success of the film can be attributed to the fact that it projects a message to which its audiences have been conditioned throughout their lives to respond positively. On the other hand, *The Matrix* does not advocate this message quite as unequivocally as a quick and superficial viewing of the film might suggest. Neo's empowerment is a fantasy of individual liberty that is undermined by the fact that the freedom from controls and boundaries that he cites here exists only within the simulated environment of the Matrix. It is only within the Matrix that Neo can fly about like Superman, while the people to whom he plans to demonstrate his power to break the rules are themselves still trapped in their battery cases in the power plants of the machines. More-over, the film has suggested that, once the people in these power plants have reached a certain age, they generally cannot be removed because the psychological shock would be too great, so that the liberation of the bulk of humanity from their slavery is not a practical possibility. Meanwhile, even *within* the Matrix it is only Neo who seems to have unlimited free-dom from boundaries and restraints. He cannot serve as a model of lib-eration for others because, as the One, he is literally one of a kind whose example cannot be duplicated.

Ultimately, of course, the phenomenon to which *The Matrix* advises resistance is not the use of human beings as batteries by far-future machines but the use of human beings as cogs in the vast capitalist machine of our own contemporary world. While many have argued that simulated life in the Matrix actually seems far preferable to life in the dystopian real world of the film, this simulated life is certainly far from ideal. Indeed, the film (or at least Smith) tells us that the machines have intentionally programmed pain and suffering into the Matrix because that is the only sort of life that human beings will accept. This notion may echo the Christian vision of humanity as a species fallen from grace and thus doomed to suffer, but Smith's explanation for the presence of pain in a simulated world also echoes the tendency of capitalism to attempt to justify its injustices and inequities as nothing more than the consequences of the natural human condition.

Importantly, the programmed pain of life in the Matrix corresponds quite closely to the negative consequences of capitalism in the real world. Thomas Anderson works at what is presumably a moderately well paying middle-class professional job, but his life as a computer programmer for a large corporation, slaving away in a tiny cubicle in a high-rise office building, seems mind-numbingly boring and routine. When we first see him on the job, he is receiving a lecture from his boss, Mr. Rhineheart (David Aston), for his lack of conformity to corporate expectations. Rhineheart himself is an embodiment of corporate conformism, a reincarnation of the gray-flanneled "organization man" of the notoriously conformist 1950s. Further, it is no accident that Rhineheart both looks and sounds like Agent Smith, the principal enforcer of rules, regulations, and conformity in the Matrix—a man who himself looks and sounds like all the other agents. Rhineheart's name may also suggest that he has a German heart, linking his strict insis-tence on obedience to corporate policy to Nazism, a link reinforced soon afterward when Neo refers to Smith's questioning of him as "Gestapo crap."

The Wachowskis reinforce this notion that life in the Matrix is driven by conformity to routine by muting the colors of this simulated world, tinting everything with a grayish-green that suggests both a lack of creativity and computer generation, recalling the green screens of early computer terminals. (Life in the Matrix is also explicitly compared to the black-and-white world of Kansas in *The Wizard of Oz*.) Meanwhile, Neo reacts to the routinization of life in the Matrix with the feeling that, as Morpheus puts it, "there's something wrong with the world," tormenting him "like a splinter in the mind." Unable fully to understand or articulate just what is wrong with the world, Neo merely has a vague sense that the world isn't right and he doesn't fit in. What he experiences, in fact, are the classic symptoms of alienation, long identified by critics of capitalism as one of the crucial consequences of life in a capitalist system. Marxist critics in particular have argued that the capitalist system is nevertheless able to ensure the necessary cooperation with this economic system through a complex system of ideological illusions designed to convince individuals that the system serves them rather than the other way around. As Morpheus continues to introduce Neo to the Matrix, he does so in terms that strikingly echo Marxist descriptions of the workings of capitalist ideology through the creation of "false consciousness." The Matrix, he explains, "is the world that has been pulled over your eyes to blind you to the truth that you are a slave, Neo. Like everyone else you were born into bondage, born into a prison that you cannot smell, or taste, or touch. A prison for your mind."

The Matrix, meanwhile, argues that this bondage through false consciousness can be broken through the revelation of the true workings of the system, just as Marxist critics believe that the best weapons against capitalism are knowledge and understanding of its true nature, which is generally heavily disguised. However, far from touting socialism as an alternative to capitalism, *The Matrix* advocates individualism, failing to see that it thereby endorses one of the principal tenets of capitalist ideology, thus reinforcing the very system it seems to want to criticize. Morpheus and his band are not Marxist theorists but individualist activists. They are, in essence, terrorists who find the power that rules the world so despicable in its suppression of individualism that they are willing to use any and all means at their disposal (including mass killings) to try to disrupt that power.

When we first meet Neo he has fallen asleep while scanning on-line newspapers for information about Morpheus, one of which describes him as a "renown [sic] terrorist." Like the rebels of the *Star Wars* saga or the alien fighters of *Independence Day*, the guerrillas of *The Matrix* tap into deeply ingrained American myths, enacting a vision of individual resistance to systemic oppression that dates back to the American Revolution but that picked up particular rhetorical power during the years of the Cold War. The fact is, however, that these rebels have far more in common with Osama bin Laden and his Al-Qaeda terrorists than they do with American heroes like George Washington or Abraham Lincoln. (Interestingly, after the screen identifying Morpheus as a terrorist, Neo's computer next scrolls to an article from *An-Nahar*, an Arabic-language newspaper from Beirut, possibly linking Morpheus with Arab terrorism.)

Like *Star Wars* and *Independence Day*, *The Matrix* was made before the 9/11 bombings and surely does not refer to them directly. However, the sequels were made after those bombings and seem to continue very much the same message as the original film. Granted, they depict the struggle of the humans against the machines as primarily defensive attempts to defend Zion from invasion by a foreign force, but then the only major offensive assaults in the war on terror in our own world have involved attacks by technologically superior American forces on strongholds of resistance to American power, not attacks by terrorists against the United States. As with the aliens of *Independence Day*, it is the machines of *The Matrix* and its sequels, not the embattled human rebels, who correspond to the role played by the United States in the global politics of our own world.

This is not to say that the Wachowski brothers are somehow attempting to drum up support for anti-American terrorist activities in their *Matrix* films. In fact, while the rebel culture of Zion does have much more of a Third World feel to it than do the oppositional cultures of *Star Wars* or *Independence Day*, it has very little of the flavor of the Islamic cultures that provide the primary opposition to the United States in our world. If anything, the political model for Zion, seems to be pre-capitalist, vaguely reminiscent of the democratic city-states of ancient Greece. On the other hand, the politics of Zion do not figure in the original *Matrix* film at all, and they are not necessarily presented as an ideal model even in the sequels. If anything, the politics of *The Matrix* are strongly antidemocratic, containing a messianic (or Nietzschean) strain that suggests a crucial need for strong, charismatic leaders on the order of Neo and Morpheus—or Hitler and Mussolini. The people of Zion are unable to save themselves from destruction, but they are able to survive their war with the machines thanks to the intervention of their superhuman leader, Neo.

One might argue that the prevailing political attitude of *The Matrix* is nostalgia. However hip and cool it might appear, there is a definite yearning for older simpler times running throughout the trilogy, whether it be in the largely antitechnological tone of the films or in this political yearning for predemocratic times of strong, paternalistic leaders, divinely endowed with the authority to rule. Similarly, the reality vs. illusion conflict of the film suggests that in our own contemporary world, we have lost touch with the kind of authenticity of experience that was presumably once available to us. From this point of view, *The Matrix* is a highly conservative film that is very much in line with the nostalgic attempts of right-wing proponents of "traditional values" to look to the past for solutions to our contemporary malaise. The structural opposition of the real world versus the simulated world of the Matrix is very much an opposition between past authenticity and present fakery, based on the assumption that a legitimate and genuine reality does exist, even if that reality may be difficult to access through the web of representations that now cloak it.

Granted, it is possible to see the "reality" of *The Matrix* as simply another simulation, perhaps one of an infinite series of such simulations, each of which is presented as a "real" alternative to the simulation before it. This possibility is explicitly suggested in "Matriculation," one of the short films included in *The Animatrix*. However, there is very little suggestion in *The Matrix* itself that this is the case. Morpheus and his crew certainly believe that their reality is "real," and most viewers of the film seem to accept that premise as well—even while believing that their own reality is truly "real" and understanding that the "real" world in *The Matrix* is a Hollywood fiction.

Then again, the real world of the viewers of the film might be seen as a Hollywood fiction as well. The film suggests in a number of ways that our own reality is a media-produced illusion, to which the film industry itself makes crucial contributions. For example, the green tint of the opening Warner Brothers logo suggests that media conglomerates like Time–Warner make crucial contributions to the distortion of reality in our own world, even as it also allows the Wachowski Brothers to lay claim to the "WB" logo for their own use. In his commentary to the DVD version of the film, special effects supervisor John Gaeta explains that "We wanted to alter the logos of the studios, mostly because we felt that they were an evil empire bent on breaking the creative juices of the average director or writer." By so doing, Gaeta goes on, the filmmakers wanted to send audiences the message that they "reject the system." He means the Hollywood system, rather than the capitalist system, but the two are not entirely separable, and this comment certainly makes it seem as if critique of the capitalist media was a major goal of the film. However, this "subversive" remark is also something of a cliché—and perhaps disingenuous, given that the *Matrix* franchise has been such a large element of the "evil" Time–Warner empire over the past several years.

In addition, when Cypher negotiates with Smith for his betrayal of Morpheus and Neo, he says that, in his new simulated life, he wants to be someone "important, like an actor." This request already indicates the prominence of the film industry in the Matrix (and, by extension, our own world). Further, when we consider that the name of Cypher in the Matrix is "Mr. Reagan," the link to President Ronald Reagan, himself a former actor, is inescapable. The fact that Reagan (like Arnold Schwarzenegger after him) could parlay his film career into a successful political career serves as an additional reminder of the power of the film industry. Finally, the fact that Reagan was often accused of having difficulty distinguishing the world of reality from the world of film (as in his frequent use of film allusions to in his political speeches) reinforces the central theme of constructed reality in *The Matrix*.

The Matrix also includes television in its media critique. Morpheus, for example, specifically mentions television in his description of institutions that contribute to the illusions of the Matrix, along with work, church, and taxes. Televisions and video screens are prominently displayed at several points in the film, and one of the favorite devices employed by the Wachowskis involves a seamless transition from viewing a scene on a video screen to being inside the scene itself—suggesting the way in which, in our own world, television plays a major role in the postmodern blurring of the boundary between reality and fiction.

Such blurring between different levels of existence is, according to critics such as Brian McHale, in his book *Postmodernist Fiction* (New York: Methuen, 1987), a central element of postmodernist culture—and of the postmodernist worldview as a whole. To an extent, the key referent here is Baudrillard and his notion that the contemporary world of late capitalism has reached a state of hyperreality, a condition in which individuals encounter nothing but "simulacra," representations that do not refer to reality, copies of originals that do not exist. Numerous commentators have acknowledged the relevance of Baudrillard to *The Matrix*, especially given the overt allusions to Baudrillard's *Simulation and Simulacra* that appear in the film, which include not only Neo's (appropriately) fake copy of the book, but also Morpheus's quotation from it when he welcomes Neo to "the desert of the real." There has, however, been considerable disagreement about whether the film demonstrates a sophisticated understanding of Baudrillard and his work or whether the use of Baudrillard is entirely superficial. (After all, Morpheus's quotation is from the first page of the book and could have been picked out without even reading it.) In his essay in the volume *Taking the Red Pill* (Dallas, Tx: BenBella Books, 2003), Dino Felluga sees *The Matrix* as an effective filmic presentation of Baudrillard's critique of postmodernism, ultimately reminding us that we are all metaphorical batteries powering the capitalist system and serving as a "commentary on the way each member of the audience is itself a coppertop, whose own fantasies are being manipulated by and thus feed capital" (83). On the other hand, Andrew Gordon argues in his essay in the same volume that the film discourages political action by encouraging viewers to wait for salvation by a messiah figure. Further, he concludes that the film waters down and distorts Baudrillard's ideas because it posits the continuing existence of a genuine reality to which one can return from the simulated world of illusions, something that Baudrillard sees as no longer possible.

The simulated reality of the Matrix may seem to correspond quite closely to the hyperreality described by Baudrillard, but the depiction of a stable alternative real world is a much more old-fashioned (and less postmodern) gesture. Nevertheless, if *The Matrix* is ultimately far less subversive than many of its proponents would like to believe, it is also the case that the film, compared to most other works of contemporary popular culture, raises an unusually large number of issues and explores an extraordinary range of ideas. Even a detractor like Gordon admits that works of science fiction that deal with virtual reality are particularly relevant today because they are "metaphors and fantasies, projections of our fears and hopes about life inside the machine or life augmented by the machine in the cybernetic age" (87). If *The Matrix* fails to strike any genuinely telling blows against the cultural, political, and economic system that surrounds it, this failure may say less about the weakness of the film and more about the strength of the system.

VIOLENCE AND VIRTUAL REALITY: THE LEGACY OF *THE MATRIX*

The Matrix is a virtual compendium of borrowings from earlier films and novels. For example, the messianic depiction of Neo recalls the role of Paul

Atreides as a messiah figure in Frank Herbert's classic SF novel *Dune* (1965), made into an oft-reviled (but actually quite interesting) film by David Lynch in 1984. Most obviously, the machine-war motif of *The Matrix* echoes the *Terminator* films, while its fight sequences recall any number of Hong Kong martial arts films, especially the films of John Woo, whose career as a director of American films probably received a sizeable boost from the success of *The Matrix*. Indeed, *The Matrix* helped Hong Kong–style fight scenes to become a staple of American cinema, as can be seen in such films as Ang Lee's *Crouching Tiger, Hidden Dragon* (2000) and James Wong's Jet Li vehicle *The One* (2001)—or even McG's two *Charlie's Angels* films (2000 and 2003). The dystopian film *Equilibrium* (Kurt Wimmer, 2002) also shows a strong *Matrix* influence in this respect.

The super-hero fight scenes of Stephen Norrington's *Blade* (1998) might also be mentioned as a predecessor to *The Matrix*, while the black-clad ass-kicking heroine of Len Wiseman's *Blade*-influenced *Underworld* (2003) draws a great deal from Trinity in *The Matrix*. Such comic book–style films provide a reminder that *The Matrix* is a super-hero film of sorts, not only recalling classics such as Richard Donner's *Superman* (1978), but also giving new life to a genre that soon produced such hits as Sam Raimi's *Spider-Man* (2002) and *Spider-Man 2* (2004) films, Bryan Singer's *X-Men* (2000) and *X2* (2003), Mark Steven Johnson's *Daredevil* (2003), Stephen Sommers's *Van Helsing* (2004), Guillermo del Toro's *Hellboy* (2004), and Jonathan Hensleigh's *The Punisher* (2004).

The Matrix is also central to a body of films dealing with either virtual reality or films that blur the boundary between reality and illusion, often due to the manipulation of perceptions of reality by the media. Important virtual-reality predecessors include *Tron* (Steven Lisberger, 1982), *Johnny Mnemonic* (Robert Longo, 1995), *Strange Days* (Kathryn Bigelow, 1995), and *Virtuosity* (Brett Leonard, 1995). *The Matrix* itself appeared in the middle of a cluster of such films, including Alex Proyas's *Dark City* (1998), David Cronenberg's *eXistenZ* (1999), and Josef Rusnak's *The Thirteenth Floor* (1999). Other important reality-bending films include *Solaris* (Andrei Tarkovsky, 1972; remade by Steven Soderbergh in 2002), *Wag the Dog* (Barry Levinson, 1997), *The Truman Show* (Peter Weir, 1998), and *Fight Club* (David Fincher, 1999).

The two sequels to *The Matrix* are themselves important SF films. *The Matrix Reloaded* (2003) begins in the immediate aftermath of the original *Matrix* film. Thanks to a budget that was approximately twice that of the original, *The Matrix Reloaded* is a great looking film, with significantly stepped-up special effects. We see lots more of the sentinels, get our first view of the human underground stronghold of Zion, and are treated to one of the most extended and spectacular chase scenes ever put on film. Meanwhile, the fight scenes that were the heart of the original film are even more spectacular here, with more action, more combatants, and more destruction.

The Matrix Reloaded also seeks to extend the mythology of the original film, though, as a sequel that merely builds on the original, it lacks the breakthrough innovation of its predecessor. The principal real-world action here concerns the advance of a sentinel army as it tunnels its way toward Zion, while the parallel action in the Matrix concerns the efforts of the crew of the *Nebuchadnezzar* (including Neo, Trinity, and Morpheus) to trace the Matrix to its source and shut it down, presumably crippling the machine world. Here Neo does indeed seem to be the One, negotiating the Matrix like a superhero—often, in fact, flying about in a mode the film itself compares to Superman. However, it turns out that the existence of the One is merely an aspect of the system itself, built in to help the system institute periodic upgrades of the Matrix software. All in all, nothing much is resolved, and in fact the film simply stops in mid-stream (with Neo lying near death after overtaxing his powers to stop an advance of the sentinels against the crew of the *Nebuchadnezzar*, which has itself been blown up).

The Matrix Revolutions (2003) picks up where its predecessor left off and is really just the second half of the film that began with *The Matrix Reloaded* (2003), very much in the mode that would be used in Quentin Tarantino's two-part film *Kill Bill* (2003–2004). On the other hand, this third *Matrix* film is in many ways quite different from the other two, largely because it takes place primarily in the real world. One half of its dual plot structure involves a massive assault on Zion by a vast army of sentinels, while the other involves a journey on the part of Neo and Trinity to the machine city to attempt to negotiate an end to the war. Perhaps the central moment in the film is a huge battle between the sentinels and the defenders of Zion, a telling scene that is spectacular in some ways, but degenerates into an orgy of computer-generated effects. This film is definitely less charged with energy than the first two. Meanwhile, Agent Smith has grown vastly stronger and essentially takes control of the entire Matrix. The film leads to a final cataclysmic good vs. evil battle in which Neo allies himself with the machines to destroy Smith, in return for which the machines call off their assault on Zion and end the war, though the exact status of humanity (and of Neo, who may or may not be dead) remains uncertain as the film—and the trilogy—comes to an end.

The other installment of the *Matrix* franchise is *The Animatrix* (2003), a collection of nine short animated films (commissioned by the Wachowski Brothers) set in the world of the *Matrix* trilogy. These films are done primarily in the style of Japanese animé, though they employ a variety of animation techniques. Though criticized by some as a mere advertisement for the sequels, they are in fact interesting in their own right and significantly help to fill in the backstory of the trilogy. Among other things, the two-part film "Renaissance" illuminates the beginning of the human–machine war, suggesting that much of the fault for the war lies in the human abuse of machines, even after the latter had become sentient.

Conclusion: Science Fiction Film and American Culture

The political and cultural relevance of the fifteen films discussed in this volume, and the popularity of science fiction films in general should be sufficient to demonstrate the prominence of science fiction film as an American cultural form. But, it is also important to note the extent to which science fiction film, by pushing the envelope of filmmaking technology, has had an important influence on films that do not themselves belong to the genre, at least not in the strictest sense. For example, such hugely successful films as *Titanic* (1997, directed by SF mainstay Cameron) and the *Lord of the Rings* trilogy (2001–2003) could not have been made without the advances in special-effects technology developed primarily in science fiction films from *Star Wars* to *The Matrix*. This same technology was also crucial to the development of a spate of recent films based on superheroes from comic books (and graphic novels), including the *Blade* trilogy (beginning in 1998), *X-Men* (2000) and *X2* (2003), *Spider-Man* (2002) and *Spider-Man 2* (2004), *Daredevil* (2003), *Hulk* (2003), *The League of Extraordinary Gentlemen* (2003), *Hellboy* (2004), *The Punisher* (2004), *Elektra* (2005), and *The Fantastic Four* (2005). Meanwhile, *Alien vs. Predator* (2004) was a vaguely science fictional action film that grew out of a comic-book series that grew out of two popular science fiction film series, further suggesting a kinship between comic books and SF film.

Special-effects technology has also been instrumental in the adaptation of a number of popular video games to film. Films such as *Mortal Combat* (1995), *Laura Croft: Tomb Raider* (2001) and *Laura Croft Tomb Raider: The*

Cradle of Life (2003), and *Resident Evil* (2002) and *Resident Evil: Apocalypse* (2004) have been directly inspired by video games. Conversely, video games themselves have been heavily influenced by science fiction film, leading to what appears to be a growing convergence of the two forms in terms of look and feel. Indeed, adaptation in this case has worked in both directions, and many science fiction films (such as the *Star Wars* series, the *Terminator* series, and *The Matrix*) have provided the inspiration for video games.

There is, however, more to science fiction film than special effects technology. Science fiction is very much a genre of ideas. As one might expect, SF films have provided the popular imagination with some of its most compelling visions of both the possibilities and the dangers of a future increasingly dominated by advanced technologies. Perhaps more importantly, such films, despite being widely regarded as mere entertainments, have often provided serious and thoughtful explorations of important contemporary social and political issues. Indeed, the very fact that genre films such as science fiction have generally not been taken as works of "serious" cinema has sometimes allowed them a special freedom to address controversial topics. For example, a film with the strong anti-nuclear arms race message of *The Day the Earth Stood Still* could almost certainly not have been made in 1951 had that message not been couched in terms of science fiction rather than straightforward drama.

While the estrangement from reality provided by the projected worlds of science fiction might make the political messages of SF film seem less threatening to some, that very estrangement also helps to provide new perspectives from which audiences can look at the world in which they live, potentially bringing into focus aspects of that world that might otherwise be less clear. Most obviously, the vivid depiction of future technologies in SF films can stimulate thought and debate about potential controversies surrounding the emergence of those technologies in the present day. For example, the appearance, beginning in the 1990s, of such "virtual reality" films as *Total Recall* (1990), *Dark City* (1998), *eXistenZ* (1999), *The Thirteenth Floor* (1999), and the *Matrix* series indicated the ability of SF film to respond to the changed sense of reality brought about by new technologies such as the internet, while addressing a broader postmodern sense of the instability of reality and individual identity. Similarly, films such as *Blade Runner*, the *Terminator* series, *Robocop*, *Artificial Intelligence: A.I.*, and *I, Robot* (2004) explore dilemmas related to the possible production of artificial humans through advances in robotics and biological engineering. In a broader sense, however, such films ask audiences to look deep within themselves to examine their own feelings about the nature of humanity and about human beings who may (racially, culturally, or experientially) be different from themselves. In this same vein, alien–invasion and alien–encounter films such as *Invasion of the Body Snatchers* and the *Alien* series address our most basic fears of otherness, while films such as *2001: A Space Odyssey, Close Encounters of the Third Kind, E.T. the Extra-Terrestrial,* and *The Abyss* encourage audiences to open their minds to new experiences and new ideas.

In addition to this ability to expose audiences to new and different aspects of the world in which they live, SF film can cast new light on social and political phenomena that we experience every day. For example, the upside-down social structure of *Planet of the Apes* may indeed at first appear to be a "madhouse," but on close examination the seemingly absurd social practices of the ape society are disturbingly similar to those of our own. SF films have also been particularly pointed in their critique of corporate capitalism, the workings of which suddenly appear strange indeed when placed in the context of the worlds projected in such films as the *Blade Runner,* the *Alien* series, the *Terminator* series, and the *Robocop* series. Even seemingly light SF films such as *They Live* (1988) and *Space Truckers* (1996) have often contained some of the most trenchant criticism of corporate capitalism to be found in American film.

In short, science fiction film, while providing some of the most rousing entertainment to be found in the American cinema, has produced some of the most important cultural reflections and expressions of popular hopes, fears, and anxieties to be found in American culture in the second half of the twentieth century and the early years of the twenty-first. As we move forward into the new century, science fiction film promises to remain one of the major forces for innovation in American cinema. The continual quest for more daring and more spectacular special effects in SF film will no doubt continue to produce some of the film industry's most important technical advances and some of the screen's most memorable images. Meanwhile, the projected worlds of science fiction cinema promise to offer film audiences a framework for the exploration of some of the most challenging and thought-provoking ideas to be found in American culture in the coming century.

Index

Klaatu addresses the Earthlings, backed up by Gort (*The Day the Earth Stood Still*).

The crew of the C57D outside their ship on Planet Altair IV (*Forbidden Planet*).

Morbius explains the workings of Robby the Robot to his new visitors from Earth (*Forbidden Planet*).

The replicant of Miles Bennell begins to emerge from its pod (*Invasion of the Body Snatchers*).

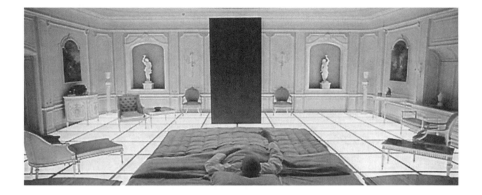

The aged Bowman lies abed in his hotel suite as another alien monolith appears before him (*2001: A Space Odyssey*).

The Star Child, waiting to be born and take humanity to the next level of evolution (*2001: A Space Odyssey*).

The members of the ape tribunal want no truck with new ideas, refusing to see, hear, or speak evil (*Planet of the Apes*).

Taylor and Nova reach the ruins of the Statue of Liberty, presumably felled in a nuclear war (*Planet of the Apes*).

The *Millennium Falcon* comes to rest inside the Death Star (*Star Wars*).

Darth Vader consults with Grand Moff Tarkin aboard the Death Star (*Star Wars*).

The alien mother ship comes to a landing (*Close Encounters of the Third Kind*).

Childlike aliens cavort outside the mother ship after its landing (*Close Encounters of the Third Kind*).

The "chest-burster" emerges from the chest of Kane (*Alien*).

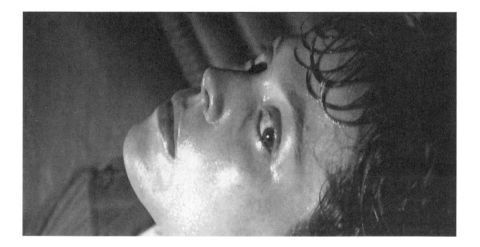

Ripley in a moment of stress (*Alien*).

Elliott and E.T. fly across the face of the moon on Elliott's bicycle (*E.T. the Extra-Terrestrial*).

The architecture of the future. Top, the dark cityscape of 2019 Los Angeles; bottom, the headquarters of the Tyrell Corporation (*Blade Runner*).

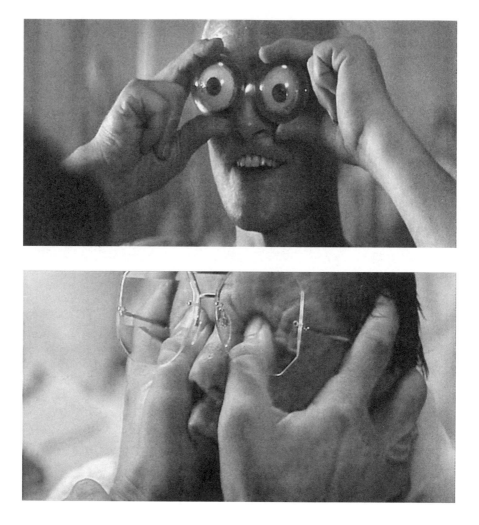

The eyes have it. Top, Roy Batty has a joke with J. F. Sebastian; bottom, Batty meets (and kills) his maker, Tyrell (*Blade Runner*).

Sarah Connor (Linda Hamilton) before and after meeting the Terminator. Top, a soft, innocent Sarah takes orders in her capacity as harried waitress (*The Terminator*); bottom, a tough, gun-toting Sarah prepares for battle (*Terminator 2: Judgment Day*).

Arnold Schwarzenegger looking tough as the Terminator, about to shoot up an L.A. police station (*The Terminator*).

Robocop (Peter Weller) prepares for action (*Robocop*).

Lindsey Brigman (Mary Elizabeth Mastrantonio) reaches out to touch the alien water probe, which has taken on the visage of her husband Bud (Ed Harris) (*The Abyss*).

A glowing, angel-like alien addresses Bud Brigman deep beneath the ocean (*The Abyss*).

An alien saucer blasts the White House (*Independence Day*).

Neo (Keanu Reeves) and Trinity (Carrie-Anne Moss) prepare to go into battle (*The Matrix*).

Neo dodges a bullet (*The Matrix*).

About the Author

M. KEITH BOOKER is Professor and Director of Graduate Studies in the Department of English at the University of Arkansas. He is the author of numerous articles and books on modern literature, film, and science fiction, including *Film and the American Left* (1999), *Monsters, Mushroom Clouds, and the Cold War* (2001), *Strange TV: Innovative Television Series from "The Twilight Zone" to "The X-Files"* (2003), and *Science Fiction Television* (2004).